The Entrepreneurial Process

The Entrepreneurial Process

Economic Growth, Men, Women, and Minorities

Paul D. Reynolds
and Sammis B. White

Q

QUORUM BOOKS
Westport, Connecticut • London

Library of Congress Cataloging-in-Publication Data

Reynolds, Paul D.
    The entrepreneurial process : economic growth, men, women, and
minorities / by Paul D. Reynolds and Sammis B. White.
        p.   cm.
    Includes bibliographical references and index.
    ISBN 1–56720–012–5 (alk. paper)
    1. New business enterprises—United States—Management.   2. Small
business—United States—Management.   3. Women-owned business
enterprises—United States—Management.   4. Minority business
enterprises—United States—Management.   5. New business
enterprises—United States—Finance.   I. White, Sammis B.
II.   Title.
HD62.5.R49   1997
658.02′2—dc21   97–19229

British Library Cataloguing in Publication Data is available.

Library of Congress Catalog Card Number: 97–19229
ISBN: 1–56720–012–5

First published in 1997

Quorum Books, 88 Post Road West, Westport, CT 06881
An imprint of Greenwood Publishing Group Inc.

Printed in the United States of America

The paper used in this book complies with the
Permanent Paper Standard issued by the National
Information Standards Organization (Z39.48–1984).

10 9 8 7 6 5 4 3 2

Copyright Acknowledgments

The authors and publisher gratefully acknowledge permission to use material from the following:

Paul D. Reynolds, "Who Starts New Firms?—Preliminary Explorations of Firms-in-Gestation." Scheduled for publication in *Small Business Economics*. Used with permission of Kluwer Academic Publishers.

Nancy M. Carter, William B. Gartner, and Paul D. Reynolds. 1996. "Exploring Start-up Event Sequences." *Journal of Business Venturing* 11: 151–66.

Over 5,000 people contributed to this research by answering questions in the five surveys that form the basis for the following analysis. Almost half completed a follow-up interview. Without their help, we would know much less about business start-ups. On behalf of both those who will analyze these data in the future and ourselves, we thank the respondents for their assistance and candor. The knowledge that develops will, hopefully, ease the path for future generations of entrepreneurs and enhance their contributions to economic growth.

Contents

Illustrations

EXHIBITS

Preface

New business organizations, the product of the entrepreneurial process, are a central feature of modern market economies. Three complementary programs of research related to the founding of new business organizations have been developed by the first author. The first research program explored the development of new firms early in their life course; it is represented by representative samples of new firms in Minnesota, Pennsylvania, and Wisconsin. The second research program was developed to explore the processes that led individuals to become involved in starting a new firm and the factors leading to a successful firm birth; it is represented by two preliminary surveys of adults in Wisconsin and the United States. A third research program is related to the effects of geographic context on firm births and is represented by cross-regional analysis of the United States (Reynolds, Maki, and Miller, 1995) and a number of other countries (Reynolds, Storey, and Westhead, 1994).

This book emphasizes the first two of these efforts, focusing on the start-up process and the early life of operating new firms. Like all data sets, the five that form the basis for the following analysis are imperfect, but the basic patterns are quite robust and provide substantial confidence on two points: (1) the same patterns will probably occur in future studies, and (2) it is possible to conduct, with substantial payoff, systematic research on the firm start-up process itself.

As there continues to be controversy regarding the importance of the role of new firms on economic growth, generally defined as job creation, a discussion of the importance of new firms is presented in Chapters 1, 2, and 9. The case that new firms provide substantial societal benefits and are worthy of both serious study and attention for public policy seems quite strong. Much of the controversy appears to reflect commitment to a "perfect competitive model" of economic activity; data provided in this analysis suggest a substantial need to revise this conception to incorporate change associated with new firms. Existing and established firms also have a role to play, but an important feature of current and future market economies will be the contributions of new firms and entrepreneurship to economic growth and adaptation. This is being more widely recognized in many international government units, such as the European Union (EIM, 1993, 1994, 1995) and the OECD (1996). If the research discussed in this book provides a new emphasis to this discussion, it is related to the importance of entrepreneurial career options for mainstream labor force participants.

The substantive core of the book is found in four chapters. Chapter 3 deals with identifying new start-ups and their critical features, emphasizing the individuals involved. Chapter 4 provides evidence, from limited pilot studies, on the start-up process and the outcomes. Chapter 5 focuses on the growth patterns of fledgling new firms, exploring a wide range of factors associated with different growth trajectories. Because the growth trajectory is one of the more salient factors affecting the persistence, or survival, of new firms, this topic is treated in Chapter 6. The contributions of Mary Williams to this work are recognized by listing her as coauthor of this chapter.

Two chapters deal with special topics. Chapter 7, written by Nancy Carter, gives special attention to the impact of gender on different aspects of the entrepreneurial process. It is both more and less than many would expect. Chapter 8 takes advantage of a unique sample of ethnic subgroups in Wisconsin to compare their participation in the entrepreneurial process. The major differences are related to those entirely excluded from the process; those involved seem very similar regardless of ethnic background.

Chapter 9 provides a summary overview and discusses some of the implications for classical conceptions of market economies, for public policy—with a presentation of the "entrepreneurial engine," and for those planning to start new firms. A postscript discusses some of the requirements that will be needed for future research on entrepreneurship if substantial progress is to be made on this topic. It seems clear that the importance of the topic justifies the resources needed for further progress.

This book should be considered a progress report on ongoing research programs. As long as the operating structure of market economies continues to change, definitive answers to the questions associated with the entrepreneurial process may never be possible. This effort, however, helps to clarify many of the important issues.

The research programs that are the core of this work have involved a wide number of colleagues and students. Steve West was heavily involved, while he was a graduate student in sociology at the University of Minnesota, in the 1984 survey of Minnesota which is not included in the following analysis (Reynolds and West, 1985). This project was the pretest for the subsequent studies of new firms. The study of Pennsylvania new firms was completed with the assistance of Steve Freeman, then a graduate student at the University of Pennsylvania Wharton School. Brenda Miller, a student in sociology, was involved in completing follow-ups on the 1984 sample of Minnesota new firms as well as supervising the 1987 sample of Minnesota new firms. (One firm was actually selected for both surveys.) The follow-up of the Minnesota and Pennsylvania new firm samples was a collaborative effort that involved Professor Richard Cardozo, University of Minnesota; Professor Ian McMillian, University of Pennsylvania; and Professor Mary Williams, Widener University.

The authors shared responsibility for the Wisconsin Entrepreneurial Climate Study, which involved surveys of both new firms and nascent entrepreneurs, those actively involved in creating new firms. A substantial team was involved in this effort, including Nancy Carter, Gary Mejchar, James Murray, Harold Rose, Tim Stearns, and Keith Tourtillott. The resources and creativity of the University of Wisconsin Survey Research Laboratory, where team member Charles Palit is associate director, contributed a great deal to the development of the procedures for locating and interviewing nascent entrepreneurs and ethnic subsamples in the adult population. Data on new firms were collected by the University of Wisconsin–Milwaukee Social Science Research Facility and the Marquette University Center for the Study of Entrepreneurship. Second-round interviews on Wisconsin new firms were a joint effort of the University of Wisconsin–Milwaukee Urban Research Center and the Marquette University Center for the Study of Entrepreneurship. Follow-ups of nascent entrepreneurs were completed by the Marquette Center.

The second study in this program was directly related to the interest and talents of James Morgan and Richard Curtin of the University of Michigan Institute of Social Research. Their efforts made the national pilot study possible. This validated the initial findings in Wisconsin and suggested that more extensive studies were feasible and justified. Follow-up interviews with the national sample of nascent entrepreneurs were completed informally from the Economic Behavior Program of the University of Michigan Institute for Social Research.

The third project in this research program will be the National Study of U.S. Business Start-ups, under development by the Entrepreneurial Research Consortium (ERC). By 1997 the ERC was composed of almost thirty research units sponsoring about 100 entrepreneurial scholars and researchers. The full data set will not become available for ERC participant analysis until 1998 and is unlikely to enter a public archive for several more years. Complementary studies are being planned in a number of other countries.

Acknowledgments

Substantial funds were required to complete the studies that form the basis for the analysis in this book. Financial support was received from the following sponsors for the these projects:

1986 Pennsylvania New Firm Survey: Appalachian Regional Commission and the Pennsylvania Department of Commerce.

1986–87 Minnesota New Firm Survey: University of Minnesota, Center for Urban and Regional Affairs; City of St. Paul, Minnesota; Metropolitan Council of the Twin Cities Area; Minnesota Chamber of Commerce; Minnesota Board of Vocational Technical Education; Minnesota Community College System; Minnesota Department of Trade and Economic Development; Minnesota Extension Service, University of Minnesota; Minnesota State Planning Agency; and the Port Authority of St. Paul, Minnesota.

Wisconsin Entrepreneurial Climate Study: Wisconsin Innovation Network, Inc. and the Wisconsin Housing and Economic Development Authority.

National Pilot Study of Nascent Entrepreneurs: Rockefeller Foundation and the University of Michigan, Institute for Social Research, Survey Research Center, Project Development Funds.

Chapter 1

Introduction

Pursuing an entrepreneurial opportunity (whether self-employment, the creation of a family business, or implementing an innovative new venture) is becoming an important option in the work careers of many. The birth and development of new businesses—the core of entrepreneurial activity—are now widely recognized as a critical aspect of market economies. Firm births, particularly new firm growth, are seen as a major source of new jobs. New firms may have a critical, causal role in economic growth. The major benefits of adaptation and innovation are associated with new firms, often leading to the creation of entirely new industries. A major mechanism for minimizing excessive profits to producers—returns greater than needed to elicit their contributions—is the threat of competition from new firms. This tends to reduce the costs for consumers and is often considered a restraint on entrenched monopolies. There is almost no government or political leader from advanced, formerly socialist, Third World, or developing countries—the entire modern world—that doesn't give substantial attention to entrepreneurial phenomena.

Despite the significance of entrepreneurship and the wide range of individuals attending to it—entrepreneurs, governments, potential employees, financiers, competitors—there is little known about the initial phases of the process. The conception, gestation, birth, and early development of new ventures are very much an uncharted territory. The following pages present an exploration of this important phenomenon—the creation of new business firms.

The presentation includes a conceptual framework for considering the entrepreneurial process and reviewing the results of several complementary studies—all based on representative samples within the United States—related to the early stages of the firm-founding process. Special attention is given throughout to the implications for public policy. Should governments intervene, and, if they do, what might be the most effective strategies for enhancing the entrepreneurial process? There is, in addition, special attention to the involvement of minorities and women in the entrepreneurial process.

CONCEPTUALIZATION OF MODERN MARKET ECONOMIES

Those studying modern market economies, particularly those who have emphasized the study of industrial organizations, have found it convenient to focus on the processes that will emerge in a "perfect market." Such markets are assumed to approach stability in terms of prices and quantities exchanged. Predicting the "steady state" of a "perfectly competitive market" with formal models is easier if a large number of assumptions are made about the products (a stable set of identical commodities) and the participants (buyers and sellers or consumers and producers). Producers are usually assumed to be profit-oriented, productive organizations using established technology to produce the commodity products. Entrepreneurial activity—the creation of new firms, products, or markets—is generally not included in these conceptual schemes (Barreto, 1989; Baumol, 1968). The result has been a series of assumptions about the workings of new and small firms that not only are poor representations of the reality of modern economies (Kirchhoff, 1994) but may actually be misleading in terms of the most appropriate public policies.

Among these assumptions are the views that (1) the entrepreneurial process leading to a firm birth is a unique and distinct event, not widespread in modern economies; (2) new and small firms have a minor role in economic growth and adaptation; (3) new firms are created by "solo entrepreneurs" acting on their own and solely for their own benefit; (4) new firms are initiated by people who are not well integrated in the modern economy, as better-trained, more competent workers pursue long-term jobs in established firms; (5) new firms appear almost instantaneously in response to new opportunities and trends; (6) there is little or no social cost to the start-up process, only riches for successful entrepreneurs; and (7) the typical new business is solely oriented toward maximizing profits or return on equity.

The following analysis of the entrepreneurial process, based largely on the exploration of two representative samples of individuals involved in the start-up process and three representative samples of those responsible for the creation and management of new firms, provides evidence relevant to all of these orientations or assumptions. Most appear to be inaccurate or misleading. This assessment of these assumptions suggests that a more complex model of modern economic growth and adaptation is required— perhaps one that gives a central role to the "entrepreneurial engine"—if policy makers are to receive useful input. This is pursued in more detail in Chapter 9.

THE SIGNIFICANCE OF NEW FIRMS

The original analysis that indicated that a majority of new jobs were created by new and small firms (Birch, 1981) has led to a substantial amount of research on the sources of gross and net (gains less losses) job growth (Armington and Odle, 1982; Birch, 1987; Kirchhoff, 1994). Despite recent controversy regarding some technical aspects of developing these estimates (Davis, Haltiwanger, and Schuh, 1993, 1996), analysis of data from twelve member countries of the Organization for Economic Cooperation and Development (OECD) indicates that gross and net job gains for the past decade are generally higher among smaller firms and *never* higher among large firms (Schreyer, 1995).

Independent firm births are one major source of job gains. For example, over the 1976–88 period in the United States, independent firm births provided 25% of gross job gains, independent firm expansions 29%, branch births 32%, and branch expansions 14% (Reynolds and Maki, 1991, Table 4.7).

In most advanced economies a downward shift in the size distribution of firms has occurred since the 1970s (Loveman and Sengenberger, 1990). A recent analysis of thirteen OECD member nations is presented in Table 1.1, indicating that the percentage of jobs in smaller firms, those with fewer than 100 employees, has increased for all countries except Japan. One major mechanism producing this shift is the founding of new firms, almost all of which are small.

As new data have become available, comparative analysis of nations, labor market changes, and economic subsectors suggests that new and small firms may have an independent, causal role in economic growth. Recent analysis of the European Union (EU) member states indicates that those states where the proportional growth in annual sales among small and medium firms exceeds that among large firms have greater growth in gross national product in the following year (Thurik, 1995). Analysis of the factors in labor market areas within the United States and Sweden indicates that higher firm birth rates have a statistically significant contribution to measures of regional economic growth in the following periods (Davidsson, Lindmark, and Olofsson, 1994; Reynolds, 1994). Comparisons of the factors leading to job growth across manufacturing subsectors in eight OECD countries have found that smaller than average firm size is a significant predictor of future subsector job growth (Schreyer and Chavoix-Mannato, 1995). A number of regional districts have been identified where specialized networks of small firms appear to be responsible for regional economic growth compared to similar regions dominated by a small number of large firms (Arzeni, 1995; Pyke, 1995).

Table 1.1

Small and Medium Enterprises (SMEs) in Advanced Economies: Shifts in Job Emphasis by Firm Size

Country	Years	Firm Size (# of employees, %)			
		1–19	*20–99*	*100–499*	*500 +*
Belgium (1)	1989–91	1.0	1.0	0.0	-2.0
Canada (2)	1984–89	0.6	6.8	-2.1	-3.7
Denmark	1988–90	9.2	-4.2	-0.9	-4.3
France (3)	1985–90	3.0	0.0	-1.9	-1.1
Germany	1988–90	2.1	-0.7	-0.4	-0.9
Greece	1984–88	-0.4	0.9	0.6	-0.6
Ireland (4)	1986–89	0.0	0.1	2.2	-0.9
Italy	1988–90	3.6	-0.8	-0.3	-2.0
Japan (2)	1988–91	-0.4	0.4	0.2	-0.7
Portugal	1986–90	2.5	2.5	-0.7	-3.5
Spain	1988–90	7.3	-3.8	-4.5	1.0
UK	1988–91	1.0	1.0	-0.5	-1.5
USA (5)	1988–90	7.4	-1.1	-1.5	-3.2

Notes: (1) Private sector only.
      (2) Manufacturing only.
      (3) Employees only, manager/owners excluded.
      (4) Does not equal 100% due to missing data by year for some firms.
      (5) Establishments, excluding agricultural sector.

Source: OECD, "Working Party on Small and Medium Enterprises, Globalization of Economic Activities and the Development of SMEs Synthesis Report," DSTI/IND/PME(95)3, 26, Table 4.

Virtually all current research finds that new and small firms have an important role in the creation of technical advances and economic innovations. While there is no question that large, established organizations and institutions (universities, government laboratories, etc.) have a major role in the creation of social innovations, new and small firms are also involved. This has become more apparent as the focus for analysis shifted from the resources devoted to research and development (always greater in larger firms) to measures of innovative activity (such as patents or new advances in specialized sectors). When the focus is on the source of innovations, new and small firms are clearly a major seedbed for advances (Acs and Audretsch, 1995).

This is consistent with the historical studies of the development of new industries or "functional niches" for organizations, either in economics or sociology, where it is referred to as (organizational) population ecology (Aldrich, 1990; Hannan and Carroll, 1992; Hannan and Freeman, 1989). These universally indicate that a large mass of new, small firms is present in the early periods of industry formation. The maturing of an industry is indicated by consolidation, as a few firms emerge from the mass of start-ups to dominate the new industry. New industries are, unfortunately, much easier to identify long after the industry birth and development have taken place.

New evidence is developing that entrepreneurship and self-employment are significant career options for many. It now appears that in the United States up to 4% of all adults, one in twenty-five, are trying to start a new firm at any given time. More details on this finding are presented in Chapter 3.

While approximately 8.6% of those in the U.S. labor force in 1993 had a primary classification as self-employed (U.S. Bureau of the Census, 1994, Table 614, 630), about 15% of heads of households report self-employment as their primary or secondary work relationship (Morgan et al., 1991). However, involvement may be much higher over the work career. The proportion of heads of household reporting periods of self-employment in a long-term panel study of household financial dynamics is presented in Table 1.2.

Older respondents, as shown in Table 1.2, were more likely to report some time in self-employment and longer periods of self-employment. Over two in five of those over forty years old reported periods of self-employment; one in five were involved for over five years. A similar finding was reported from a statewide sample of Minnesota adults; 43% were found

Table 1.2
Self-Employment over the Work Career

Age of Head of Household	Any Self-employment	Self-employment Duration	
	(%)	1–5 years (%)	6 or more years (%)
Less than 20 years old	5	5	—
20–29 years old	13	13	—
30–39 years old	28	22	6
40–49 years old	42	22	20
50–59 years old	40	20	20
60–69 years old	43	17	26

Source: Morgan et al., 1991, special tabulations.

to have some involvement in entrepreneurship (or self-employment) during their work career (Knudsen and McTavish, 1989).

In summary, new and growing small firms have important roles in (1) gross and net job contributions, (2) economic growth, (3) technical advances and innovation, (4) the formation of new industries, and (5) providing work career options for a large proportion of U.S. adults. Given the significance of new firms to so many areas of economic life, a careful treatment of their development—the entrepreneurial process—seems justified.

THE ENTREPRENEURIAL PROCESS

The entrepreneurial or firm start-up process, presented in Exhibit 1.1, is considered to begin when one or more persons initiate a firm start-up and ends, some time later and following much effort, when a viable new business is in place. The process of creating new firms, analogous to biological creation, is marked by three transitions.

The first transition begins when one or more persons first commit time and resources to founding a new firm. It is convenient to call the individuals involved "nascent entrepreneurs." Once "conception" has taken place, gestation occurs as the business structure develops, and the operational procedures emerge. The more important new terrain to be mapped includes the details associated with the events and their timing within firms-in-gestation.

The second transition occurs when the nascent entrepreneurs (alone or as a team) complete the gestation process. The more positive outcome is the successful launching of the new firm. But a more common result may be withdrawal from the effort, in which case no firm birth will occur. The general parameters associated with each outcome are now available.

The third transition marks the fledgling new firm's successful shift to an established new firm. If business activity for five years is considered an indication of a transition from firm infancy to adolescence, then recent analysis suggests that from half to three-quarters of new firms successfully complete the third transition (Kirchhoff, 1994; OECD, 1994, Table 3.10).

It is now possible to consider the proportion of adults actively involved in a new business start-up, the definition of firm conception. As mentioned before, preliminary evidence suggests that one of twenty-five U.S. adults is so involved. For the first time, perhaps, it is also possible to identify what

Exhibit 1.1
The Entrepreneurial Process

Adult	Nascent	Fledgling	Established
Population—(I)→	Entrepreneur(s)—(II)→	New Firm—(III)→	New Firm
(Conception)	(Gestation)	(Infancy)	(Adolescence)

types of persons are willing to take the steps required to launch a new firm. We have various descriptions of those who successfully launch new firms (Shaver and Scott, 1991). But we have not known—until these studies were completed—whether those who successfully start new firms are in any way different from those adults who do not become nascent entrepreneurs. Such information is important if governments want to encourage more people to start new firms.

More should be known about the second transition, as start-ups complete gestation, are born, and become fledgling new firms. What ingredients distinguish successful firm births from start-up efforts that are abandoned? Do specific steps increase the odds that a new firm will emerge from gestation? Do characteristics of the individuals make the difference in the rates of transformation from nascent entrepreneur to new firm owner, or has it more to do with the context in which the gestation process takes place? Learning what affects the rates of transformation can direct efforts toward increasing the number of firms in gestation that lead to firm births. Similar information may also help us to better understand what characteristics of the transition lead to a longer life for a new firm.

There has been some information about the third transition, but it tends to be ambiguous. Two portrayals of the early life course of firms have developed. Some analyses support the "liability of newness" argument that firm mortality declines constantly following firm birth. In the earliest years the firm death rates are the highest (Stinchcombe, 1965; Carroll, 1983; Freeman, Carroll, and Hannan, 1983). Other evidence supports the inverted U-shaped pattern, referred to as the "liability of adolescence," where death rates are highest after a brief period—perhaps of several years—where they are very low (Ben-Ner, 1988; Bruderl and Schussler, 1990; Bruderl, Priesendorfer and Ziegler, 1992; Finchman and Levinthal, 1991; Preisendorfer and Voss, 1990; Reynolds and Miller, 1992). The controversy centers on the presence of high or low risk of death early in the life of the new firm. As much of the analysis has been done with a wide range of data sets with varying definitions of firms, "firm births," and "firm deaths," it can be resolved only with the development of a panel of firm start-ups that can track the developments utilizing all definitions of a "firm birth." The following chapters provide some evidence in this regard.

Some would argue (Boeker, 1989) that actions during the gestation stage "shape" or "imprint" the firm such that the ability to react to market forces is severely constrained. Decisions on the allocation of resources during gestation may make it difficult to deploy these resources later in the firm's life. Thus, the fate of the "established" new firm may depend as much on actions taken during gestation as on market forces. The ensuing chapters attempt to fill in some of the gaps in our knowledge of the impact of this impressionable period on subsequent outcomes, be they firm birth or firm growth and development.

EFFECTIVE PUBLIC POLICY

Given the substantial impact on society from a vigorous entrepreneurial sector, government officials may wish to affect its level and intensity. Such intervention may be considered as affecting the transitions, shown in Exhibit 1.1, that are central to the process.

- Encourage more individuals to initiate start-up efforts, becoming nascent entrepreneurs working with firms in gestation.
- Assist start-up efforts, to improve the rate at which firms in gestation become fledgling new firms.
- Nurture fledgling new firms, to increase the proportion that survives the early years to become established new firms.
- Promote and encourage high-growth new firms, known to be a disproportionate source of new firm jobs.

The programs or policies that would be more effective at each stage of the process may differ not only in terms of their content or emphasis but in terms of their costs and political feasibility.

The following analysis considers the relative significance of alternative public policies for enhancing the yield from the entrepreneurial process.

DATA SOURCES

The ideal procedure to explore the entrepreneurial process would be a complete census of all individuals who decided to create a new firm and systematic tracking of their efforts until they succeeded in launching an established new firm or abandoned their efforts. This would, however, be very expensive—to track all adults in their work years to locate nascent entrepreneurs—and take a considerable period of time—as it would probably take six to ten years for the successful efforts to be completed.

There have been, however, efforts to study parts of the process. A number of studies have explored the third transition, from fledgling new firm to established new firm, usually with samples of "newly registered firms" or, using retrospective historical analysis, with all firms located in a given economic sector after it is clear that a new industry has emerged. As mentioned, these results have been inconsistent. There have also been a number of efforts to describe "entrepreneurs" by utilizing samples of those in the labor force who report they are self-employed, although there is some question if this is an appropriate criterion for identifying efforts to initiate new firms. As discussed later, the majority of nascent entrepreneurs identified in representative samples have an established role in the labor force, usually a full-time job.

An alternative procedure for locating nascent entrepreneurs and firms-in-gestation is emphasized in the following analysis. It is based on a representative sample of those eighteen years or older who are asked if they are trying to start a new firm. If those who respond "yes" indicate an appropriate level of activity, they are considered nascent entrepreneurs. Once identified, their efforts are described, and their success is tracked in follow-up studies. This procedure has been utilized twice, once with a representative sample of Wisconsin adults obtained in 1991–92 and once with a representative sample of adults from the forty-eight contiguous U.S. states in fall 1993. Follow-up interviews were conducted with those identified as nascent entrepreneurs eight to eighteen months after the initial interviews.

Three other data sets on new firms are also involved in the analysis. Two are based on representative samples of new entries in the Dun and Bradstreet Dun's Market Identifier File, one from Pennsylvania in 1986 and the other from Minnesota in 1987. The third is based on a representative sample of new listings in the Wisconsin unemployment insurance file in 1992. Follow-up interviews were completed for all three samples. The same procedure was used in data collection in all three new firm surveys: representative samples of new listings were obtained from a census of new listings, all listings were screened for suitability in an initial phone call (only half qualified), and a combination of mailed questionnaires and phone interviews was used to obtain high response rates (60–76%), limited only by the time and resources available.

The relationship of the data sets to the entrepreneurial process is presented in Exhibit 1.2. It should be clear that they cover different transitions. The surveys of nascent entrepreneurs and the follow-up interviews cover the first two transitions. The three data sets on the new firms primarily deal with the third transition. While no single cohort has been tracked over all three transitions, much of the information developed from all the data sets has used the same interview items and the same structure, considerably simplifying comparisons over time and across data sets.

All five data sets with complete documentation on sampling procedures and interview schedules are now in a public archive, the University of Michigan Inter-University Consortium for Political and Social Research (ICPSR), and available for analysis by others.[1] Data on nascent entrepreneurs are part of the Wisconsin Entrepreneurial Climate Study data sets (Reynolds and White, 1993b) and a segment of the survey of consumer attitudes data for two months (Economic Behavior Program, 1993a,b). New firm data are provided in two data sets and part of the Wisconsin Entrepreneurial Climate study data (Reynolds, 1987b, Reynolds, Freeman, and Oshana, 1987, Reynolds and White, 1993b). No follow-up data have been, as yet, included in these public archives.

In both types of data sets—two on nascent entrepreneurs and three on new firms—the same general results have been obtained. There has been little evidence among the three new firm samples, once geographic context and economic sector are taken into account, that there are substantial and

Exhibit 1.2
Data Sets and the Entrepreneurial Process

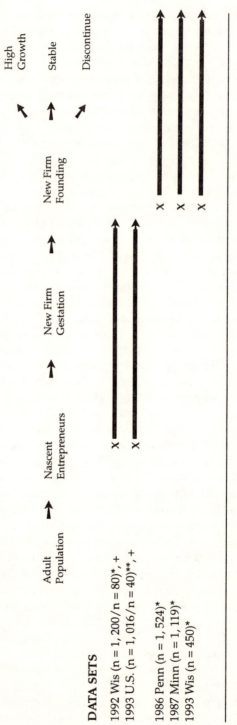

* ICPSR, University of Michigan, as specific data sets.

** Included in ICPSR, University of Michigan, as part of monthly Survey of Consumer Attitudes.

+ First figure is the size of the adult population sample; second figure is the number of nascent entrepreneur, identified in the screening.

sustained differences among the three states: Minnesota, Pennsylvania, and Wisconsin. Indeed, some of the descriptive information is almost identical among the different samples. The two surveys designed to identify nascent entrepreneurs indicate some differences, but these may be due to the use of slightly different interview schedules and the difference in the composition of the U.S. and Wisconsin adult populations.

In most important respects, these different samples are very similar, which provides strong evidence that other U.S. samples will provide the same types of results. Extrapolation to other countries—where cultural values regarding entrepreneurship, the economic structure, and the relationship between business and government may all be quite different—should be done with considerable caution, at least until comparable data from others countries are available.

CONCEPTIONS OF MODERN MARKET ECONOMIES

Of the previously cited seven assumptions about entrepreneurship and new firms in modern economies, the preceding discussion has provided evidence with regard to several. First, it would appear that new-firm births are not a unique and distinctive event. Second, there is substantial evidence that new and small firms have a very substantial role in economic growth and adaptation. Third, it would appear that participating in a new or small firm as an owner/manager is an important work career event for a substantial proportion of the labor force. It may, however, may be one of many work activities pursued between labor force entry and retirement.

ORGANIZATION OF THE BOOK

This book is organized around four topics: (1) the entrepreneurial process; (2) the transformation of both nascent entrepreneurs to fledgling new firms and fledgling new firms to established new firms; (3) the entrepreneurial participation of two specific groups, women and minorities; and (4) the implications of findings for public policy.

An overview of the entrepreneurial process and its impact on economic growth is presented in Chapter 2. Chapter 3 reviews the participation of adults in the entrepreneurial process and how they go about the start-up process. Chapter 4 reviews what has happened to the start-up efforts described by the nascent entrepreneurs identified in the initial survey, specifically, which have become new firms and what makes these efforts unique.

Chapter 5 explores the status of new firms, which have substantial variation in size. The analysis is oriented around factors associated with different new firm growth trajectories. Chapter 6 considers the persistence of new firms in some detail, considering those factors that lead some new firms to complete the third transition to become established firms.

Chapter 7 explores gender differences in the entrepreneurial process. It covers both nascent entrepreneurs and new firm owners. Chapter 8 examines differences between whites and nonwhites in their entrepreneurial participation and experiences.

Chapter 9 provides an overview of the entrepreneurial process and a commentary on the assumptions about modern market economies. In this context the "entrepreneurial engine," the recurrent contributions to economic well-being provided by a continuous flow of new jobs through the entrepreneurial process, is introduced. It concludes with a discussion of implications for public policy and what new entrepreneurs might expect as they participate in the entrepreneurial process. A postscript discusses the major implications for future research on the creation of new firms.

NOTE

1. Data sets may be acquired by contacting the Inter-University Consortium for Political and Social Research, University of Michigan, P.O. Box 1248, Ann Arbor, Michigan 48106. Descriptive material is provided on a Web site, "http://www.icpsr.umich.edu," which includes code books for most data sets. Reference numbers are as follows: Minnesota New Firm Survey, 1986: ICPSR No. 6505; Pennsylvania New Firm Survey, 1979–84: ICPSR No. 6526; Wisconsin Entrepreneurial Climate Study: ICPSR 6241; U.S. Survey of Nascent Entrepreneurs included as Part F of Survey of Consumer Attitudes, October and November, 1993: ICPSR Nos. 6765 and 6766.

Chapter 2

Economic Growth and Entrepreneurial Activity: Symbiosis in Action

Entrepreneurial activity generating new businesses prevents employment declines and leads to economic growth. Market economies are dynamic: firms are born and die. Jobs are created and destroyed. Unless there are continuing sources of new businesses, it is unlikely that a region can prosper for long. Growing regions, however, also encourage entrepreneurial activity. There is clearly a circular relationship—entrepreneurship creates economic growth and economic growth begets entrepreneurial activity. But do the contributions of new firm start-ups and entrepreneurial activity justify more careful attention to the start-up process? This issue alone is worth some attention.

Answering this question justifies attention to two aspects of the relationship between context and entrepreneurial activity. The first focuses on the evidence regarding economic growth associated with autonomous, independent firm births and their early development. The second considers the extent to which a typical region, in this case Wisconsin, promotes—and is seen to encourage—entrepreneurial activity. To what extent is the perception of Wisconsin as a "good place to start a business" important to those involved in the entrepreneurial process? Does it affect their entrepreneurial behavior?

NEW FIRMS AND ECONOMIC GROWTH

A great deal of attention has been given to the role of new firms in creating jobs. Because of the significance of this topic, several different estimates will be developed regarding the job creation contributions of new firms. There is, in addition, attention to the quality of the jobs provided by new firms and further analysis of the role of new firms in providing exports outside a region.

New Firms in Job Generation

An important question is the role of new firms and small firms in job generation. Many researchers (Birch, 1979 and 1987; Manson, Howland, and Peterson, 1984; White, et.al. 1994; White, Binkley, and Osterman, 1993) have wanted to learn which firms are responsible for the new jobs appearing in the economy. A major question has been: To what degree do new firms contribute to economic growth?

The stumbling block to answering such a question has been the lack of comprehensive business registries, or lists of all firms, new and established, that incorporate longitudinal records of firm sales and employment. While the perfect data set does not exist, several efforts to provide approximate estimates have been developed. A variety of definitional problems must be overcome. What is to be considered a new firm? How are jobs to be counted? When is a firm "new" versus "established"? Which jobs are associated with a firm birth, and which from early growth? How can one determine the net job creation from a given sector—say, small firms—that is the source of both job creation and job destruction? How can one ensure that the measures have covered all of the businesses, new and established? Are independent operating units separated from branches owned by a multisite firm? Should this extend to self-employment or only firms with employees? Are all new firms entrepreneurial, or only those with innovative products and high-growth trajectories?

Different answers to these technical issues can lead to different answers regarding the contributions of entrepreneurship to economic growth. As a result, we provide several answers, which are similar with regard to the most important points.

U.S. National Data. Job counts are one measure of economic activity, one that does not need to be corrected for inflation. One federal government effort has been tracking jobs for each U.S. county since 1969; it provides a good measure of annual changes in the total number of jobs (U.S. Department of Commerce, 1995). Measuring economic growth with jobs has a unique feature. Because of the number of part-time positions and people doubling up with several jobs, the number of jobs is usually 10–15% higher than the number of employed persons.

A complementary effort by the U.S. Small Business Administration tracked the sources of business job gains and losses for six two-year periods, from 1976 through 1988.[1] Extensive editing of a commercial credit rating register for the entire United States (Dun's Market Identifier File) allows individual business locations (called establishments) to be classified as single-site businesses or as branches of a firm with headquarters located in the same county, same state, or outside the state. By comparing the national registers for successive years, it was possible to determine the changes in jobs provided by different types of businesses due to establishment births, expansions, contractions, or deaths.

The results are presented in Table 2.1 for the United States as well as Minnesota, Pennsylvania, and Wisconsin. These states have been the context for surveys of new firms discussed in the following analysis. This comparison helps to indicate to what extent they are typical of patterns in the United States.

Over the 1976–88 year period, as shown in Table 2.1, the number of jobs grew about 30% for the United States, Minnesota, and Wisconsin and about 20% for Pennsylvania. This is reflected in the annual rate of job increase, slightly higher than 2% for the United States, Minnesota, and Wisconsin, slightly less for Pennsylvania. The annual rate of job churning, the percentage of jobs created or lost each year, was slightly higher for the United States (19%) than for the three states, where it was about 17%. Still, at least one in six jobs was created or destroyed each year.

The sources of job creation indicate that about one in five new jobs came from the birth of autonomous new firms. This would include all jobs created up to the first two years of operation. Further, one-third or more of the new jobs were produced from local firm expansions: expansion of a single-site firm, or expansion or birth of a branch owned by a headquarters located in the same county.

The smallest proportion of new jobs, about one in ten, came from the birth or expansion of branches owned by a firm headquartered elsewhere in the same state. Finally, about three in ten of all new jobs were provided by the birth or expansion of branches owned by a firm headquartered outside the state.

Several conclusions are justified by this analysis. First, there is a substantial level of job churning in the United States and the three states selected for analysis. Second, the birth of autonomous firms and their local expansion (either at a single site or a branch within the same county) provide over half of all job creation; the other major source is the births and expansions of branches owned by firms with a multistate presence. Third, there are no dramatic differences between the patterns found in the United States and those of the three states selected for analysis. Hence, it seems appropriate to assume that the patterns found in Wisconsin, Minnesota, and Pennsylvania are probably similar to those found across the United States.

Other features of the relationship of firm births and job creation can be explored with this information, as presented in Table 2.2. The average values over the twelve-year period can be used to get an overall estimate of annual firm birthrates, per 1,000 human population. This is 1.6 for the entire United States, and the three states are in the same order of magnitude, although Pennsylvania is the lowest with 1.17 annual new firm births per 1,000 human population.

The last column in Table 2.2 indicates the average number of jobs provided by these new firms during their birth period, which averages one year for this data set. The four estimates are remarkably close, varying from

Table 2.1
Job Growth and Sources: U.S. and Selected States, 1976–88

Year	1976	1978	1980	1982	1984	1986	1988	Average Job Growth (1976–88)
Private sector, nonagricultural jobs (1,000):								
United States	101,376	109,608	113,726	114,152	120,769	126,616	134,063	32%
Minnesota	1,971	2,122	2,244	2,195	2,334	2,443	2,579	31
Pennsylvania	4,483	4,716	4,767	4,666	4,799	4,987	5,297	18
Wisconsin	1,740	1,910	1,958	1,900	1,990	2,072	2,213	27
								Average (1976–88)
Job change (annual rates):								
United States		4.1%	1.9%	0.2%	2.9%	2.4%	2.9%	2.4%
Minnesota		3.8	2.9	-1.1	3.2	2.3	2.8	2.3
Pennsylvania		2.6	0.5	-1.1	1.4	2.0	3.1	1.4
Wisconsin		4.9	1.3	-1.5	2.4	2.1	3.4	2.1
Annual job churning (% job gains + losses):								
United States		19%	18%	18%	18%	20%	21%	19%
Minnesota		17	16	16	16	18	18	17
Pennsylvania		16	16	16	16	17	18	17
Wisconsin		17	17	15	17	17	18	17
Sources of job creation (% from each source)								
Autonomous firm births:								
United States		28%	21%	24%	27%	22%	23%	24%
Minnesota		31	20	23	27	20	18	23
Pennsylvania		29	18	22	27	23	22	23
Wisconsin		26	21	21	22	22	19	22

16

Year	1978	1980	1982	1984	1986	1988	Average (1976–88)
Autonomous firm expansions, county-owned branch births, expansions:							
United States	31%	35%	36%	34%	36%	34%	34%
Minnesota	35	42	44	42	41	49	42
Pennsylvania	31	36	36	36	37	34	35
Wisconsin	38	36	39	40	39	43	39
Stated owned branch births and expansions:							
United States	11%	11%	11%	10%	10%	11%	11%
Minnesota	11	17	9	10	12	10	11
Pennsylvania	11	12	11	11	12	11	12
Wisconsin	12	13	12	11	12	11	12
Out-of-state owned branch births and expansions:							
United States	30%	33%	29%	28%	32%	33%	31%
Minnesota	23	21	24	21	26	22	23
Pennsylvania	29	33	31	26	28	32	30
Wisconsin	23	30	29	27	27	27	27

Notes: Data on total jobs from U.S. Department of Commerce, Regional Economic Information System: CD-ROM, May 1995. Data on sources of job gains and losses from special tabulations of Small Business Data Base, U.S. Small Business Administration.

Table 2.2
Estimates of Annual Firm and Job Births

	Total Human Population Avg: 76–86 (1,000s)	Annual Firm Births Avg: 76–88	Firm Births per 1,000 Human Population	Firm Births New Jobs Avg: 76–88 (1,000s)	Jobs/Firm Birth
United States	229,097	365,578	1.60	2,409	6.58
Minnesota	4,090	6,398	1.57	41	6.41
Pennsylvania	11,845	13,910	1.17	99	7.09
Wisconsin	4,689	6,263	1.34	41	6.53

Notes: Population data from U.S. Department of Commerce, Regional Economic Information System: CD-ROM, May 1995. All other data from special tabulations of Small Business Data Base, U.S. Small Business Administration.

6.41 to 7.09, with the U.S. average at 6.58. This is further evidence that the patterns found in any one state are likely to be present in the others.

Wisconsin, Unemployment Insurance Registry Estimate. Another data set that can be used to estimate the sources of net Wisconsin employment growth is the state unemployment insurance file. All employers of one or more persons are required to file quarterly with the state unemployment insurance office. These records, known as the ES202 file, can be used to track individual establishments as well as firms with more than one location to determine quarterly or annual changes in employment and payroll.

A recent analysis of eight metropolitan economies in Wisconsin for 1991 to 1994 was based on this information (White, 1995). It was found that the percentage of employment attributable to autonomous, single-site employers was 51% in 1994. In metropolitan areas of the state the percentage of employment attributable to single-site employers varied from a low of 42% to a high of 67%. In some cases the absolute change in single-site employment was positive for the three-year period. In others it was decreasing. Overall, though, single-site employers in the eight areas collectively lost almost 44,000 jobs, while the multisite employers added over 114,000. Thus, single-site firms, while still responsible for over half of all employment, are currently becoming increasingly less important. It was not possible, in this case, to separate locally owned branches from those owned by firms with headquarters outside Wisconsin; some branches may have been part of local or state multisite firms. What these data do not contain, however, are the self-employed and others who do not report to the state unemployment agency. With numerous reports of growing self-employment, multisite employment may not be quite as important as these numbers imply.

If we examine recent years in Wisconsin (1991–94) and calculate the average number of actual new firms appearing on the unemployment insurance rolls and the number of employers associated with their appearance, we get another estimate of the role of these new endeavors for Wisconsin. We find that approximately 12,600 new, autonomous, single-site employers appear annually on the unemployment insurance rolls. They added an average of 82,400 employees to the state each year.

While new listings of employers appear annually, the entries are not always new firms. The new listings may include older firms that failed to report earlier, established employers that were small but decided to add employees, established employers that migrated from outside the state, and employers that had more than one location but reported all employment from one location inside the state. To explore the nature of the entries on the new listings, in 1992 we telephoned about 1,000 of these new listings and found that not all represented autonomous, Wisconsin-based, new businesses. In fact, about 50% of these respondents were new, independent, Wisconsin-based firms. We, therefore, divide the 82,400 employees by two to generate an estimate of the annual contribution of new, independent firms. This estimate, 41,200, is extremely close to the twelve-year average of new firm births of 41,000 reported in Table 2.2. The closeness of two estimates from two independent sources increases confidence in the overall result.

Wisconsin: New Firm Survey Estimate. To complete our triangulation to determine the employment contribution of new firms, we need to examine what we think may be the most accurate of the estimation methods available, survey results. The third estimate is based on the survey of a representative sample of new, autonomous firms in Wisconsin. More details of the survey follow in succeeding chapters. We can use the numbers derived from the survey to estimate the job contributions of new firms. The numbers are taken from the survey of 449 new firms that started business January 1, 1987, or later and were in existence in 1992.

We created this third estimate by computing just how many employees the average new firm had in its first year, as illustrated in Table 2.3. (This estimate applies only to new businesses with employees and does not include the newly self-employed.) We then added to that average the number of owners/managers who were involved in starting and operating the firm who were not reported as employees of that firm. In this instance, because of different reporting requirements for firms with different legal construction, we add a portion of the average number of firm owners/managers.

The big news is that a first-year firm that starts with employees, as opposed to others started by those who become self-employed on their own, creates, as shown in Table 2.3, 5.28 positions. This is slightly less than the 6.5 presented in Table 2.2, but this higher figure covers more years in the early life of the firm, providing more time for growth. Survey sample firms grow to an average of 8.14 positions per firm by the fourth year. If we multiply the average new firm size by the estimated number of new,

Table 2.3
Annual New Firm Job Creation in Wisconsin

First Year of Operation	Average per New Firm (1)	Total for 6,300 New Firms (2)	Distribution
Employees (avg.)	4.33	27,279	82%
Owner/managers (avg.)	0.95 (3)	5,985	18
Total positions	5.28	33,264	100

Notes: (1) Based on a representative, weighted sample of 398 Wisconsin new firms with initial sales occurring after January 1, 1987. Details of the sample and data collection are discussed later in the report.

(2) The 1992–1994. Wisconsin unemployment insurance filings register includes 12,392 listings initiated in 1992; 12,813 in 1993; and 12,673 in 1994. These are firms that are single-site and autonomous. Phone verification of a sample of these listings has determined that about one-half are independent, Wisconsin-based, new starts, or about 6,300 per year. Analysis of these numbers was completed by University of Wisconsin Urban Research Center for this project.

(3) The average team consists of 1.7 persons. Because sole proprietorships and partnerships have different reporting requirements for owner-workers, the average owner/manager number is reduced to take into account those individuals already appearing in the "employee" count.

autonomous, Wisconsin-based firms, we find that these firms create over 33,000 new jobs in their first year. If we add the average start-up team size to the employee total, we find the average number of positions is 6.06, and the total number of first-year jobs created is 38,178.

The total number of positions estimated from this survey (33,264), reported in Table 2.3, is relatively close to the annual average (41,000) based on the small business data set, reported in Table 2.2, and the 41,200 figure derived earlier from the unemployment insurance registry[2] analysis. When three independent estimates provide the rather similar result, it increases confidence that all reflect the same phenomenon and that the phenomenon is accurately described. These figures all indicate that the contribution to the state economy of new, single-site firms is important. In fact, in the early 1990s, these new, independent firms accounted for somewhere between 41% and 50% of the net annual employment growth experienced in the state. Those figures indicate the importance of new firm starts to the economic health of the region.

Job Quality

Obviously, the most basic concern with regard to economic development is the number of jobs created by new business activity. But related to this is a concern for job quality. For example, do the jobs bring new income into the area? That is, are they "export-based" jobs? A related question is how much the new jobs pay. Are they low-wage or high-wage jobs? Previous surveys of new firms in Minnesota and Pennsylvania found that three-fourths of jobs created by new firms required post-high school education and training (Reynolds and Freeman, 1987; Reynolds and Miller, 1988). The Wisconsin survey was able to provide additional information on average earnings per worker.

In their first year of operation the average annual earnings per worker for all reported workers in the new-firm sample was $15,900. For the state as a whole in 1992, a roughly comparable year, the average figure was $22,100. New firms in the sample pay less for the typical job, about 72% of the state average for all jobs. This is, however, above the minimum wages, which would be $12,000 per year for a person working fifty, forty-hour weeks at $6 per hour. By the fourth year of operation, average earnings per worker in current dollars had risen to $20,000. This is a 26% gain and shows that as firms mature, their payroll should contribute more to the local economy.

Examining the distribution of low- versus high-wage jobs requires the use of a surrogate; the "average earnings per worker" is created by dividing the total payroll in a firm by the total number of workers reported at the firm. Among first-year firms, we find that 15% of the employers have annual average earnings per worker of $25,000 or greater. This is considerably higher, over 40%, for all employers in the state. By the fourth year 19% of the new firms had average earnings per worker above $25,000. Over time new firms will increasingly move to higher levels of earnings, but the process appears to be a slow one.

Sales and Out-of-State Exports

Another way of measuring the regional contribution of new firms is through sales volume and the proportion of sales that are to buyers from outside the region. The higher sales level or the higher the proportion of sales to outsiders, the greater the contribution of new firms to the regional economy. Exports generate new income for the exporting region.

In their first year the average sales per Wisconsin new firm was $190,500. If we assume that is true for the 6,300 new firms born each year, their collective first-year sales were over $1.2 billion. For the 72% that will survive to year five with average sales of $500,000, their aggregate annual sales will be about $2.3 billion. If the self-employed, sole proprietors, and numerous family-owned businesses that do not have to submit unemployment tax payments were to be included, these average figures would be a little smaller. On the other hand, both the number of new businesses and the number of jobs generated by new business activity would be enhanced if these other types of firms were included.

In terms of export activity, a small proportion of firms tended to provide the majority of the out-of-state exports. To illustrate this pattern, firms were classified in terms of a focus on a national market (including international sales), a regional market, with a focus on exports into the adjacent states, or an internal or local market. The patterns developed from the surveys of new firms in Minnesota, Pennsylvania, and Wisconsin are presented in Table 2.4. In this case, the analysis is based on the data assembled in the year in which the survey was conducted, including firms one to six years old.

The same general patterns are found in all three states: four-fifths of all new firms emphasize the local, intrastate markets. In all three states, about 10% of the new firms have a strong emphasis on national markets (including Canada and other international sales). Beyond this, there is more commerce with adjacent states among Pennsylvania new firms, and there is less for those in Minnesota and Wisconsin. This no doubt reflects the slightly more remote geographic situation of these north-central states.

Of the $2.4 billion annual sales among Wisconsin new firms in their fifth year, about 20%, or $450 million, involved sales outside Wisconsin, exports that enhanced Wisconsin's relative economic well-being. Only 2% of the total is estimated to have been direct sales to foreign customers, although undoubtedly a higher proportion found its way out of the country as part of final products assembled by others elsewhere.

Regardless of whether one considers participation in the entrepreneurial process or contributions of new firms to job growth, the entrepreneurial process should be considered an important aspect of any region's economic well-being, as Wisconsin's experience demonstrates.

Variations across Regions

Another issue for any state is whether new economic activity is uniformly distributed across it or whether, as in the past, certain areas of the

Table 2.4
New Firm Sales and Exports: Minnesota, Pennsylvania, and Wisconsin

	Survey Year	Annual Sales ($1,000)	Annual Exports ($1,000)	Export Focus		
				National	Regional	Local
Minnesota	1986	$514	$106	10%	6%	84%
Pennsylvania	1985	698	126	8	12	80
Wisconsin	1992	596	84	12	14	84

Notes: National Exporter: 50% or more total sales or $100,000 or more per year shipped outside state or adjacent states.
   Regional Exporter: 50% or more total sales or $100,000 or more per year shipped to adjacent states.
   Local: All other firms.

Source: Minnesota data from Reynolds and Miller, 1990, pg. 37; Pennsylvania data from Reynolds and Freeman, 1987, pg. 52; Wisconsin data tabulated for this presentation.

state benefit more than others. To analyze this issue, one must select a geographic area for study. This area must then be subdivided to measure the distributional impact of new firm activity on the subparts. For the purposes of this analysis, Wisconsin was divided into seven subareas, presented in Exhibit 2.1. Selected characteristics of these regions are presented in Table 2.5.

The seven subareas can be considered of three types. The four-county Milwaukee metropolitan area is the single, major, urban area. Three subareas are considered local economic centers, areas with a significant centralized population but fewer people than Milwaukee. These subareas include the central region, several counties around Madison (host of the state capital and a major campus of the University of Wisconsin); the southeast subarea, which includes the corridor between Milwaukee and Chicago; and the counties from Fond du Lac to Green Bay. The remaining three subareas—Northeast, Northwest, and Southwest—are considered predominantly rural.

Exhibit 2.1
Seven Regions of Wisconsin

Table 2.5
Selected Characteristics of Wisconsin Regions

Major City	Metropolitan		Regional Centers		Rural			State Total
	Milwaukee	Central	Fox Valley	So-East	No-East	No-West	So-West	
	Milwaukee	*Madison*	*Fond du Lac*	*Kenosha/ Racine*				
Human population, 1990 (1)								
Whites	1,157,877	516,797	874,916	531,210	499,957	516,934	364,375	4,461,066
American Indians	8,001	2,077	8,082	1,739	9,728	8,108	1,652	39,387
Asians	18,782	9,179	10,174	3,439	4,480	4,131	3,398	53,583
Blacks	197,183	11,295	3,941	29,575	725	981	839	244,539
Hispanics	51,306	7,489	8,110	19,545	2,695	2,327	1,722	53,586
Total	1,432,149	546,837	905,223	585,508	517,585	532,481	371,986	4,891,769
Whites	80.78%	94.51%	96.65%	90.73%	96.59%	97.08%	97.95%	91.20%
American Indians	0.56	0.30	0.89	0.30	1.88	1.52	0.44	0.80
Asians	1.31	1.68	1.12	0.59	0.87	0.78	0.91	1.10
Blacks	13.77	2.07	0.44	5.05	0.14	0.18	0.23	5.00
Hispanics	3.58	1.37	0.90	3.34	0.51	0.46	0.46	1.90
Total	100.00	100.00	100.00	100.00	100.00	100.00	100.00	100.00

	Metropolitan	Regional centers			Rural			State Total
		Central	Fox Valley	So-East				
Major City	Milwaukee	Madison	Fond du Lac	Kenosha/Racine	No-East	No-West	So-West	
Business population								
Autonomous firm births								
Annual avg., 1986–88	1,755	675	960	552	602	555	347	5,446
Total establishments, 1986	32,924	12,919	19,062	11,147	11,679	10,034	7,443	105,208
Proportion autonomous	77%	77%	77%	80%	80%	80%	78%	78%
Industry distribution:								
Agr. services/mining	1%	3%	2%	3%	3%	3%	4%	3%
Manufacturing	12	9	11	13	9	10	9	11
Business services	19	17	12	11	9	9	9	14
Distribution services	16	13	16	13	15	16	18	15
Local market	51	58	59	59	63	61	61	57
Total	100	100	100	100	100	100	100	100
Autonomous firm Birth rates, 1986–88:								
Per 100 establishments	5.3	5.2	5.0	5.0	5.2	5.5	5.2	5.2
Per 10,000 total population	12.3	12.3	10.6	9.4	11.6	10.4	11.6	11.1

Note: (1) Data based on 1990 U.S. Census data by county for Wisconsin. Hispanic estimates were developed by assuming all "other" ethnic categories were Hispanic and then subtracting the remaining Hispanic totals for the white count. This was justified by the pattern, which indicated that for Wisconsin over 90% of "other" ethnic categories were also included in the Hispanic category.

The business population is represented by the distribution of 105,208 establishments across the seven subareas. These establishments, defined as each single site where business is conducted, can be divided into autonomous (or independent) firms and headquarters and branches of other firms. Approximately four of five establishments are autonomous firms in Wisconsin, which is fairly constant across the seven subregions. The percentage of establishments in each of five types of industry categories is fairly similar for each subarea except for the largest, Milwaukee. Approximately three-fifths of all establishments are in industries oriented toward the local markets (construction; retail; consumer service; health, education, and social services). Only in Milwaukee does this ratio drop to about half of all establishments. Distributive services, which include all transportation as well as wholesale businesses, are about one in six of all establishments. Business services, including law firms, consulting firms, financial and real estate activities, as well as a range of photocopying, secretarial services, and the like, are about one in seven establishments but rise to one in five in the Milwaukee area and are less than one in ten in the rural subareas. Manufacturing establishments are about one in ten of all establishments. They constitute a slightly greater proportion in Milwaukee, Kenosha-Racine, and the Fox Valley and slightly less in other subareas. Agricultural services and mining are a small proportion (3%) in all subareas and hardly noticeable in Milwaukee (1%).

An important measure of entrepreneurial activity is birthrates of independent firms. Autonomous firm birthrates can be computed in terms of all existing establishments (autonomous firms and branches) or in terms of the human population. About five autonomous establishments appear each year for every 100 existing establishments, according to the Small Business Administration (SBA) data set. Little variation seems to exist across the subareas of the state. During 1986–88, about eleven autonomous firms appear annually for each 10,000 persons in a subregion. This varies somewhat across the subregions, ranging from 9.4 to 12.3 firms. This variation in pattern is related to the differences in the average size of the business establishments in the different areas. Subregions with low firm birthrates per population but higher firm birthrates per existing businesses, such as the Kenosha-Racine area, tend to have more businesses per human population because they have smaller businesses.

The homogeneity of both the industry structure and new firm births across the seven subregions of Wisconsin is more striking than the differences. The differences appear to reflect subtle variations associated with urban and regional centers. Given this overview, major differences in the entrepreneurial process related to different regions would not be expected. New businesses seem to form at fairly uniform rates across the state regardless of the rural or urban nature of the place. Thus, we can largely dismiss subregional location as a major factor in determining rates of entrepreneurship in Wisconsin. This is not, however, generally true across the United States, where there is substantial regional variation in birthrates of both autonomous firms and branches (Reynolds, Maki, and Miller, 1995).

SUPPORT FOR ENTREPRENEURSHIP: THE WISCONSIN EXAMPLE

There are two aspects to support for new firms and the entrepreneurial process. The extent to which there are special efforts to provide assistance to firms is one critical arena. The other is the perception of a context as a good location to start a business.

Programs to Assist New, Small Firms

One factor that may play a role in fostering entrepreneurial activity or its outcomes is the level of support provided for nascent entrepreneurs, business start-ups, and fledgling firms. Areas with more and better assistance programs may encourage people to come forward as nascent entrepreneurs and move successfully through the start-up process. The analysis of assistance programs in Wisconsin included two relevant activities. First, an inventory of all existing business assistance programs in the state was completed. The second involved asking nascent and discouraged entrepreneurs as well as new firm owners about their experience with these programs. We sought to learn not only their knowledge of such offerings but also their reaction to them.

In the summer of 1992, it was possible to identify at least 456 programs providing assistance in twenty-eight different categories, for a total of 752 distinct offerings in Wisconsin. As shown in Table 2.6, about half were offered statewide by a variety of state and federal agencies; the remaining half were provided within the seven regions, often by county or city governments or local, nonprofit organizations.

Among the services provided, technology-development assistance (198 providers) and information on financial resources (131 providers) were clearly the most popular. Together they accounted for 44% of all forms of assistance. The next most popular form of assistance was help in locating sites, with 38 providers accounting for 5% of the total. Other types of assistance included business incubators (32), a variety of continuing education courses (26 providers), general business management assistance (25 providers), marketing assistance (23 providers), and personnel management assistance (23 providers). Among those services least commonly available were minority business assistance programs (3 providers), retail/service business location assistance (5 providers), and women's business assistance (6 providers).[3]

Information on the knowledge, use, and reaction to these services was gathered from nascent and discouraged entrepreneurs and from new firm

Table 2.6
Wisconsin Assistance Programs by Type

	State-wide Offerings	Regional Offerings	Total Offerings
Accounting	4	17	21
Business advocacy groups	12	2	14
Business feasibility	4	4	8
Business plan	7	5	12
Business start-up, expansion	10	5	15
Continuing education	9	17	26
Financial counseling	13	8	21
Financing, information on sources	25	106	131
General business management	6	19	25
Government procurement (1)	6	3	9
Incubators	0	32	32
Information on laws and regulations	8	1	9
Information systems	7	7	14
International trade	11	6	17
Manufacturing systems technical	5	17	22
Marketing-demographic information	2	9	11
Marketing planning	5	18	23
Marketing research	8	10	18
Minority business	2	1	3
Networking	9	3	12
Patent and trademark	6	2	8
Personnel management	7	16	23
Retail/service business location	3	2	5
Site location	8	30	38
Technology development	181	17	198
Tourism business	4	2	6
Venture capital (2)	0	12	12
Women's business	4	2	6
Total	365	377	752

Notes: (1) Assistance in meeting government procurement guidelines and procedures.
(2) Includes small business development companies.

owners, discussed in the following chapters. The analysis appears to indicate a positive relationship between use of these assistance programs and entrepreneurial outcomes.

The Entrepreneurial Climate

There has been much discussion, particularly among politicians and the business press, about the extent to which some regions may have a positive "entrepreneurial climate." It is widely assumed that regions that are more hospitable for entrepreneurial activity will elicit more efforts to start new firms and, in turn, a higher level of firm births. This leads directly to efforts to measure the perception of a region as supportive for entrepreneurship. The initial question we ask, however, is: How does one define and measure the entrepreneurial climate? Following this, a variety of analyses is developed, including the entrepreneurial climate ratings of different groups of individuals, how this judgment may change over the start-up process, factors affecting the perception of the entrepreneurial climate, and how such judgments about the entrepreneurial climate may affect future business plans.

Measuring Perceptions of the Entrepreneurial Climate. A number of different strategies may be used to measure regional entrepreneurial climate. Each reflects a different conception of this feature. More global conceptions include the presence of special programs or government policies, the nature of the infrastructure, costs of doing business, and the like (Grant Thornton; *Inc.* Magazine; Center for Enterprise Development). In this analysis, the focus is on the perception of the individuals who are likely to be affected by the entrepreneurial climate, those who would actually take the initiative to pursue a new firm start-up and be responsible for launching a new business enterprise. The focus, then, is on developing a reliable measure of the perception of the local context as a good place for entrepreneurial activity.

The result was the development of a multi-item measure regarding judgments about the region as a good place to do entrepreneurship. While the initial list had eighteen items, it was found that a set of nine provided the best overall index. These nine are presented in Exhibit 2.2. They were chosen because of the high level of internal consistency in answering these items. By using a set of nine, the irregularities associated with the measurement procedure are minimized. The actual entrepreneurial climate score was the average response to these nine items.[4]

For each item, the respondent had four choices: strongly agree, agree, disagree, and strongly disagree. They were given values from 4 to 1 so that the higher the number, the more positive the response about their location as a place to start a new business. A neutral response would be the average of 4 and 1, or 2.50. Thus, if respondents thought that there was positive support for men and women starting new businesses, that new business

Exhibit 2.2
Entrepreneurial Climate Measure Items

Those with successful businesses get a lot of attention and admiration.

Young men are encouraged to be independent and start their own businesses.

Young women are encouraged to be independent and start their own businesses.

State and local governments provide good support for men starting new firms.

State and local governments provide good support for women starting new firms.

Bankers and other investors go out of their way to help new firms get started.

There are many examples of well respected people who made a success of themselves starting new businesses.

Among my family and friends . . . many of the men have started new firms.

Among my family and friends . . . many of the women have started new firms.

Note: Response alternatives: strongly agree (4), agree (3), disagree (2), strongly disagree (1).

owners were well regarded, that the state and local governments provided useful services, and that individuals knew others who had successfully started new businesses, then the climate should reflect a higher index score than for someone else who had just the opposite judgments.

The average for all typical adults in Wisconsin was 2.48, almost exactly neutral. Wisconsin adults, as a group, have neither a significantly positive nor negative attitude about the state as a place to start a new business. As no comparable data are available from any other state, it is not possible to compare Wisconsin with its neighbors—Illinois, Iowa, Minnesota, or Michigan—or with some of the more exotic locations—California, Florida, or Texas.

Participation in the Entrepreneurial Process and Reactions to the Climate. The greater the involvement in the entrepreneurial process, the more negative the judgment about the entrepreneurial climate. This is reflected in comparisons of those with different levels of involvement in the entrepreneurial process in Exhibit 2.3. Comparisons are provided of the standardized judgments of typical adults (n = 1,278) compared to nascent entrepreneurs (n = 93), discouraged entrepreneurs (n = 44), and those who have started new firms in the past six years (n = 426). The brackets indicate the 95% confidence interval. This is the range expected to include the true value for 95% (or nineteen out of twenty) of the samples. If two brackets do not overlap, the difference between the groups would be considered statistically significant (likely to occur 95% of the time). Data were gathered from new firm owners in two ways, by phone interviews (n = 131) and with a self-administered mail questionnaire (n = 295), using the same items to measure the entrepreneurial climate. There is apparently a difference in the response, with new firm owners completing the mail questionnaire on their own being more negative than those answering an interviewer's questions over the phone.

Exhibit 2.3
Entrepreneurial Climate Judgment by Participation in the Entrepreneurial Process

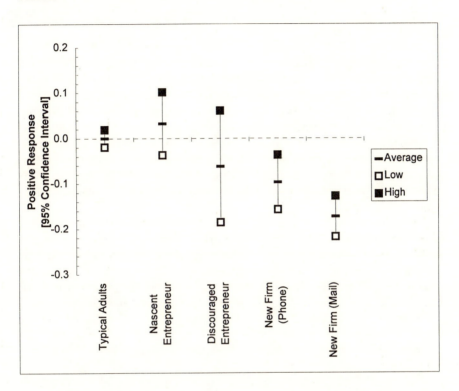

There is little question about the basic pattern, although the differences are not all statistically significant. Nascent entrepreneurs, those trying to start a new business, are more positive than typical adults. Discouraged entrepreneurs, those who tried to start a new business but gave up, are more negative. Those who tried to start a new firm and succeeded in putting a new business in place are the most negative.

This is consistent with a broader assessment of Wisconsin adults (Reynolds and White, 1993a, Exhibit 1.6). A positive judgment is more likely to occur among those who have less contact with the business world in Wisconsin: those not in the labor force, women, those over seventy years old, and those who have not gone beyond high school. Those with more contact with the world of work in Wisconsin—men, those in their middle years or with higher levels of education or higher household incomes—are less positive about the entrepreneurial climate.

Changes over the Entrepreneurial Process. The preceding results seemed to indicate that experience with starting a new business tended to decrease judgments about the region as a "good place to start a business."

However, this was a comparison of different individuals with different experiences. Confidence that the experience of starting a firm was the critical factor in creating a more negative judgment would be increased if the same individuals responded at different points in the entrepreneurial process.

This information is available from follow-ups from two different groups of participants: nascent entrepreneurs and new firm owners. Twelve to eighteen months after the initial interview, a second interview was completed with fifty-three of the ninety-three nascent entrepreneurs (described in Chapter 4). A second round of follow-ups was completed with 368 of the firms contacted in the first interview (described in Chapter 6). In both cases, the same items were asked in the second interviews, providing an opportunity for a second assessment of judgments about the entrepreneurial climate. Unfortunately, only eighty-three of the new firm principals completed both interviews by phone, so the number with valid comparisons is small (see Table 2.7).

Even with the small number of cases, the patterns are instructive. Those most heavily involved in the start-up process become more negative over time, which is true for the nascent entrepreneurs and, in particular, those with firms that have been discontinued. Those who have given up on the start-up, the discouraged entrepreneurs, seem to become more positive. Those with fledgling new firms become, relative to those with established new firms, even more negative. Those with established new firms (in business four or more years) may become, over time, less negative about the entrepreneurial climate. Perhaps there is hope for recovery.

Factors Affecting Entrepreneurial Climate Perception. Given the dramatic pattern found regarding changes in the entrepreneurial climate judgments, a number of analyses were implemented to explore potential sources of

Table 2.7
Changes in Perception of the Entrepreneurial Climate

Entrpreneurial Process Status	Number	Initial EC Score	Follow-up EC Score	EC Score Change
Discouraged entrepreneurs	22	2.43	2.50	0.07
Nascent entrepreneurs	30	2.49	2.37	0.13
Discontinued new firms	13	2.43	2.28	-0.16
Fledgling new firms	30	2.34	2.32	-0.02
Established new firms	40	2.37	2.40	0.03

Notes: Only new firm principals interviewed by phone in both interviews included in last three rows. No differences between interviews are statistically significant.

negative judgments. These included detailed examination of various aspects of the multi-item measure, individual attributes of the respondents, and features associated with the new businesses.

For example, there is a clear pattern associated with two of the nine items, presented in Table 2.8. Both are related to judgments about government support for new business and have the U-shaped pattern presented in earlier analysis. Discouraged and nascent entrepreneurs are very similar in their assessment on this feature of the environment. The rating is much lower for those with fledgling new firms and increases significantly for those whose firms are at least four years old, the established new firms. This is strong evidence that it is a direct assessment of government support that varies among those at different stages of the entrepreneurial process.

Personal background factors did not seem to have a major impact. Men were slightly more negative than women. Midlife adults had lower scores than young or older adults. There was some impact associated with educational attainment, but it was not systematic. Overall, personal characteristics were not associated with major differences in perceptions associated with the entrepreneurial climate.

Among the new firm owner/managers, a number of business characteristics were considered. There was some variation due to economic sector, with lower scores associated with agriculture, mining, and restaurants/bars (2.20) and higher scores in wholesale, retail, and health education and social services (2.45). Those with larger firms, presumably more successful, tended to have a slightly more positive perception of the entrepreneurial climate. However, there was no consistent pattern with annual sales, an alternative measure of firm success.

One factor that deserved more attention was the nature and extent of start-up problems associated with the new firm. There were some differ-

Table 2.8
Reaction to Selected Items by Participation in the Entrepreneurial Process

Agree/ Strongly Agree	Discouraged Entre's	Nascent Entre's		Fledgling New Firms	Established New Firms	
State and local governments provide good support						
for men	52%	47%	(NS)	22%	39%	(*)
for women	59%	43%	(NS)	26%	54%	(***)
starting new firms						

Notes: Samples weighted. Only phone interview respondents among new firm principals included. Statistical significance compared only within type, entrepreneurs or new firm principals: * = 0.05; *** = 0.001.

ences for seven of the forty-four start-up problems associated with the interviews. These are reported in Table 2.9, ranked in terms of the effect of the severity of the problems on differences in entrepreneurial climate scores. Those where major problems were associated with a more positive view of the entrepreneurial climate are placed at the top of the list.

Examining the problems reported in Table 2.9 indicates that problems with financing are the only ones that provide a significant negative impact on the entrepreneurial climate score. As difficulty with establishing a banking relationship or obtaining long-term funding increases, the judgments about the entrepreneurial climate become more negative. In contrast, those with more problems with government rules and regulations seem to have more positive judgments about the entrepreneurial climate. This may reflect positive experiences with government officials or satisfaction associated with managing more substantial new firms. In contrast, Table 2.8 indicates that the percentage agreeing that there is general support from government for those starting new firms is the lowest among those with fledgling new firms, increasing among those with established new firms.

Two types of direct contact with government were assessed in the interview. Only 43% of those with new firms reported special contact with a government: 25% with federal or state and 17% with county or local

Table 2.9
Start-up Problems and the Perception of the Entrepreneurial Climate

Problem	EC Score by Severity of Problem			Major-Never Difference
	Never	*Minor*	*Major*	
Coping with government regulations	-.09	0.22	0.23	0.14 (**)
Finding qualified technical/ professional staff	-.19	0.15	-.13	0.06 (NS)
Finding qualified managers	0.08	0.12	-.04	-.12 (NS)
Finding qualified employees	0.08	0.11	-.09	-.17 (NS)
Obtaining equity investments	0.09	0.14	-.16	-.25 (NS)
Establishing banking relationship	0.31	-.20	-.28	-.59 (***)
Obtaining long-term debt finance	0.45	-.11	-.22	-.77 (***)

Notes: Comparison based on standardized scores of all new firm principals, which allowed consolidation of phone and mail interview responses. Statistical significance from one-way analysis of variance: 0.01 = **; 0.001 = ***.

governments. While two-thirds considered this a helpful contact, one in six rated it negative. Overall, this small proportion with negative experiences did not seem to affect the aggregate assessments of the entrepreneurial climate.

Knowledge, use, and reaction to business assistance programs were another matter. Those who knew about programs, contacted them for assistance, and received help had a relatively high entrepreneurial climate score of 2.43. Those who made contact with a program but failed to receive the help they needed had a somewhat lower score of 2.27. But those who needed help and could not find a suitable source of assistance had a very low score of 2.06. Furthermore, both the type of assistance and the ratings of the assistance provided were associated with the entrepreneurial climate score.

We conclude from this examination that the experience with business assistance programs does materially influence one's perception of the entrepreneurial climate. It appears that if an effort were to be made to better acquaint new business owners and nascent entrepreneurs with the availability of these services, the entrepreneurial climate ratings of new business owners would rise. This may positively affect the message new business owners transmit to potential nascent entrepreneurs. This could, in turn, increase the rate at which nascent entrepreneurs transform into new business owners.

Entrepreneurial Climate Perceptions and Future Business Plans. Do judgments about the entrepreneurial climate make any difference? That is, are they related to the conduct of the business? A preliminary answer is provided by considering the relationship between the future plans of those with new businesses and their assessment of the entrepreneurial climate. "Future," in this case, refers to the next two to three years. Table 2.10 provides a list of future activities for new firms and distinguishes between those who say they are planning each activity and those who are not. The difference in their judgments regarding the entrepreneurial climate has been computed, and the list of future activities is ranked by this difference. That is, actions with the greatest positive difference between "with plan" and "without plan" are placed at the top; those with the greatest negative difference, at the bottom.

There does indeed seem to be a consistent relationship between plans and assessments of the climate. Those with no changes planned are slightly more positive than those with plans to change. Those employers who plan on expanding employment are more positive (modestly) than those who do not. Those who want to get out of the business, sell the business, change the product/service mix, reduce employment, relocate, or expand elsewhere are all considerably more negative than those who do not share such plans.

Two findings give credibility to the multi-item measure of the perception of the entrepreneurial climate. First, as discussed earlier, is systematic

Table 2.10
Perception of Entrepreneurial Climate and Future Plans

Changes Planned	% with Plan	Entrepreneurial Climate Score		
		w/o plan	*With plan*	*Difference*
No major change	34%	-0.6	0.12	0.18 (#)
Significant increase in employees	12	-0.3	0.20	0.23
Significant change in production process	4	0.00	0.10	0.10
Expand firm in other city	4	0.01	-.17	-.18
Change mix of products/ services	14	0.04	-.21	-.25
Get out of business	2	0.01	-.39	-.40
Relocate firm	3	0.01	-.48	-.47 (#)
Sell firm	5	-0.4	-.78	-.74 (***)
Significant decrease in employees	2	0.02	-1.24	-1.26 (****)

Notes: Comparison based on standardized scores. Statistical significance: # = 0.10; *** = 0.001; **** = 0.0001.

relationship between judgments about the entrepreneurial climate and future plans for the business. Second, is the overall pattern of change in the measure as individuals move through the entrepreneurial experience, high for nascent entrepreneurs just getting into the start-up process, lowest for those in the middle of the new firm birth transition, and then an increase among those whose firms survived the infancy period and have entered adolescence.

OVERVIEW AND IMPLICATIONS

There is substantial evidence that new firms have a significant contribution to job growth. There is evidence for the United States, as well as Minnesota, Pennsylvania, and Wisconsin, that in their first year new firms provide one-fifth of gross new jobs. The jobs provided by new firms may be equal to 40–50% of net, new job growth. Further, new firms appear to provide a substantial level of new sales as well as major out-of-state exports, although this is concentrated among 20% of the new start-ups. Further, the salaries paid by new firms exceed those expected from minimum wage positions, although they are somewhat less than the wages paid by established firms.

There is evidence that judgments about the entrepreneurial climate may vary and may have an impact on the start-up process. Use of a multi-item index to determine the extent to which individuals considered Wisconsin a "good place to start a business" found a distinctive pattern among those moving through the entrepreneurial process: positive judgments as they first become involved with a firm start-up, substantially more negative judgments as they reach the critical stage of the process—launching a new business—and a more positive view as the firms become established and survive the "liability of newness." Further, judgments about the entrepreneurial climate were affected by the ability to locate and receive assistance from programs designed to help new and small firms succeed. New firm owners with more negative perspectives on the entrepreneurial process, moreover, were more likely to plan reduction or abandonment of the business.

Given the contributions of new firms to economic well-being, the impact of government programs on the judgments about Wisconsin as a good place for entrepreneurial activity, and the relationship between judgments about the entrepreneurial climate and the conduct of the firm management, there seems to be a strong justification for more careful attention to the entrepreneurial process. Improved understanding—the focus of the ensuing chapters—may enhance the efficiency of public programs promoting economic growth and the effectiveness of those trying to initiate new firms.

CONCEPTIONS OF MODERN MARKET ECONOMIES

Regardless of how one approaches or analyzes the data, it is clear that two of the assumptions underlying the "perfect competition" market model are inconsistent with the data. First, new firm births are clearly not a rare and unique event. Second, new and small firms clearly have a major role in economic growth. Just how significant may vary, but it is clearly not negligible.

NOTES

1. The Small Business Data Base was developed for the United States for 1976–88 by the U.S. Small Business Administration (Office of Advocacy, U.S. Small Business Administration, *Handbook of Small Business Data* Washington, D.C.: U.S. Government Printing Office, 1988.). Special versions of these data, based on new entries in a commercial credit rating and marketing register (Dun and Bradstreet's Marketing Identifier files), can be used to estimate the number of jobs created or lost by establishment births, expansions, contractions, or deaths. A version of this database was developed to allow determination of whether an establishment was an autonomous firm (single location, independent business), a branch owned by a headquarters within the same state, or a branch owned by a headquarters outside the state. Data from this special version were provided by Regional Economic Development Associates, Inc. of Edina, Minnesota. The presentation covers about 80% of all jobs, excluding those in agricultural production, governments, and most self-employment.

2. In Wisconsin this file excludes certain categories of firms, such as those with only family employees, agricultural enterprises with fewer than ten employees, and the like, which may actually underestimate counts compared with the sample survey data.

3. It was not possible, with limited resources, to determine the size or scope of these different programs. This would have required gathering systematic information on staffing or budget of each provider. Further, it was not possible to gather information from the different providers regarding the amount of assistance provided—in terms of number of clients served or the amount of time given to each client.

4. Eighteen items were used to determine perceptions of Wisconsin's entrepreneurial climate. A factor analysis completed with a sample of adults, weighted to be representative of the population, indicated one dominant dimension composed of these nine items. The nine-item scale had a Chronbach's alpha, a measure of reliability, of 0.65.

Chapter 3

Nascent Entrepreneurs
and Business Start-ups

N ew businesses make a considerable contribution to regional development. But where do new businesses come from? There has been
substantial progress in predicting new firm birthrates on the basis of the
contextual features (Reynolds, Storey, and Westhead, 1994) and understanding how general processes—legitimation and competition—can influence the existence of organizations such as new firms (Hannan and Carroll,
1992). Contextual features and general processes, however, do not start new
firms; people start new firms. Individuals acting alone or with a team are
responsible for launching new businesses. Despite the importance of this
activity, how individuals create new firms is one of the least-understood
features of modern societies.

Knowledge about this process would be of considerable value to two
important constituencies involved in the entrepreneurial process: (1)
those implementing and managing these new businesses and (2) those
who develop public policies related to them. In terms of improving public
policy, it has not been possible to provide reliable empirical descriptions
of the start-up process for those seeking to create a more supportive
context for entrepreneurship. This hiatus may have created or maintained
barriers to the development of effective public policy. For those active in
attempting to start new firms, more complete information may encourage
more participation as well as improve the outcomes for those in the
start-up process.

This chapter answers some of the questions about the entrepreneurial
process. It focuses on those individuals who, at the time of the survey, were
attempting to start a new business ("nascent entrepreneurs"). Following a
discussion of how they are located, there is attention to their unique
characteristics, the types of firms they are working on, reactions to the

immediate context, financial needs and aspirations for the new firms, and the use of services to assist business start-ups.

NASCENT ENTREPRENEURS

Nascent entrepreneurs are those persons currently taking explicit steps to start a new business. One of the most fundamental issues is to determine the proportion of the adult population involved in a business start-up at any given time. Once these persons are identified, the focus shifts to learning more about them, the businesses they are attempting to start, and features of the start-up experience.

The interview schedule also identified those in other stages of the entrepreneurial process. Closely related to nascent entrepreneurs are "discouraged" entrepreneurs, individuals who have taken steps to start a firm but have decided, by the time of the interview, not to follow through. These individuals are similar to nascent entrepreneurs, and, where appropriate, they are included in the analysis.

Identifying Nascent Entrepreneurs

The major stumbling block to a precise estimate of the percentage of adults involved in the entrepreneurial or firm start-up process has been locating nascent entrepreneurs. The procedure identified a representative sample of households, and, in each, an adult was randomly selected for the interview. During the telephone interview, these persons were asked a number of details about their work activity, such as whether or not they had a full-time job, a part-time job, were self-employed, student, homemaker, retired, or disabled. A number were simultaneously involved in several ways. Regardless of their response, all were asked, "Are you, alone or with others, *now* trying to start a business?"

Those who answered "yes" to this question were then asked about "serious thought" related to the business and a number of activities associated with the start of a new firm. This list, in the order of popularity, is presented in Table 3.1. For each activity reported as initiated, the respondent was asked the month and year work began on this particular start-up behavior.

Start-up Activities

A frequent observation about entrepreneurship is that many people talk about it but do little to follow up. One bad day on the job may result in claims that a person will start his or her own business. To avoid concern that the emphasis was given to those who only talked about entrepreneurship, the basic measure of whether a respondent was indeed serious about starting a new business was whether the individual had taken at least two

Table 3.1
Firm Start-up Events

	Order Asked	U.S. Oct–Nov. 1993	Wisconsin Spring, 1993
Number of respondents		40(1)	42(2)
Percent reporting each gestation activity			
Serious thought about business	1	99%	91%
Looked for facilities/equipment	4	75	68
Initiated savings to invest	16	68	62
Invested own money in the new firm	7	66	79
Organized start-up team	3	58	50
Written business plan	2	56	49
Bought facilities/equipment	5	50	56
Sought financial support	8	41	26
License, patent, permits applied for	14	38	43
Developed first model or prototype	10	35	14
Received money from sales	12	33	45
Achieved positive monthly cash flow		22	NA(3)
Devoting full time to new business	13	32	19
Received financial support	9	29	15
Other start-up behaviors initiated	17	22	12
Rented or leased facilities/equipment	6	15	13
Created a new legal entity	15	14	22
Hired employees to work for wages	11	11	12
Incorporation with lists of businesses			
Know that firm on Dun & Bradstreet lists	18	2%	3%
Paid state unemployment insurance taxes	19	16	5
Paid federal social security taxes	20	15	NA
Filed federal income tax return	21	18	NA

Notes: (1) Initial respondents only. (2) Initial respondents plus others nominated, and interviewed, as potential nascent entrepreneurs. (3) Not asked.

explicit steps to start a firm. If only one had been taken, that was not thought to be sufficient, and such individuals were excluded from further analysis. More than one step indicates some seriousness of purpose.

As it turns out, almost everyone (95% of the U.S. sample and 94% of the Wisconsin sample) who reported starting a new business had begun at least two of the start-up activities. In fact, for the U.S. sample, the median number of steps taken was 7.0, and the average was 6.7 (with a range of 1–15). In Wisconsin the median number of reported behaviors was 7.0, while the average was 6.6.

Virtually all of the U.S. sample (99%) report giving "serious thought" to the new business, while 91% of the Wisconsin respondents did so. As shown in Table 3.1, the most prevalent gestation behaviors, reported by more than half of the respondents in each sample, are looking for facilities, equipment, or locations; investing money in the business; purchasing some type of asset such as equipment or a building; beginning to save money for an investment; organizing a start-up team; or preparing a written business plan. Less frequently reported are seeking financial support; devoting full time to the business; licenses, patents, or permits applied for; development of models or prototypes (applicable to a small proportion of new firms); setting up a formal, legal entity; receipt of financial support; renting facilities, equipment, or property; or hiring employees. Only 12% of our initial respondents in Wisconsin reported actions not on our survey list, suggesting it was a comprehensive inventory of gestation behaviors.

Based on the Wisconsin results, one additional question was added to the national interview schedule for the national survey. Those reporting income to the business were asked if and when the monthly income exceeded monthly expenses. This allowed determination of when significant revenue began to develop. It had not developed for three-fourths of the start-up firms.

All respondents were also asked whether they had (1) been included in the Dun and Bradstreet credit rating files of businesses or (2) filed a state unemployment insurance tax payment. Further, the respondents in the U.S. survey were asked if they had filed a federal Social Security (FICA) payment or an annual federal income tax statement. The results are very similar for the two analyses, with a very small percentage included in the Dun and Bradstreet files and a somewhat larger proportion in registers based on tax filings. This suggests that analyses of firm births based on new entries in the Dun and Bradstreet files should result in a smaller number of firms, firms that are further along in the start-up process, and new businesses that may be slightly larger when first identified as a "D&B birth."

It is convenient to treat firm start-ups as similar to biological gestation; indeed, the same type of language has been used in this analysis. However, the analogy is not accurate with regard to several critical features (Reynolds and Miller, 1992). First, there is wide variation in the time of gestation, which is discussed later. Second, there is no uniform sequence of events required to create the birth of a fledgling new firm. Third, there is no fixed set of gestation events. Variation in the gestation process may reflect differences associated with different industries, regional contexts, and resources available for initiating a new firm, such as start-up team skills, time, physical resources, and financial reserves. Indeed, the only feature that is required for a business birth appears to be "sales"; it is hard to conceive of a viable business without income.

Some gestation events are more common than others. But the prevalence of start-up activities is different from the sequence of start-up activities. Does it matter whether specific steps are taken first or early in the process? Will nascent entrepreneurs who take specific steps or steps in specific order be more likely to transform into a new business owner or have greater likelihood of success once they have launched their new business? These are questions we would like to answer. But before we can do so, we must learn whether there are steps that are more likely to occur early in the start-up process.

A preliminary effort to determine those activities most likely to occur early in the start-up sequence was completed by identifying activities reported in the first month. The results are presented in Table 3.2. As a more extensive list of start-up activities was included in the follow-up interviews, this analysis is confined to those respondents contacted a second time and reporting an autonomous start-up or franchise, excluding those sponsored by another firm or involving the purchase of an ongoing business.

In both samples, one in six (17%) reported engaging in start-up activities before giving serious thought to the new business; the majority, 83%, reported serious thought occurring before, or as they began to pursue, start-up activities.

Almost every activity is reported in the first month, except hiring employees. Some are, however, more likely to occur early in the start-up, such as investing money in the firm, saving to invest, or preparing a written business plan. More than 10% actually report that money was received by the new firm in the first month; some even report positive monthly cash flow at the beginning of the process. One behavior very rare early in the start-up is devoting full time to the new firm. This is consistent with the finding that 60-80% of the individuals starting new firms also have another established work role (full- or part-time work or self-employment).

A curious finding is that between 13% and 17% attempted to organize the start-up team in the first month. This is curious because the average new firm has 1.73 founders, and some 49% of new firms are founded by two or more individuals. It appears that the thought of teammates does not always come at the outset. The many benefits of a cooperative approach may become apparent as the complexities of creating a new firm begin to unfold.

Table 3.2
Firm Start-up Events: Frequency of First Occurrence

	United States Oct.–Nov. 1993	Wisconsin Spring 1993
Number of respondents	24 (1)	46 (1)
Thought-behavior sequence		
Behavior first	17%	17%
Simultaneous (same month)	46	31
Thought first	37	52
Thought among first	83	83
Totals	100%	100%
Prevalence in the first month (2)		
Invested own money in the new firm	25%	35%
Initiated savings to invest	25	22
Written business plan	25	15
Sought financial support	17	20
Looked for facilities/equipment	13	30
Bought facilities/equipment	13	26
Organized start-up team	13	17
Received money from sales	13	17
Achieved positive monthly cash flow	13	9
Provided salary for owner(s)	8	NA (3)
Received financial support	8	13
License, patent, permits applied for	8	7
Other start-up behaviors initiated	8	7
Developed first model or prototype	8	4
Devoting full time to new business	8	4
Acquired separate phone directory listing	8	NA
Rented or leased facilities/equipment	4	4
Developed marketing program	4	NA
Installed separate phone line	4	NA
Acquired Federal Employer Identification Number	4	NA
Created a new legal entity	0	4
Hired employees to work for wages	0	0

Notes: (1) Respondents who, in the follow-up interview, reported starting an autonomous firm or franchise. (2) As more than one event could occur within the first month of the gestation period, or start-up window, the totals exceed 100%. (3) Not asked.

PREVALENCE OF NASCENT ENTREPRENEURS

How many nascent entrepreneurs pursuing new firm start-ups are there? Using the procedure described earlier to locate representative samples of adults trying to start new firms, it is possible to determine the prevalence within the total adult population. The various background characteristics can be used to explore the personal attributes or contextual factors that encourage individuals to become nascent entrepreneurs and pursue a new firm start-up. These are presented in Table 3.3. Here again, the results of two survey samples—the United States and Wisconsin—are the basis for discussion. It should be noted that low rates of prevalence (almost all are below 10%) and samples in the hundreds are associated with very wide standard errors of the mean. We present our findings with the caveat that our statements are based on small samples that may not adequately represent the population at large. Our findings illustrate, however, the types of analysis that would be possible with adequate samples, and the results have implications for public policy and individual entrepreneurs.

Examination of Table 3.3 makes it clear that both age and gender have a major impact upon the tendency of individuals to report they are engaged in a business start-up. Because these samples are small, there is the possibility that they are not fully representative of the total population on these critical personal attributes. As a result, the prevalence for various categories of respondents by age and gender is used with a more precise estimate of the gender and age distribution for the total adult population to provide an adjusted estimate of the prevalence of nascent entrepreneurs. The result is presented in Table 3.4.

This correction slightly reduces the prevalence in both samples, from 4.4 to 4.3 per 100 adults for Wisconsin and from 3.9 to 3.7 for the entire United States. Hence, it seems reasonable to treat 4 per 100 (or 4%) as a good first estimate for discussions of the prevalence of nascent entrepreneurs in the U.S. adult population. The most significant difference is the prevalence rates for men fifty-five and older, which is 8 per 100 for the Wisconsin sample and 0.5 per 100 for the U.S. sample. Clearly, larger samples will be required to resolve this problem. The other major patterns, men twice as likely as women to report involvement in a new firm start-up and a higher level of involvement among those twenty-five to forty-four years old, are present in both samples.

Regardless, the 4%, or one in twenty-five estimate means that participation in the entrepreneurial process is a major activity for those in the U.S. adult population. At any time, about 7 million U.S. adults are involved in the start-up process. This number is larger than the annual number of adults who get married or who have children. Just as with marriage and childbearing, however, new firm start-ups are concentrated among younger adults.

If one assumes even a small replacement flow of the adults in the "start-up pool," then a substantial proportion of adults may be involved in

Table 3.3
Prevalence of Nascent Entrepreneurs, United States and Wisconsin: By Selected Characteristics

		United States: 1993			Wisconsin: 1993	
		No. of Cases	Nascent Entre's		No. of Cases	Nascent Entre's
Overall		1,016	3.9%		683	4.3%
Gender	Men	431	4.6%		292	5.6%
	Women	585	2.7		364	3.4
Age	18–24 yrs. old	106	3.3%		79	2.6$
	25–34 yrs. old	290	9.7		182	3.6
	35–44 yrs. old	174	3.0		143	7.0
	45–54 yrs. old	95	2.1		116	3.2
	55–up yrs. old	349	0.3		133	4.8
Ethnic status	White	798	3.6%		226	4.3%
	All other	204	5.6		463	3.6
Educational attainment	Less than high school	151	1.4%		55	0.0%
	High school degree	383	2.3		237	4.8
	Post-high school	223	6.4		167	4.3
	College degree	168	6.2		137	4.5
	Post-college experience	85	5.1		60	6.9
Household income	Up to $10K per year	216	3.3%	Up to $10K per year	57	0.2%
	$10K–34K per year	490	3.7	$10K–29K per year	170	4.0
	$35K–49K	111	3.6	$30K–49K per year	189	6.9
	$50K+ per year	160	5.6	$50K+ per year	160	3.1
County tenure	0–5 years	234	5.2%		138	1.6%
	6–15 years	180	4.9		109	4.1
	16–30 years	257	5.6		189	3.0
	31+ years	320	1.4		217	7.5
State tenure	0–5 years	65	2.8%		58	3.7%
	6–15 years	62	7.0		53	0.9
	16–30 years	130	6.9		213	2.8
	31+ years	238	0.7		329	6.1

		United States: 1993		Wisconsin: 1993	
		No. of Cases	Nascent Entre's	No. of Cases	Nascent Entre's
Region of U.S.	Northeast	200	6.0%		
	South	356	2.7		
	North central	262	2.1		
	West	197	6.6		
Type of region	Metropolitan	288	4.2%	195	3.9%
	Mixed / Regional center	627	3.6	282	4.9
	Rural	101	5.0	200	3.8
Labor force status	Full-time job	388	3.3%	390	3.5%
	Part-time job	131	3.9	67	4.5
	Self-employed	115	12.1	36	5.7
	Unemployed	37	7.6	29	0.2
	Homemaker	66	0.9	38	8.4
	Retired	149	0.4	82	7.8
	Student/disabled/other	111	3.9	40	0.8
Occupational status	Professional-technical	160	3.0%		
	Manager-administrator	151	6.5		
	Clerical-sales	241	3.3		
	Foreman-craftsman	107	5.5		
	Operators-unskilled work	160	2.4		
	Service-household work	150	5.3		
Consumer confidence index	High	305	4.9%		
	Medium	352	2.0		
	Low	346	5.2		
Business confidence index	High	332	5.0%		
	Medium	327	2.4		
	Low	332	4.4		
Entrepreneurial climate index	Positive			262	3.5%
	Neutral			211	5.8
	Negative			210	3.6

Notes: Missing data reduces the total number of cases in some categories. State tenure obtained only for November 1993 U.S. sample.

Table 3.4
Prevalence of Nascent Entrepreneurs: Adjusted Population Estimates

	Total Adults (x 1,000)		Prevalence of Nascent Entres (per 100)		Total Nascent Entres (x 1,000)		Prevalence of Nascent Entres (per 100)
	Men	Women	Men	Women	Men	Women	Total Population
Wisconsin (1)							
18–24 years old	253	254	5.2	0.0	13	0	
25–34	410	415	6.2	2.7	26	11	
35–44	366	361	5.5	8.5	20	31	
45–54	236	243	0.7	5.3	2	13	
55 and up	464	599	8.4	0.0	39	0	
	1,730	1,872			99	55	
Totals		3,602				154	4.3
United States (2)							
18–24 years old	13,217	12,703	4.8	1.4	628	183	
25–34	21,247	21,215	11.7	8.1	2,494	1,718	
35–44	19,768	20,136	4.7	1.5	935	296	
45–54	13,399	14,018	3.7	0.6	501	77	
55 and up	22,958	30,254	0.5	0.2	117	76	
	90,589	98,326			4,675	2,350	
Totals		188,915				7,026	3.7

Notes: (1) U.S. Census counts for 1990.
(2) 1992 estimates, *Statistical Abstract of the U.S.: 1994*, Table 20, p. 20.

a firm start-up over a couple of decades. This is consistent with the patterns presented in Table 1.2, which indicated that over a work career 40% of male heads of households had a period of self-employment. Self-employment or entrepreneurial endeavors are mainstream activities, not a peripheral action taken by a limited few.

CHARACTERISTICS OF NASCENT ENTREPRENEURS

There is a substantial gender difference in both samples, with men about twice as likely as women to become involved in the new firm gestation process. There are striking differences associated with age in the U.S. sample, with those twenty-five to thirty-four over twice as likely to be involved as the typical adult and those over fifty-five very unlikely to be involved at all; see Table 3.3. In Wisconsin it appears that the peak involvement may be among those thirty-five to forty-four years old, while those over fifty-five years old seem to have an enhanced interest.

Different patterns are found between the two samples with regard to ethnic comparisons, with the white majority having a lower prevalence in the U.S. sample and a higher prevalence in the Wisconsin sample. It should be mentioned that differences among minority groups (American Indians, Asian Americans, blacks, and Hispanics) are substantial in Wisconsin (Reynolds and White, 1993a), and treating them as an undifferentiated agglomerate is inappropriate. There is, in particular, diversity within the American Indian and Asian-American groups. More precise comparisons will require larger samples. (The subject of minority participation in Wisconsin is the topic of Chapter 8.)

The relationship between level of education and being a nascent entrepreneur is quite similar for the two samples, with those adults (both samples excluded respondents under eighteen years old) who have not completed high school being very unlikely to become involved in starting a new firm. Equally important, there is no dramatic surge of participation among those with graduate experiences.

The pattern associated with household income is slightly different for the two samples. There is little effect of household income on prevalence among the U.S. sample, except for a slight increase among those with annual household incomes in excess of $50,000 per year. In the Wisconsin sample, virtually no individuals in households with incomes below $10,000 per year are involved in new firm gestation, and the rate of participation is highest among those with annual incomes in the $30,000-$50,000 range. Larger samples will be needed to confirm the impact of household income.

Differences are also found in the length of time individuals had lived in their current county of residence. At issue is the degree to which entrepreneurs are persons who recently moved into a community to initiate a new business. Are they a mobile population or a stable group that has built up a network of friends and acquaintances over time?

Duration of county and state residence also reflects a different pattern in the two samples. In the U.S. sample longer duration of residence, over thirty years in the same county or state, is associated with a sharply reduced tendency to be a nascent entrepreneur. The opposite is true for the Wisconsin sample. While it is clear that the majority of nascent entrepreneurs are not recent arrivals to a state, there may be some substantial regional variation on this factor. It may take longer for a newcomer to Wisconsin, a state with a stable, established population, to establish the contacts, networks, and credibility required to establish a new firm.

Although it is not shown in Table 3.3, the Wisconsin interviews included an elaborate procedure to measure the size of the respondents' social network and, in addition, the extent to which their family and friends were involved in the entrepreneurial process (Palit and Reynolds, 1993). Those who identified sixteen or more family and friends in their social network were three times as likely to be nascent entrepreneurs as those with fewer than six (Reynolds and White, 1993a). Smaller social networks would be expected among newcomers.

Nationally, regional differences are surprisingly strong, given the scope and diversity of the four U.S. regions. It appears that the tendency to pursue new firm gestation is somewhat higher in the more urbanized Northeast and West, and somewhat lower in the South and north-central regions. There are not strong differences related to type of region (metropolitan, mixed, rural), but the measure of region type was very crude for the U.S. sample.

The relationship between labor force status and participation reflects some important similarities between the two samples. A substantial proportion of individuals with established roles in the work-force (full-time job, part-time job, self-employment) in both samples is participating in new firm gestation as nascent entrepreneurs. It should be mentioned that careful attention was given to ensuring that those reporting self-employment or the management of a small firm were actually trying to start *another* new firm.

Some (Storey, 1991, 1994; Reynolds, Storey, and Westhead, 1994) have hypothesized that unemployment has led many individuals to pursue starting a new business. The results of our two surveys, especially the results from Wisconsin, raise some questions about the validity of that hypothesis. Even given this difference between the prevalence of nascent entrepreneurs among the unemployed, it is clear that the low percentage of unemployed adults, especially in Wisconsin, means that a very small percent of nascent entrepreneurs (7% or less) will be unemployed. In other words, despite the fact that those involved in the labor force are less likely to start new firms, the vast majority of new firms are started by those actively involved in the workforce.

Another background characteristic of interest is occupation. We can hypothesize that persons who are currently managers might be more prone to starting a new business because they already have experience operating one. Others who may have a higher probability of starting a new business could be craftspeople who can develop new products and professional and technical workers who have the skills and training to develop new products and processes. The results of the surveys support some of these contentions.

There are some differences in the U.S. sample related to professional background. Those considered managers or administrators and forepersons or craftspeople are more likely to be nascent entrepreneurs. Lower rates of participation are indicated for operators and unskilled workers, as expected. But somewhat surprisingly, those in professional and technical occupations have a relatively low incidence of nascent entrepreneurs within their ranks. Perhaps these workers have enough rewards from their current endeavors that they see less reason to attempt to start new businesses.

Indexes of consumer[1] and business[2] confidence reflect judgments about future economic conditions. The prevalence associated with both indexes in the U.S. sample is quite similar. Those with high or low levels of confidence are more likely to be classified as nascent entrepreneurs. These are individuals who either (1) see a promising economic future and, perhaps, are encouraged to initiate a new firm or (2) consider the future bleak and feel pushed into implementing a new firm. As discussed in Chapter 2, the Wisconsin interviews included a nine-item index reflecting the respondent's judgment about the "entrepreneurial climate," whether or not Wisconsin was a good place to start a new business. Those in the Wisconsin sample who have a neutral judgment about Wisconsin as a place to pursue entrepreneurial options are most likely to be nascent entrepreneurs. Those with positive or negative judgments are less likely to pursue a new firm start-up. Such a result is difficult to explain. The entire subject of entrepreneurial climate is discussed at some length later.

Additional information was gathered on yet another dimension of potential entrepreneurs (see Table 3.5). Adults at large and nascent entrepreneurs were asked a series of questions to determine whether or not they viewed certain elements of work differently. Respondents were read a series of statements with which they were to strongly agree, agree, disagree or strongly disagree. A four-point scale was attached to the range of responses. These statements were the basis for four multi-item indexes related to different aspects of work, including the importance of autonomy and independence, work in which they can pursue ideas they find interesting, ability to build wealth for their family, and a desire to stay in the community.

There was a statistically significant difference between nascent and discouraged entrepreneurs when compared to typical adults in Wisconsin, as shown in Table 3.5. The nascent entrepreneurs were more likely to be motivated by autonomy in work, having specific task interests that they could pursue, and having greater interest in building wealth. Most striking, however, was that those involved in firm start-ups reflected a greater interest in all three aspects of work; no single factor was dominant. There was also a slightly higher interest in staying in the community, but this was not statistically significant.

Table 3.5
Work Values: Typical Adults and Entrepreneurs in Wisconsin

	Typical Adults	Discouraged Entrepreneurs	Nascent Entrepreneurs
Number of respondents	940	42	81
Autonomy, independence	3.14	3.43*	3.42*
Task interest	3.21	3.33*	3.57*
Wealth, income	2.81	2.76*	2.99*
Staying in community	2.87	2.95	3.01*

Notes: Scale range: 1–4; higher values indicating more positive orientation. *Indicates a statistically significant difference compared to typical adults.

WHO STARTS NEW FIRMS?

It is clear that a number of factors are related to the tendency to pursue a new firm start-up: age, gender, educational background, residential location, household income, interest in work activity, and so on. The problem, as always, is how to combine these individual elements into a composite. The most widely used strategy is to develop an additive model based on the assumption that the various factors can be summed to create a portrayal of a "typical" nascent entrepreneur. This is facilitated by the use of multiple regression procedures, which allow identification of the factor with the impact considered statistically most significant, followed by the second most significant factor, and so on. A number of analyses have used this technique with large-scale population samples, where reported self-employment has been considered an indication of entrepreneurial activity (Blanchflower and Meyer, 1991; Blanchflower and Oswald, 1990; Dolton and Makepeace, 1990; Evans and Leighton, 1989; Storey, 1994).

When this procedure is used with the national sample of nascent entrepreneurs, using a regression procedure designed for dichotomous dependent variables, the results are as presented in Table 3.6. There are two ways to complete the analysis—the forward procedure enters variables sequentially until an "optimal model" occurs, and the backward procedure removes variables sequentially until an "optimal model" occurs—and the outcomes are slightly different. Three background characteristics are retained as significant in both cases: age—which reduces the tendency to start a new firm—and self-employment and divorce, both of which increase the tendency. A number of other factors are present in one or the other of the analyses.

Perhaps most significant is the overall success of the models, which are identical at 96% correct predictions. On a case-by-case basis, this is achieved by predicting that none of the 1,016 individuals in the sample are trying to start a new firm. This results in an incorrect judgment for only those 4% of the individuals that are actually involved in the firm start-up process. These results do not provide a very useful interpretation regarding those starting new businesses.

This analysis replicates the type of findings reported in other studies using the same procedure. Others have used this technique to provide very low predictive success, 0.3% of the explained variance in one analysis (Evans and Leighton, 1989). Further, the underlying conceptualization of the decision to start a new firm is, to say the least, bizarre. One seldom encounters an entrepreneur, nascent or otherwise, who reports a decision based on youth, a divorce, or current self-employment. Those with experience with business start-ups almost always talk about a combination of circumstances and opportunities that led them to take action.

The alternative is to develop a procedure that considers the potential impact of interaction among the various factors. Rather than simply add the effects together, the procedure seeks unique combinations of back-

Table 3.6
Linear Models Predicting Nascent Entrepreneurs: Logistic Regression Analysis

	Forward Stepwise		Backward Stepwise	
	Beta	*Sign*	*Beta*	*Sign*
Constant	-.7944	0.16	-1.9761	0.002
Gender			0.7507	0.05
Age	-.0757	0.0000	-.0837	0.0000
North-central resident	-1.0848	0.03		
West resident			1.0963	0.008
Northeast resident			1.0920	0.010
Self-employed	1.6137	0.0000	1.5463	0.0001
Unemployed			1.2638	0.07
Managerial-administrative occupation			0.8408	0.05
Consumer confidence			-.3702	0.10
Divorced	1.0175	0.01	1.3445	0.001
Overall chi-square	55.634	0.0000	70.031	0.0000
Percentage correct predictions	96.02%		96.02%	

Note: SPSS PC 5.0.2 logistic regression with standard defaults.

ground, contextual, and personal attributes. The desire to analyze this type of substantive problem led to the development of the Automatic Interaction Detection (AID) technique (Sonquist and Morgan, 1964; Sonquist, 1970). The procedure involves two stages. First, an initial analysis (such as found in Table 3.3) is used to create nominal or ordinal independent variables. A staged analysis is then completed. At each stage the independent variable that provides the most statistically significant relationship to the dependent variable is used to divide the sample—one subgroup for each independent variable category. Each subgroup is then examined to determine which of the remaining independent variables will provide the most significant divisions among the further subgroups. This procedure is continued until no further statistically significant divisions of the sample are possible. Different independent variables may be involved in different paths of the analysis hierarchy. The procedure does not assume a linear impact or any particular form of interaction (SPSS CHAID, CHi-square Automatic Inter-action Detection, is used in this application; Magidson, 1992). The second stage involves using a one-way analysis of variance utilizing the resultant sub-groups to determine the extent to which subgroup differences are statistically and substantively significant.

This procedure was carried out with the U.S. sample and is presented in Exhibit 3.1. Age is clearly the dominant factor affecting decisions to start a new firm. The impact of age, however, is not monotonic but curvilinear, with the highest proportion, almost 10%, occurring among those twenty-five to thirty-four years old. The rate is one-third this level, about 3%, among those eighteen to twenty-four or thirty-five to fifty-four years old. Nascent entrepreneurs are virtually nonexistent among those fifty-five and older. The impact of other factors varies with the age of the respondent, indicating the significance of these interactions. Among the youngest adults, eighteen to twenty-four years old, the presence of other adults in the household is critical. Among the oldest respondents, fifty-five and up, the availability of financial reserves is critical. Among the midlife adults, their occupational status has a major effect, with self-employment substantially increasing the probability of attempting to start a new firm. But for those young adults, twenty-five to thirty-four years old with full- or part-time work, educational attainment is critical, for almost one-in-eight who have completed high school are also attempting to start a new business. Among those in later middle years, thirty-five to fifty-four years old, and *not* self-employed, those new to a county (the United States has 3,124 counties) are more likely to be starting a new firm, particularly if they are men.

While two of the variables with great emphasis in the univariate analysis (Table 3.3) or the linear models developed from logistic regression (Table 3.6) have a major impact in this search for interaction—age and self-employment—it is also important that a number of others do not. For example, gender does not appear in this model, partially because those fifty-five and over who are *not* trying to start new businesses are dominated by women. Two-thirds (67.4%) of those fifty-five and over are women; one-third (38.1%) of all women in the sample—and the adult population—are fifty-five and over. In all other age categories the genders are relatively evenly balanced.

The second phase of the analysis, comparing the twelve subgroups developed in the first stage, is presented in Table 3.7. When the groups are ranked on the basis of the prevalence of nascent entrepreneurs, and a one-way analysis of variance is completed, the results are statistically significant beyond the 0.0000 level, and about 12% of the variance is accounted for.

The ranking presented in Table 3.7 demonstrates the extent to which efforts to start new firms are concentrated in unique groups in the adult population. Seven in ten new firm start-ups (69%) are provided by one-sixth (17%) of the adult population: those twenty-five to thirty-four that are self-employed, unemployed, or students (group A) or those with employment and more than a high school degree (group B). If those thirty-five to fifty-four reporting self-employment (group C) are added, five-sixths (83%) of start-ups are provided by less than one-quarter (23%) of the adult population.

Exhibit 3.1
Interaction of Factors and Prevalence of Nascent Entrepreneurs

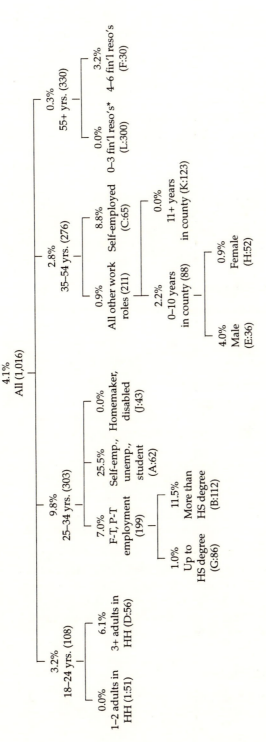

Notes: Based on U.S. random sample from October–November 1993 Survey of Consumers. Number of cases in each group in parentheses. Letter appearing before the number of cases identifies category in next exhibit. Collapsing sample weights into nine categories for use in the CHAID analysis procedure slightly increased the overall prevalence from 3.9% to 4.1%. For this exploratory analysis, CHAID was allowed to develop a six-level analysis and use chi-square values of 0.20 for both predictors and significance of categories, and subgroup sizes were limited to fifty before splits and twenty-five after splits.

* Count of different types of financial resources available to respondent.

Table 3.7
Population Groups and Prevalence of Nascent Entrepreneurs

	Proportion of Nascent Entre's	% Total Nascent Entre's	% Sample
A 25–34 yrs; self-employed, unemployed, student	26%	38%	6%
B 25–34 Yrs; full or part-time employment; more than H. S. degree (cumulative proportions)	12	31 (69%)	11 (17%)
C 35–54 yrs; self-employed (cumulative proportions)	9	14 (83%)	6 (23%)
D 18–24 yrs; 3 or more adults in household	6	8	6
E 35–54 yrs; not self-employed; 0–10 yrs in county; male	4	3	4
F 55–up yrs; 4 or more financial reserves	3	2	3
G 25–34 yrs; full or part-time employment; up to H. S. degree	1	2	9
H 35-54 yrs; not self-employed; 0-10 yrs in county; female	1	1	5
I 18–24 yrs; 1–2 adults in household	0	0	5
J 25–34 yrs; homemaker, disabled	0	0	4
K 35–54 yrs; not self-employed; 11 or more years in county	0	0	12
L 55–up yrs; 0–3 financial reserves	0	0	29
Total	4%	99%	100%

Note: This is a weighted sample of 1,016. Using a one-way analysis of variance (SPSS PC 5.0) the total explained variance is 11.6 %, statistically significant beyond the 0.000 level.

Equally dramatic is identifying that 50% of the adult population that fail to generate any efforts to start a new firm are those fifty-five and over with no financial reserves; those thirty-five to fifty-four not self-employed and with over ten years in a county; twenty-five to thirty-four year-olds who are homemakers or disabled; and those eighteen to twenty-four living in households with one or two adults.

TYPES OF START-UP FIRMS

Because these are firms in development, little can be said about these new businesses. It is possible, however, to consider the economic sectors in which these start-ups may operate. The type of business can be compared with the active businesses in the United States. The distribution across economic sectors of all existing business enterprises (i.e., all forms of businesses, not just autonomous establishments) compared to the distributions of the start-up firms is presented in Table 3.8.

As shown in Table 3.8, the distribution among the new firms is very similar to that of the existing enterprises. For example, 70% of existing U.S. business enterprises are in construction, retail, or services, compared to 74% of the sample of U.S. start-ups and 70% of the sample of Wisconsin start-ups. When the distribution across economic sectors of active new firms in Minnesota, Pennsylvania, or Wisconsin is considered, the same result is obtained; the distribution of new firms is largely a reflection of existing firms (Reynolds and Freeman, 1987; Reynolds and Miller, 1988; Chapter 5). Even though our sample sizes are small, there is no justification for considering the economic sectors of the start-ups as different from the existing structure of U.S. businesses. It also suggests that the sample of new Wisconsin firms, discussed in Chapter 5, will be similar to those start-up efforts that become active new firms.

Table 3.8
Economic Sector of New Firm Start-ups

Economic Sector	Active Firms	Start-up Firm Samples	
	U.S. Total(1)	U.S.	Wisconsin
Agricultural, forestry, fishing	2%	8%	—%
Mining	1	—	—
Construction	11	5	9
Manufacturing	6	5	6
Transportation, communications, utilities	3	2	7
Wholesale	7	5	4
Financial, insurance, real estate	8	—	6
Retail, including restaurants, bars	22	27	34
Services	37	42	27
Other, can't classify	2	5	9
Total	100%	99%	102%

Note: (1) Table 2.1, Office of Advocacy, U.S. Small Business Administration, *Handbook of Small Business Data: 1994*, based on 4,991,474 firms (not establishments) with employees in 1988.

REACTION TO THE CONTEXT

Nascent and discouraged entrepreneurs in the Wisconsin sample were asked to consider the community in which their business would be located, be it an urban area, regional city, small town, suburb, or whatever. They were asked to consider the importance (very, somewhat, or not) and their satisfaction (very, somewhat, or not) with twenty-five characteristics of the immediate context for their new firm. These are listed in Table 3.9. Contextual factors included access to such things as customers, suppliers, insurance coverage, bank loans, research and development (R&D) facilities, skilled workers, education and training; location attributes such as crime, property taxes, local regulations, transportation, energy, infrastructure (sewer, water, roads); and general qualities, such as the quality of life, government support for business, labor costs, personal and business taxes, and state regulations.

The variation in the reaction to these factors is quite striking. Three in four (77%) consider access to customers very important, while only one in six (15%) consider the availability of skilled workers very important. (This difference could be attributable to the small number of nascent entrepreneurs who are attempting to start either manufacturing or construction firms.)

Six of the contextual features (access to customers, crime, property taxes, capital availability, quality of life, and state regulations) are considered very important by over half of the nascent/discouraged entrepreneurs; twenty-one of the twenty-five characteristics are considered very important by at least one in three.

The rank order of these features makes it clear that access, availability, and quality of various features take precedence over business costs. The only costs that are in the upper half of the list are those associated with taxes (property, business, household and personal), which are not the major cost factors for any business. The upper half of the rankings are dominated by the availability or access (to customers, capital, insurance) or the quality of the context (crime, quality of life). Three items related to government control (state regulations; local [city, county] regulations; zoning and land use) are in the upper third of the rank order. For those starting a new business the most important factors are the access to quality inputs and coping with various government controls.

In general, the more important a contextual feature, the more satisfied the nascent and discouraged entrepreneurs. About three of five are very satisfied with access to customers and the quality of life, the factors rated first and fifth in importance. Half are very satisfied with the level of crime in the area of their new business, and this is considered very important by three out of every five respondents. These same patterns—high satisfaction with most contextual features considered important and high dissatisfaction with taxes and regulations—were found in the surveys of new firms in Minnesota and Pennsylvania (Reynolds, 1989).

Table 3.9
Ratings of Context: Importance and Satisfaction

Feature	Important	Satisfied with Current	
	Very	Not	Very
Access to customers	77%	12%	57%
Crime (level of)	57	20	48
Property taxes	51	55	7
Capital availability	51	31	18
Quality of life	51	5	61
State regulations	51	15	23
Local (city, county) regulations	49	17	26
Zoning and land use	47	14	23
Business taxes	45	36	14
Personal or household taxes	45	49	9
Transportation (highways, railroads)	45	2	46
Availability of insurance coverage	44	14	31
Access to bank loans and support	44	39	16
Land purchase or rental costs	42	15	30
Building space availability	41	11	37
Access to suppliers	40	4	47
Energy availability	39	2	44
Infrastructure (roads, water, sewer)	39	4	45
Energy costs	37	16	23
Building space expenditures	35	15	19
Government support for business	33	69	5
Education & training opportunities	31	10	40
Land availability (for expansion)	27	8	30
Labor costs	23	6	37
Access to R & D facilities	21	16	33
Availability of skilled workers	15	14	31
Overall average	41%	19%	31%

Note: As there was no difference between nascent and discouraged entrepreneurs, their responses are combined for this analysis.

A factor considered very important and associated with a high level of dissatisfaction could be considered a major warning sign. This is clearly the case for all items related to taxes. Half of the respondents report they are not satisfied with personal or household and property taxes. One in three is not satisfied with business taxes. This is in contrast to the factors associated with government regulations, generally considered very important but not associated with high levels of "not satisfied." Only one in six is "not satisfied" with local regulations, state regulations, or zoning and land use.

The other features considered high in importance that receive high levels of "not satisfied" are related to the availability of financial support. More than two in five consider access to bank loans and support or capital availability "very important," and more than two in five are "not satisfied" with these features of their immediate context.

FINANCIAL NEEDS AND FIRM PROJECTIONS

If nascent entrepreneurs were not happy about the availability of financial support, how much did they think they needed? Wisconsin nascent entrepreneurs (not the discouraged entrepreneurs) were asked to identify the amount of loans (borrowing) or equity (ownership investments) their new firm would require. Quite surprisingly, when asked initially about the amount of money they expected for their business, 61% expected to have no external support of even personal equity in the business. Those who did anticipate some form of financial support expected it to be quite modest. The average of equity and debt for eighty-nine start-up firms was about $1,500. Twelve percent expected to require up to $10,000; 13%, from $10,001 to $50,000; and 13%, over $50,000. Only one firm out of the eighty-nine that provided information will require more than $500,000.

These small amounts reflect some naiveté on the part the respondents, many of whom are just beginning to develop their financial projections. As discussed in Chapter 5, new firm owners have found their financial requirements to be significantly greater. New firms with employees and in operation for three to seven years require, on average, close to $200,000 of capital from both equity and loan sources. The sample of nascent entrepreneurs contains a number planning self-employment, rather than a business organization, and their financial requirements may be very modest. Even so, there is some reason to suspect that many of the nascent entrepreneurs are not well informed about the resources required to start a new firm.

The respondents actually showed somewhat more realism as they were led through a series of specific questions on equity and loan needs and sources. The major results are shown in Table 3.10. When queried about specific sources and amounts, some 80% claimed that they expected some type of ownership or equity funding, and over 60% expect to borrow

Table 3.10
Expected Sources of Financial Support: Wisconsin Nascent Entrepreneurs

	Ownership (Equity)	Loans (Debt)
Percent that expect some amount	80%	62%
Owner/respondent expects to contribute	49%	24%
Other start-up team members	18	7
Total start-up team family/kin	9	7
Friends or business associates	7	6
Banks or other financial institutions	12	25
Private investors, venture capitalists, stockholders	3	6
Government agency, government guaranteed loans	6	8
Other sources	2	1

Note: Totals may exceed 100% as respondents could select more than one source.

some money. The most popular source of equity funding is from the respondent/owner themselves. The other start-up team members and banks/financial institutions are considered a weak, secondary source of funds. About one-quarter of the respondents expect to make loans to the new firm, and another one-quarter expect to borrow from banks or other financial institutions.

Equally important are the sources not considered of significance. Few of the nascent entrepreneurs anticipate support from family, friends, private investors, or government agencies. This may reflect the small-scale aspirations for most of the endeavors. For example, one-half of the nascent entrepreneurs expect their firms to have sales of less than $30,000 the first year (and one employee); $100,000 in the fifth year (with three employees); and sales of no more than $200,000 in the tenth year (with four employees). A small percentage, however, have more significant aspirations: 4% of the nascent entrepreneurs expect sales to exceed $1 million in the first year, $4 million in the fifth year, and approach $10 million in the tenth year. Eight percent expect to have fifty or more employees in ten years. As with other analyses of new firms, the majority have modest plans, and a small minority are planning for bigger things.

AWARENESS AND USE OF SERVICES FOR ENTREPRENEURS

A substantial amount of information was obtained from nascent and discouraged entrepreneurs to assess their knowledge of, use of, and reaction to the diversity of services available for those starting new firms. They were asked about the twenty-eight different types of services, discussed in Chapter 2 and listed in Table 2.6. For each type of service, the respondents were asked (1) if they knew of them; (2) if they considered them relevant to the business they were trying to start; or (3) if they simply were unaware that the service existed.

The average responses of those with experience in the start-up process are provided in Table 3.11. The percentage of nascent and discouraged entrepreneurs making contact or not knowing of the type of service is presented. The forms of assistance are rank-ordered by the percentage of respondents who made contact. This varied from two in five for assistance related to laws and regulations to one in twenty for assistance regarding international trade. In general, one in six made contact regarding a type of assistance, and one in three was not aware of a service. The remainder, about half of the responses, reflected a judgment that the service was not relevant to the start-up business activity.

The major patterns are quite clear. The majority of the potential clients for the majority of the programs are unaware of the existence of a program or did not consider it relevant. If all of the potential clients for the typical type of assistance used that assistance, the workload would triple. Stated another way, for each client served by the typical form of assistance, two are not served because they didn't know such help was available.

There were some differences in this regard between nascent and discouraged entrepreneurs. For an average of 41% of the services, discouraged entrepreneurs were unaware of the service, compared to 28% among nascent entrepreneurs. This lack of awareness, which may have led to a lack of assistance, may have led some to withdraw from the start-up effort.

Nascent and discouraged entrepreneurs were also asked about their most recent experiences with service or assistance from a program. If they had been clients in several programs, they were asked to comment on only the most recent "assistance experience." Presumably, they would remember this one with greater accuracy. Over seven in ten respondents considered the assistance an extremely or very helpful experience. The assessment was slightly higher for nascent entrepreneurs (eight in ten) and slightly lower for discouraged entrepreneurs (six in ten). About 16% considered the assistance only "somewhat helpful." None of these individuals considered the experience harmful, although a small proportion, from 1% to 11%, may not have considered it a good use of their time.

Given the evidence developed in this project, which utilized randomly selected samples of individuals, the majority of the evidence suggests that nascent and discouraged entrepreneurs (1) were unaware that most services were available and (2) were quite satisfied with the services that were provided.

Table 3.11
Knowledge of and Use of Assistance for Entrepreneurs

Category of Assistance	Percentage That:	
	Made Contact	*Did Not Know About Service*
Information on laws and regulations	44%	24%
Networking, or making contacts	30	40
Continuing education courses	30	15
Accounting assistance	29	29
Information on financial resources	29	31
General business management	24	35
Financial counseling	21	33
Business start-up or expansion assistance	18	46
Retail/service business locations	16	27
Business plan development	16	51
Demographic profiles of customers	35	14
Venture capital	14	43
Personnel management assistance	13	25
Business advocacy groups	13	44
Marketing program assistance	12	35
Manufacturing systems tech assistance	12	19
Marketing research assistance	10	36
Technology development assistance	9	25
Assistance in selling to governments	9	46
Minority business assistance	9	28
Information systems assistance	9	45
Patent & trademark assistance	8	16
Tourism business assistance	8	22
Site location assistance	7	38
Business feasibility review	6	70
Women's business assistance	6	29
Business incubator	6	61
International trade assistance	5	25
Average	15%	35%

Note: Each row would sum to 100% if the percentage that did not consider the service relevant to their business was included.

OVERVIEW AND IMPLICATIONS

The procedure developed to identify nascent and discouraged entrepreneurs appears to have successfully identified individuals who are, or have been, engaged in behavior to implement a new firm. At any given time about one in twenty-five adults, in Wisconsin or the United States, are nascent entrepreneurs, involved in a business start-up. Most of these individuals are younger (twenty-five to forty-four years of age), have graduated at least from high school, are likely to have incomes over $30,000 per year, are more likely to live in the more urbanized East or West Coasts, and have a large number of friends and family in their social networks. Further, it is likely that some of their family or friends are active participants in the entrepreneurial process. If they differ from typical adults in their work interest, it is due to a greater desire to be independent and work autonomously, and a somewhat stronger interest in the substance of the work itself. There is a slightly greater interest in financial rewards.

As a group, nascent and discouraged entrepreneurs are quite satisfied with the context provided by the state of Wisconsin. The overall assessment of the entrepreneurial climate is about the same as for typical adults. They are satisfied with the current status of a number of contextual features considered important. For example, access to various factors (customers, insurance, suppliers) is considered important and satisfactory. Measures related to the quality of various factors (transportation, infrastructure, research and development [R&D] facilities) indicate a high level of satisfaction; most important is the high rating given to the quality of life. Surprisingly, there is an absence of dissatisfaction with measures related to regulations from the state, city, or county. This may be because the nascent entrepreneurs have not put their businesses into full operation and, hence, have not had much contact with governmental regulations.

Warning signs would occur when there are factors considered important but for which there is indication of high dissatisfaction. Two areas fit this category. One is the availability of capital or financial support, and the other is related to any type of taxes (business, property, or personal).

A large number of services have developed to serve nascent entrepreneurs. For every nascent entrepreneur now served by the existing services, two eligible clients go without service. This is because they are unaware of its presence. Once they receive services, the majority of the clients consider the assistance very helpful. Only a small minority (one in eight) consider it a waste of time. None consider the service to have damaged their business.

For three of four nascent entrepreneurs, the amount of financing required is small, certainly less than $10,000; but about 10% expect to need more than $100,000 in initial funding. This distribution reflects, in part, the modest aspirations many have for their new firms. About half expect sales to remain below $200,000 in the tenth year, with no more than four employees. An optimistic minority (4%), however, expect sales to approach $10 million in ten years and anticipate over fifty employees.

CONCEPTIONS OF MODERN MARKET ECONOMIES

This chapter has covered a number of features associated with conceptions of modern market economies. Perhaps most important, efforts to start new firms are neither unique nor distinctive; indeed, they are a pervasive feature of economic life. One in twenty-five adults—and one in eight men twenty-five to thirty-four years old—is attempting to start a new firm at any one time; two in five heads of households report self-employment during their work careers. In the United States, more adults are involved in starting new firms than in creating families (through marriage) or new citizens (as parents).

Second and equally important, these are not marginal individuals, not "misfits cast off from wage work" (Evans and Leighton, 1989),[3] but mainstream adults seeking new options in their work careers. In fact, the evidence is quite clear in this section and more dramatic in Chapter 8 that marginal individuals without education, income, work experience, jobs, or community ties are the least likely to become involved in starting new firms. Nascent entrepreneurs tend to be very well established in their careers, life, and communities.

Third, the personal objectives associated with starting a new firm are very mixed. While nascent entrepreneurs show some interest in financial gain, autonomy and task interest are also significant (Table 3.5).

NOTES

1. This index has been used as an indicator of economic well-being for the United States since 1948 and is now reported semi-monthly (Curtin, 1982). The items for the index are (1) We are interested in how people are getting along financially these days. Would you say that you (and your family living there) are better off or worse off financially than you were a year ago? Why would you say so? (2) Now looking ahead—do you think that a year from now you (and your family living there) would be better off financially, or worse off, or just the same as now? (3) Now turning to business conditions in the country as a whole—do you think that during the next 12 months we'll have good times financially, or bad times, or what? (4) Looking ahead, which would you say is more likely—that in the country as a whole we'll have continuous good times during the next five years or so, or that we will have periods of widespread unemployment or depression, or what? (5) About the big things people buy for their homes—such as furniture, a refrigerator, a stove, television, and things like that. Generally speaking, do you think now is a good or a bad time for people to buy major household items? Why do you say so? Responses for each item are on a scale from 1 (positive) to 5 (negative). The index was created by standardizing each item with a zero mean and standard deviation of 1 and then taking the average of the responses for each respondent. Any respondent answering

three or more of the five items was included. Standardized Chronbach's alpha, a measure of reliability, was 0.54 for this sample.

2. The items used in this index of business confidence, constructed for this analysis, are: (1) Now turning to business conditions in the country as a whole—do you think that during the next 12 months we'll have good times financially, or bad times, or what? (2) Would you say that *at the present time* business conditions are better or worse than they were a year ago? (3) And about a year from now, do you expect that in the country as a whole business conditions will be *better*, or *worse* than they are at present, or just about the same? (4) As to the economic policy of the government—I mean steps taken to fight inflation or *un*employment—would you say the government is doing a good job, only fair, or a poor job? Responses for each item are on a scale from 1 (positive) to 5 (negative). The index was created by standardizing each item with a zero mean and standard deviation of 1 and then taking the average of the responses for each respondent. Any respondent answering three or more of the four items was included. Standardized Chronbach's alpha, a measure of reliability, was 0.71 for this sample.

3. This may be an example where inferences about the entrepreneurs and the start-up process based on reported self-employment have led to serious errors of interpretation. Given the paucity of appropriate indicators of entrepreneurial behavior or measures of firm start-ups in standardized government data, some researchers have utilized reported self-employment as a primary occupational role, as a surrogate for entrepreneurial activity. The systematic efforts to identify, first, start-up efforts and, second, current labor force activity of those starting new firms indicate that most have full-time work until the firm is considered a going concern. It is also true, however, that about a third of firm start-ups are initiated by individuals who are owner/managers of an existing firm, although most owner/managers are not trying to start another new firm.

Chapter 4

Transformation of Business Start-ups to Fledgling New Firms

M any people are trying to start many firms. That is the major conclusion from the discussion of the first transformation—initiating the firm start-up process. Two groups have a major interest in the second transformation—where start-ups become fledgling new firms. First, the individuals involved, the nascent entrepreneurs, would like to know the most efficient or most productive techniques for creating a viable new firm. Second, public policy makers—those promoting new firms as a way to enhance economic growth—would like to know where to devote their attention. Should they focus on encouraging more to become nascent entrepreneurs—initiate start-up efforts—or try to assist those who have already completed that transition and may need assistance in completing firm gestation to create a live firm birth? If assistance to start-up efforts is to be the focus, what types of help might be the most effective or efficient for public policy?

We begin with an analysis of the two fundamental features of the second transition. First, what proportion are able to complete the gestation process with the founding of a new firm? Second, how long does it take to reach a resolution? The preliminary analysis is able to provide only approximate answers for these questions, partly because the samples are small and partly because it turns out that simple, precise answers are difficult with this phenomenon. To determine if these preliminary findings are reasonable, an effort is made to check their accuracy through a comparison with estimates of new entries into established business registries.

This is followed by a comparison of different features of start-up efforts with different outcomes. Start-up efforts that result in new firms are compared to those with other outcomes on the basis of the characteristics of the teams, investments in time and money, and the nature and sequence of start-up activities. The results provide some implications for both policy-makers and future nascent entrepreneurs.

OUTCOME OF THE START-UP PROCESS

Efforts were made to contact all nascent entrepreneurs in both the Wisconsin and U.S. samples to determine the outcomes—or at least the current status—of the start-up efforts. The results are summarized in Table 4.1.

The first survey, in Wisconsin, actually involved three different procedures for locating nascent entrepreneurs. Because it was expected that the prevalence of nascent entrepreneurs would be in the range of 1–2%, a special technique, called multiplicative sampling, was used to locate nascent entrepreneurs among all respondents' social contacts (Palit and Reynolds, 1993). As a result, there was a total of ninety-two candidates for the follow-up interviews from the Wisconsin project. In the U.S. sample,

Table 4.1
Start-up Firm Outcomes

	U.S.	Wisconsin
Total receiving initial interview	65 (1)	92 (2)
Name and phone number available	65	69
Time to follow-up interview (months)	6–8	12–18
Phone interview length (minutes)	30–40	30–40
Total full or partial completion of follow-up	43	52
Percent follow-up completed	66%	75%
Incomplete interview	2	—
Unable to classify business activity	1	1
Purchase of existing business	1	3
Business-sponsored, subsidiaries, or spin-off	11	2
Franchises	2	3
Independent start-ups	26	43
Total franchises or independent start-ups	28	46
Reported outcomes		
New firm established (self-report)	43%	46%
Actively working on the start-up	25	30
Temporarily inactive	18	6
Given up on new business	14	17
Totals	100%	100%

Notes: (1) This includes all those who were asked details of start-up activities; only thirty-nine qualified as current start-ups.

(2) Includes all respondents in three procedures involving systematic scans of the respondents' social network to locate eligible nascent entrepreneurs.

sixty-five individuals were asked the detailed questions about their start-up efforts, although only thirty-nine qualified as currently in the start-up phase. Efforts were made to locate and interview all sixty-five.

There is always attrition in panel studies, and the experimental nature of these efforts leads to more than usual losses. For example, an oversight led to the loss of twenty-three respondents from the Wisconsin effort because their names and phone numbers were not retained from the first procedure. Further, it turned out that some start-up efforts were sponsored by existing businesses and were not independent efforts. This was determined, however, only in the follow-up interviews. While the proportion of nascent entrepreneurs who were contacted and interviewed a second time was reasonably high, 66% for the U.S. sample and 75% for the Wisconsin sample, the total for whom data are available for independent start-ups, including franchises, was reduced to seventy-four.

There are a number of possible outcomes for this procedure, and the results are presented in Table 4.1. The similarity between the two samples is striking: when the two samples are combined, 45% report that the new firm is established, 28% report they are still working on the start-up, 11% report they are "temporarily" inactive with regard to the start-up of this business, and 16% claim to have given up entirely. Stated differently, the *least* likely response (one in six) was that they had decided to give up on this new firm. It appears that once individuals have made the commitment to start a new firm—a commitment reflected in behavior—it is difficult for them to abandon these efforts, at least psychologically.

The high proportion that reports an active business is surprising on two counts. First, the time lag between the first and second interviews was twice as long in Wisconsin (twelve to eighteen months) as for the U.S. sample (six to eight months). Yet the proportion of successful start-ups reported for Wisconsin is only slightly higher (46%) than that reported for the national sample (43%). Why is not the proportion of successful start-ups higher in Wisconsin, as they have more time to put a firm in place? The answer, to be elaborated later, is that most successful start-ups occur so quickly, within six to nine months, that the process was completed before the second interview was conducted with either the Wisconsin or U.S. samples of nascent entrepreneurs.

A second problem is with the high level of successful start-ups reported in both samples: nascent entrepreneurs report that almost half of the firms in gestation result in live firm births. Just as the prevalence of nascent entrepreneurs was two to three times greater than expected, the proportion of new firm births is two to three times greater than expected. Two factors may account for this high proportion of firm births. First, this includes a wide range of business entities, from part-time self-employment to new business organizations with management teams, employees, and substantial sales. Further analysis will be needed to separate the hobbies from "real" new firms. Second, there was some attrition in the follow-up process.

Substantial effort went into trying to locate individuals for the follow-up interview. If the start-up efforts reported by those not interviewed a second time are considered abandoned, this would reduce the proportion of successful start-ups. In the analysis that follows a figure of 30%, rather than 50%, is used as an approximation of the proportion of start-ups that leads to firm births.

HOW LONG IS THE START-UP PROCESS?

Estimating the length of the gestation process requires two operational definitions: a criterion and a date for the start of the process and a criterion and a date for the conclusion of the process. There are a number of alternatives for each. All are based on the dates reported for the initiation of gestation events listed in Table 3.1.

The same inventory of start-up activities, including the date of initiation, was asked of all respondents for a second time in the follow-up interviews. The answers were then compared, and the earliest reported date for each behavior was determined. The "date of conception" was, then, the date at which the first reported activity was initiated. It may have been any start-up activity—saving to invest, organized start-up team, looked for sites, and so on. "Serious thought," however, was not considered a start-up "activity."

A criterion for the end of the start-up process is harder to establish. This is due, in part, to the range of outcomes. A different criterion is needed for those who give up compared to those who establish a new firm. Those who reported giving up were simply asked, "When did you give up?" Their answer established that date. The date for founding a new firm is somewhat more problematic, and four measures were developed: date of first hire, date of first sales, date of first positive monthly cash flow, and date the respondent "knew" the firm would become operational. For those still involved in the gestation process, the time from the initial behavior to the date of the interview was calculated to provide information on the length of involvement in the process.

These various times, in months, are presented in Table 4.2. This provides evidence regarding the time spent on the gestation process by respondents whose firms in gestation have taken these different outcomes. Because of missing data and variation in the occurrence of some types of activity, the number of respondents is somewhat less than the total of seventy-four reported in Table 4.1.

Despite the small samples, there are some patterns in Table 4.2 worth attending to. Firms are put in place in slightly less than a year, regardless of the measure of "firm birth." The average is less than twelve months and as low as ten months for three measures. In every case the median is less than the average, suggesting a large proportion of nascent entrepreneurs put firms in place rather quickly. It takes slightly longer, however, for nascent entrepreneurs to give up and become discouraged entrepreneurs.

Table 4.2
Measures of the Start-up Window (Months)

	United States					Wisconsin				
	No.	Mean	Median	Minimim	Maximum	No.	Mean	Median	Minimum	Maximum
New firm founded										
First behavior										
to first hiring	3	17.9	15.2	7.1	31.4	6	10.5	7.6	2.1	25.4
to first sales	11	9.2	7.1	0.0	26.4	20	10.4	4.1	0.0	78.1
to positive monthly cash flow	3	4.1	0.0	0.0	12.2	13	10.6	8.1	0.0	24.4
to "know" it will be successful	11	10.6	7.1	0.0	43.6	20	11.8	9.6	0.0	43.7
to first filing of:										
D&B report	0	—	—	—	—	2	7.6	7.6	4.0	11.2
unemploy. insurance	2	8.6	8.6	5.1	12.2	6	25.5	12.6	0.0	80.1
FICA	4	11.4	8.6	0.0	30.4	12	14.2	5.6	0.0	71.1
federal taxes	7	12.9	14.2	0.0	30.4	17	13.1	7.7	0.0	71.1
Quit—gave up										
First behavior to gave up	1	23.2	—	—	—	6	63.3	32.2	14.7	185.9
Still active										
First behavior to interview date	7	18.8	17.3	12.2	30.4	13	47.5	32.9	16.8	143.3
Temporarily inactive										
First behavior to interview date	2	152.0	152.0	10.1	293.0	3	30.3	29.1	18.0	43.8

All measures report several years of attempting to start a firm after the first activity is reported. Those who are still active in trying to put a firm in place also report years of attention to this start-up.

This pattern, then, suggests that most new firms are put into place in about a year and that after two years nascent entrepreneurs are beginning to lose interest. There is, however, a small proportion of people who are quite tenacious about their entrepreneurial ambitions, working on the establishment of a new firm for three or four or five years—some for a decade.

This has substantial implications for cross-sectional surveys of a general population. Any random sample of nascent entrepreneurs reporting on start-up efforts will include a proportion that has been working on the effort for an extended period. Those engaged in organized and deliberate efforts may have a much shorter start-up period. As a result, great care in the interview will be required to determine which nascent entrepreneurs are reporting on a serious start-up and which are hobby start-ups, pursued in a more casual manner.

VERIFICATION OF THE PROCESS: ARE THE ESTIMATES REASONABLE?

The results of this research suggest that about one in twenty-five adults is involved in trying to start a new business and that 30-50% of these businesses are launched within a year. Although this research represents preliminary efforts utilizing small samples, the procedure is designed to provide an estimate of new entries in established databases. Hence, there is considerable interest in determining the correspondence between the sample and established business registries. If there is a rough agreement between the two figures, it will increase confidence in the general applicability of the results. If the two estimates are widely divergent, there would be a strong reason to question the entire procedure used in this survey research.

Several data sets in the United States are considered to be relatively complete listings, or registries, of business entities (although the definition of "entity" varies): Dun and Bradstreet files, data based on the state filings of unemployment insurance tax payments, data based on filings of federal Social Security (FICA) payments, and the annual federal income tax filings. Using the data assembled so far, it is possible to compare the results of these preliminary studies with those from another source, as demonstrated in Table 4.3. This is, however, a complicated comparison because a number of issues need to be taken into consideration.

Estimates are developed in Table 4.3 for both Wisconsin and the United States. The procedure is as follows. First, the total adult population is taken from the 1990 census of the human population. The prevalence of nascent entrepreneurs is used to estimate the total number in the population, following the analysis in Table 3.4. Most firms in gestation are being

Table 4.3
The Entrepreneurial Process and Incorporation in Business Registries

		Wisconsin		United States
Adult population (18 yrs and older) (1)		3,600,000		187,000,000
Prevalence in sample (per 1,000)		43		37
Total in Population		155,000		6,920,000
Start-up team size (2)		2.2		2.2
Firms in gestation (3)		70,400		3,145,000
Annual proportion fledgling firm births	30%	21,100	30%	563,000
Proportion reporting filing: (4)				
D&B credit	9%		0%	
State unemployment insurance	29	6,100	18	170,000
FICA payments	57		36	
Federal tax return	81		64	
Annual new entries in unemployment insurance tax files (5)		6,300		370,000

Notes: (1) U. S. and Wisconsin populations for 1991 from Table 27 of *Statistical Abstract of the United States: 1992.* (Washington, DC: U.S. Government Printing Office, 1992).

(2) Both estimates based on responses of nascent entrepreneurs in the interviews to the question, "Counting yourself, in total how many people are active in trying to start this business?" Estimates based on responses of ninety-seven nascent entrepreneurs in the Wisconsin project (which includes data from those contacted in pretests prior to the main survey) and thirty-nine in the U.S. sample. One outlier, with twenty-five on the start-up team, was dropped for the U.S. sample of nascent entrepreneurs.

(3) Computed by dividing the average start-up team size into the estimated number of nascent entrepreneurs in the population.

(4) Percentages based on reports of principals of autonomous new firms or franchises reporting these behaviors in the follow-up interviews.

(5) Wisconsin estimate based on annual counts of new entries into the state unemployment insurance files. Hence, the new entries into these files are reduced by 50%. The U.S. estimate is based on data received and edited by the Office of Advocacy of the U.S. Small Business Administration from the Employment and Training Administration, U.S. Department of Labor. It reflects new entries in all state unemployment files not considered successors. As with the Wisconsin counts, this U.S. count has been reduced by 50%.

developed by teams, with an average size slightly greater than two (2.2). Hence, the total number of start-up firms is less than half the total of nascent entrepreneurs (assuming that no two respondents in these surveys are working on the same start-up).

Two estimates from the pilot follow-ups discussed earlier are critical for the next stage: (1) the percentage of firms in gestation that become new firms, assumed to be 30%, and (2) the length of time required to complete the gestation of a new firm, assumed to be twelve months. If the average gestation period was substantially longer or shorter, additional adjustments would be necessary. The final step is to utilize the data from the follow-up interviews to estimate the proportion of new firms that have filed the reports required to enter the major registries. In this case, 29% of the Wisconsin respondents and 18% of those from the U.S. sample claim they have filed their first unemployment insurance payment with the state tax authorities.

The annual number of new firms, with employees, is available for both Wisconsin and the United States. Both estimates are based on the reports of new entries in the state unemployment insurance files, the national data prepared by the U.S. Department of Labor. The estimates from the survey research would be 6,100 new firms listed for Wisconsin, which compares favorably with the 6,300 annual new entries in the Wisconsin state data. The estimate from the survey results for the entire United States would be 170,000 new listings, half the 370,000 from the official reports. If the true proportion of U.S. start-ups filing unemployment taxes for the first time is the same as for Wisconsin, 29% rather than 18%, then the estimated first-time filings for the United States would be 274,000, about three-fourths of the U.S. annual figure.

Two conclusions seem reasonable from this comparison. First, larger samples are needed in panel studies of the start-up process. More reliable estimates of all the figures associated with the comparison (proportion of nascent entrepreneurs, length of the start-up process, proportion of start-ups that become new firms, and proportion of new firms entering standardized business registries) would be of great value. Second, the current comparisons are not that far off. They are, given the small sample sizes, relatively close. It seems reasonable to conclude that the survey procedure and the mechanisms for incorporating new start-ups into business registries are reflecting the same phenomena, albeit at different points in the start-up process.

START-UP ACTIVITIES AND GESTATION OUTCOMES

Nascent entrepreneurs reported four outcomes in the follow-up interview: the firm was started, they are still working on the start-up, the start-up was temporarily inactive, or they abandoned the effort altogether. What factors known about the start-up teams and their efforts might differentiate these outcomes? Three types of factors are considered in this comparison: characteristics of the respondent—considered a lead nascent entrepreneur; selected features of the business effort; and, finally, attention to the activities pursued in starting the business. In all cases, the two samples have been combined, and the major focus is on the outcome reported by the respondent at the time of the second interview. These results might change if another criterion was used for a "business birth," such as filing a first federal tax return.

Does the Person Make a Difference?

The major features of the respondent associated with a successful start-up are presented in Table 4.4. They include gender, age, ethnic background, educational attainment, household income, labor force status, and length of residential tenure in the county and state. As 45% of the seventy-four respondents reported that the firm was a "going concern" in the second interview, the major attention is to factors that increase or decrease this proportion.

As in previous analysis, gender seems to play a major role, with men twice as likely as women to report the business is operating. As a consequence, three-fourths of the new start-ups are reported by men, as indicated in the far right column of Table 4.4.

The other factor that has a dramatic—and unexpected—effect is educational attainment. Slightly more than 70% of those who did not go beyond high school, although most had a high school degree, reported starting a new business. In contrast, not a single person out of eight with some graduate training (including a postcollege degree) reported starting a new firm. The pattern is, in fact, clearly linear and negative, with a systematic decrease in the proportion of start-ups reported as educational attainment increases. As a result, less than one in five of the new firm start-ups is reported by those with a college degree.

Other patterns are of some interest. The proportion of business births is highest for those with intermediate levels of income, and three-fourths of the firm births are reported from households with annual incomes between $20,000 and $60,000 a year. The highest proportion of starts is reported by those who are self-employed, followed by those with full-time jobs; together these individuals account for three-fourths of all reported firm births. There is a distinctive pattern related to length of residence in the area, for while 53% of the firm births are reported by those who have lived in their county less than ten years, 75% are reported by those who have lived in their state for over ten years. Clearly, many are operating within familiar territory at the same time they are starting businesses.

There is some indication that black respondents are less likely to report a business birth, but the slight reduction among other ethnic groups is not statistically significant. The results of the effect of ethnic background are inconclusive with these small samples.

Several measures of attitudes or orientations were available from the initial interviews. The measures of consumer or business confidence for those in the U.S. sample or the measure of judgments about the entrepreneurial climate for the Wisconsin sample were unrelated to the start-up outcome. In addition, four indexes of work interest—autonomy/impact; task or type of work; wealth and prestige; staying in community—available for the Wisconsin sample were unrelated to the outcome of the start-up effort.

Table 4.4
Background Characteristics and Fledgling New Firms: Combined Samples

Proportions		No. of Cases	Give Up	Start-up Hiatus	Start-up Continues	Firm Birth	Row Total	Bus. Births
				Outcome				
Overall		74	16%	11%	28%	45%	100%	—
Gender	Men	44	9%	7%	27%	57%	100%	76%
	Women	29	28	14	31	28	100	24
	Column total							100%(*)
Age	18–34 yrs. old	34	9%	12%	29%	50%	100%	51%
	35–44 yrs. old	19	16	5	32	47	100	27
	45–54 yrs. old	11	27	9	36	27	100	9
	55–up yrs. old	9	33	11	11	44	100	12
	Column total							100%
Ethnic status	White	48	15%	6%	27%	52%	100%	76%
	Black	10	20	30	30	20	100	6
	Other, don't know	16	19	13	31	38	100	18
	Column total							100%
Educational attainment	Up to H.S. degree	30	10%	0%	20%	70%	100%	66%
	Post-high school	14	21	14	29	36	100	16
	College degree	19	15	21	32	32	100	19
	Post-college exp.	8	25	12	63	0	100	0
	Column total							100%(*)
Household income	Up to $19K per year	8	25%	25%	13%	38%	100%	9%
	$20K–29K per year	10	0	0	40	60	100	18
	$30K–49K per year	13	15	0	15	69	100	27
	$50–59K per year	20	25	5	25	45	100	27
	$60K+ per year	18	11	17	39	33	100	18
								100%
Labor force status	Self-employed	17	12%	6%	29%	53%	100%	27%
	Full-time job	37	14	14	30	43	100	48
	Part-time job	8	38	0	25	38	100	9
	Other, don't know	12	17	17	25	42	100	15
	Column total							100%
County tenure	0–5 years	22	5%	14%	32%	50%	100%	39%
	6–10 years	10	10	20	30	40	100	14
	11–20 years	10	20	20	30	30	100	11
	21+ years	23	30	0	26	43	100	36
	Column total							100%
State tenure	0–5 years	13	8%	8%	46%	39%	100%	18%
	6–10 years	6	17	17	33	33	100	7
	11–20 years	10	20	20	20	40	100	14
	21+ years	36	19	8	25	47	100	61
	Column total							100%

Notes: Missing data reduce total cases in some categories.

    * Indicates chi-square test of statistical significance exceeds 0.05 level.

This lack of relationship between most individual attributes, as well as measures of judgments or attitudes, and the start-up outcome is a major justification for considering other features of the start-up process, particularly the activities involved.

Does the Business Make a Difference?

Several features of the new business are considered in Table 4.5: the size of the start-up team, the economic sector, and, using data only from the U.S. sample, the strategy emphasized by the start-up firm. Team size seems to have some effect, a higher proportion of one-person efforts reporting a firm birth and a larger proportion of those with three or more on the team in a start-up hiatus, perhaps waiting to get organized.

Some economic sectors seem to be of major significance, as four of five of the start-up efforts in agriculture and construction report a firm birth. At the opposite extreme is the retail sector, where less than one in six reports a business birth. On the other hand, there is little variation among the other sectors, the context for two-thirds of the start-ups.

Previous studies of business strategy, utilizing three samples of new firms, have found seven dimensions of emphasis useful in assessing the presence of distinctive strategies (Carter et al., 1994). While the original procedures utilized over twenty items, factor analysis produced seven major dimensions of strategy. The item with the highest loading on each factor was chosen for inclusion in the U.S. sample follow-up interview schedule. For each of the seven items, the respondent indicates the appropriate emphasis on a four-point scale (4 = critical, 3 = important, 2 = marginal, 1 = insignificant). The overall emphasis on strategy is indicated by adding together the average response to all seven items.

Two results emerge from this analysis. First, when the relative emphasis on the seven strategy dimensions are rank-ordered, the provision of quality products and services receives the greatest emphasis. Second, it would appear that those in a start-up hiatus give less emphasis to any strategy emphasis than those reporting any other outcome. This may reflect one reason these efforts are stalled—lack of a coherent business focus. Or because this start-up effort has stalled, they may have forgotten what they intended to do.

The weak patterns in the analysis of business characteristics, combined with those related to characteristics of the entrepreneur, give even more reason to attend to what goes on in the start-up process.

Does the Start-up Activity Make a Difference?

The answer is yes—and in spades. In fact, actions deserve a more extended discussion, for not only the presence of action but the cumulative development seem to be of considerable consequence, in the sense that they

Table 4.5
Selected Business Characteristics and Fledgling New Firms

	No. of Cases	Outcome				Row Total
		Give Up	Start-up Hiatus	Start-up Continues	Firm Birth	
Overall	74	16%	11%	28%	45%	100%
Start-up team size						
One	26	19%	4%	15%	62%	100%
Two	27	11	7	48	33	100
Three or more	11	18	36	9	36	100 (*)
Economic sector						
Agriculture, construction,	10	10%	0%	10%	80%	100%
Manufacturing, transportation, wholesale	13	15	15	23	46	100
Financial, insurance, real estate, business services	15	27	0	33	40	100
Retail, restaurants, bars	16	19	19	50	13	100
Consumer service: health, education, social service	11	9	18	9	64	100
Other, cannot classify	9	11	11	33	44	100
						All Cases
U.S. sample only (no cases)		4	5	7	12	28
Strategy emphasis (4 = HI, 1 = LO)						
Overall emphasis		2.36	1.97	2.97	2.86	2.65 (*)
Quality products, services		3.00	3.40	3.43	3.67	3.46
Serve those missed by others		2.50	2.00	3.14	3.42	2.96 (*)
Contemporary products		3.75	1.80	2.71	2.83	2.75
Lower prices		2.50	1.60	3.14	2.75	2.61 (*)
Product technology		3.50	1.40	3.71	2.17	2.61 (#)
Superior location, convenience		2.00	2.00	2.71	2.93	2.54
Process technology		3.75	1.60	2.57	2.33	2.46

Notes: Missing data reduces the total cases in some categories.

(*) Indicates test of statistical significance exceeds 0.05 level.

(#) Indicates test of statistical significance between 0.05 and 0.10 level

distinguish those start-ups efforts that lead to fledgling new firms from the others.

Investments. A comparison of three aspects of the start-up process—initial activities, total time invested, and total team financial investments—is presented in Table 4.6. The first is based on activities reported in the first interview, as presented in Table 3.2. Those who report a firm in place in the second interview have produced about 50% more of these start-up behaviors

Table 4.6
Start-up Investments and Start-up Outcomes

	Outcome				
	Give Up	Start-up Hiatus	Start-up Continues	Firm Birth	All Cases
Combined samples: No. of cases	12	8	21	33	74
Start-up behaviors reported in first interview					
Minimum	0.00	0.00	0.00	1.00	0.00
Median (50 percentile)	4.50	4.50	5.00	7.00	6.00
Average	4.33	4.75	4.95	6.93	(***)5.72
Maximum	8.00	10.00	9.00	13.00	13.00
U.S. sample only: No. of cases	4	5	7	12	28
Total team time invested (hours)					
Minimum	160	60	160	60	60
Median (50 percentile)	700	300	300	1,900	375
Average	810	1,030	700	3,110	1,810
Maximum	1,700	4,000	1,840	8,000	8,000
Total team financial investment ($1,000)					
Minimum	0	0	0	0	0
Median (50 percentile)	10	100	200	85	85
Average	55	188	376	458	332
Maximum	200	470	1,000	2,000	2,000

Note: *** Statistically significant beyond the 0.01 level.

by the time of the first interview. The follow-up interviews with the U.S. sample included questions about the total amount of time each member of the start-up team had "invested" in the new firm. Those who reported a successful firm start reported, on the average, *three to four* times as many hours as those without a new firm. (This approaches but does not reach statistical significance, due to a small number of cases and substantial dispersion within each outcome.) The patterns are similar for differences related to the total financial investment by the start-up team, which is the largest for the start-ups that became new firms. The differences among the various start-up outcomes, however, are smaller. This type of financial data is difficult for analyses, due to extremely wide dispersion and the small samples.

In brief, there is strong evidence that those able to put a new firm in place put in much more time, complete half again as many behaviors, and invest more of their own funds in the new firm, when compared to those who are not able to get the firm established. But what about the specific activities associated with a start-up?

Start-up Activities. The differences in the specific activities associated with a new firm birth are presented for the combined samples in Table 4.7. The percentages that reported that different activities were initiated, though not necessarily completed, are indicated for the four outcomes. The far right column indicates the level of statistical significance associated with comparisons across the four outcomes.

These behaviors, which occurred within five years of the first behavior, are placed in five categories. The top group lists those that most strongly

Table 4.7
Start-up Events: Prevalence and Outcomes

Start-up Behavior (1, 2)	Outcome				All Cases	Stat. Sign
	Give Up	Start-up Hiatus	Start-up Continues	Firm Birth		
Strong differentiators						(3)
Bought facilities and equipment	45%	43%	53%	88%	67%	**
Hired employees	9	0	11	33	20	#
Received financial support	18	14	26	52	36	#
Weak differentiators						
Invested own money	64	71	84	94	84	#
Asked for funding	18	29	32	55	40	
Devoted full time to business	36	29	16	48	36	
Applied for license or patent	45	71	42	70	59	
Created a legal entity	27	14	21	45	33	
Uncommon, no differentiation						
Developed models/prototypes	36	29	26	18	24	
Leased facilities or equipment	9	29	26	24	23	
Common, no differentiation						
Gave serious thought to start-up	91	100	100	94	96	
Looked for facilities	64	71	74	82	76	
Saved money to invest	55	57	74	67	66	
Organized start-up team	55	57	58	67	61	
Prepared business plan	55	57	47	58	54	
Start-up indicators						
Money from sales	55%	43%	53%	97%	73%	***
Positive monthly cash flow	27	14	16	52	34	*
First filing of:						
Federal income tax	14	0	17	86	50	****
FICA	0	0	0	57	28	***
State unemployment insurance	0	0	0	24	12	
Knowledge firm in Dun & Bradstreet files	0	0	0	5	2	

Notes: (1) All but last four rows base on reports of behaviors that had occurred in the first or second interview for both samples.

(2) Last four rows based only on reports in follow-up interview.

(3) Statistical significance based on one-way analysis of variance F-test: # = 0.10; * = 0.05; ** = 0.01; *** = 0.001; **** = 0.0001.

differentiate between the start-ups that became firm births and those with other outcomes. These include the purchase of facilities and equipment, hiring employees, and the receipt of outside financial support. These differences are, in most cases, statistically significant. The next group differentiates between the outcomes, but the results are weaker. These include a decision by the nascent entrepreneur to invest in the firm, formal requests to outsiders for funding, the decision to devote full time to the start-up effort, an application for a license or patent, or taking steps to create a legal entity (corporation or partnership). With larger samples, these differences would probably be statistically significant.

Two groups of events fail to differentiate between the outcomes. Behaviors in the first are uncommon and include the development of models or prototypes and leasing facilities or equipment. The other group includes those behaviors that are common among all start-ups, regardless of outcomes. These include searching for facilities or equipment, saving money to invest in the new firm, organizing a start-up team, or preparing a business plan. Given all the attention to a formal business plan by training and educational programs, it is to be noted that it is not associated with differential outcomes of start-up efforts. Perhaps the development of a business plan leads to more confidence in the outcome decision.

The final group is composed of those that would be considered universal indicators of a business start, and all are much more prevalent for the business births. These include income, positive monthly cash flow, first federal income tax filing, first FICA filing, first state unemployment insurance filing, and knowledge that the firm is in the Dun and Bradstreet files.

Sequence of Start-up Activities. The data collected on these business start-ups were gathered at two points in the process. The timing of the interviews was, from the point of view of the process itself, arbitrary. Random selection of pregnant women would select women at different stages of the human birth process. Analysis of human pregnancy, however, generally starts by trying to identify the date of conception and tracks progress from that event. In a similar fashion, a "gestation period" was established for each firm, with conception defined as the month the first start-up behavior occurred. Each subsequent behavior was then tracked in relation to this initial event.

The cumulative number of behaviors could then be tracked for the firms with different outcomes. This is presented in Exhibit 4.1. For this analysis, those not actively trying to start a business, who have permanently or temporarily withdrawn from the process, have been combined into one group. The results are quite striking.

Those who report a firm birth and those who have given up have similar patterns, particularly in the first year. Compared to those "still trying," these individuals report more activity from the very first month, an average of 2.5 activities compared to 1.5, with almost twice as many completed in the first year.

This provides a clear answer to the question posed earlier, why the longer follow-up for the Wisconsin sample was not associated with a substantially higher proportion of successful firm births. It was because the events that determine a successful birth are determined six to twelve months from the first behavior. A follow-up interview more than six months after the initial interview does not increase the proportion of start-ups that become fledgling firms.

Events during the first year of the start-up appear to be critical in determining the outcome. This justifies more careful attention to the activities during the first twelve months. Given the diversity of economic sectors, locations, and types of businesses found in this sample, identifying any systematic pattern is a challenge. A preliminary effort, however, has been initiated by considering the median time five or more start-ups were

Exhibit 4.1
Cumulative Start-up Activities Initiated by Start-up Outcome

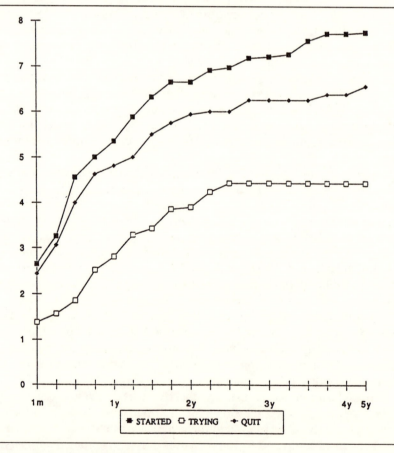

Source: Carter, Gartner, and Reynolds, 1996.

associated with a given activity for each outcome. The sequence for the first year is presented by outcome in Table 4.8.

The differences, tentative because of the small samples, are intriguing. For example, those who gave up were more uniform in their early activities and were more often focused on a physical model or prototype. It may be that the commercial viability of the start-up was easier to determine when a new physical product was the focus of the business. Those who are "still trying" are more diffuse—represented by the lack of entries in this column—and take much longer for events to appear.

Those who report a business birth are more consistent in the completed activities. While the presence of a business plan may not ensure a successful firm birth, those with successful firm births and a business plan started working on the plan early in the process, within the first three months.

The low level of effort among the "trying to start" group presented in Exhibit 4.1 is mirrored in the patterns in Table 4.8, which reflect a gradual buildup of activities. This suggests, once again, that in repeated surveys these "hobby start-ups" will continue to recur as part of a sample of business start-ups.

OVERVIEW AND IMPLICATIONS

For those involved in the start-up process, the outcome is a critical transition. In two samples of nascent entrepreneurs where a second interview was completed, almost half report a firm birth, although this would be reduced to 30% if those not contacted are included in the base. A majority of the others claim they are still working, or plan to work, on putting a business in place. One in six claims to have abandoned the start-up initiative. It would appear that it takes about a year for a firm to be established, somewhat longer to abandon the effort. Estimates of annual rates of new firm entries into business registries based on the survey data approximated the annual rates of new entries into the registries, suggesting that both—survey data collection and new entries in firm registries—are tracking the same phenomenon.

In exploring those factors associated with a firm birth, individuals' characteristics, with a few exceptions—gender and educational attainment—did not have major impacts. There were some small effects associated with the economic sector in which the firm operated: firm births were higher in construction and lower in retail. The actual level of effort and investments in the start-up, as measured by start-up activities initiated, hours invested by the start-up team, and financial contributions from the team, was substantially greater for start-ups that resulted in a firm birth. Particularly striking was the intensity of effort early in the process, which was found for both firm births and those who abandoned the effort.

These findings have implications for those interested in becoming involved in a new firm start-up. Those who see the start-up process itself as

Table 4.8
First-Year Activity by Start-up Outcome

Time in First Year	Started Firm (n = 34)	Gave Up (n = 16)	Still Trying (n = 21)
1st month	Looked for facilities or equipment	Asked for funding Developed models or prototypes Saved money to invest Organized start-up team	
1st quarter	Invested own money Asked for funding Got financial support Prepared business plan	Invested own money Got financial support	Saved money to invest
2nd quarter	Formed legal entity Organized start-up team Bought facilities or equipment Devoted full-time to new business	Prepared business plan Bought facilities or equipment	Prepared business plan Organized start-up team
3rd quarter	Hired employees	Looked for facilities or equipment	Invested own money Looked for facilities or equipment Applied for license or patent
4th quarter	Saved money to invest Rented facilities or equipment Applied for license or patent	Devoted full-time to new business Applied for license or patent	Bought facilities or equipment

Note: Timing based on median values of those initiating activity. Event included only if reported by five or more start-up activities in each outcome category.

Source: Carter, Gartner, and Reynolds, 1996.

their major interest and are not sure about an actual firm birth will find they have lots of company. For those serious about starting a new firm, it is clear that they should expect an intense experience that moves quickly. They should expect to devote a great deal of time to the effort at the very beginning, as they simultaneously initiate a number of start-up activities. Financial investments will also be required, which may range from thousands to hundreds of thousands of dollars. A team may also slow the start-up process, but slowness may be a major asset for more complex endeavors or after a new firm is operating, and diverse skills are needed to manage a fledgling firm, particularly one on a high-growth trajectory. A study of the 1% of new firms with the highest growth rates found that such firms were implemented very quickly and had larger start-up teams than typical new firms (Reynolds, 1993).

Policymakers interested in promoting new firm births should realize that some groups appear to have problems successfully completing the start-up process. There seem to be more losses in the start-up process among women, perhaps minorities, and those with more formal education. They may need special attention or may have an unrealistic conception of what is involved in starting a new firm. They may need help in understanding how to coordinate and implement the various components in a firm start-up in a timely fashion. Training and educational programs may need to emphasize both the advantages of a business plan and the capacity for reacting to new information and changing circumstances in the start-up process. Above all, those starting new firms need to be aware of the intense personal commitment required in the initial stages.

From the perspective of society, it is clear that a great deal of funds and person-years of work are associated with the start-up process. Much of this investment does not result in a firm birth. For example, assume an average of $50,000 is required for each start-up (this is somewhat less than the figures reported in Table 4.6). If there are 3 million start-ups each year, this is an annual total of $150 billion. Seventy percent may be associated with start-up efforts that do not result in a firm birth. Each dollar associated with a start-up that leads to a firm birth, then, represents another two dollars in start-ups that were abandoned. The allocation of sweat equity, however, is more equitable, for it is clear that the majority of sweat equity goes into start-ups that become new firms. If 1.2 billion hours (3 million start-up firms, 400 hours each), or 600,000 person-years, are devoted to firm start-ups each year, three-fourths are probably devoted to those that become new firms. Whether or not public policy and programs may be modified to increase the efficiency of the process is, at this time, an open question. Policymakers encouraging more persons to engage in entrepreneurial activity should be aware, however, that they may be increasing the societal costs if these new recruits merely increase the proportion of unsuccessful start-up efforts.

CONCEPTIONS OF MODERN MARKET ECONOMIES

This small, representative sample of firms in the start-up process makes it quite clear that the appearance of a new firm is neither instantaneous nor without social costs. First, while some firms are put in place in a few months, the average from conception to birth is a year. While a short time in terms of all of human history, it is a significant part of the work life of those involved.

Second, there is a considerable aggregate or social cost associated with each new firm birth. One new firm birth may represent three start-up efforts. The major social cost of each successful firm birth may be borne by the teams—and the families of the teams—of the start-ups that were abandoned. The direct benefits, however, will be achieved by those whose start-ups were successful in leading to a new firm. In short, the major social costs are borne by those with unsuccessful start-ups; the major personal benefits are received by those who successfully launch a new firm.

Chapter 5

Fledgling New Firms:
Growth after Birth

Nothing about new firms is more dramatic than their substantial variation in size. The postbirth variation in growth trajectories is one of the two most critical features of new firms and is the focus of this chapter. The other major feature, persistence or survival, is explored in Chapter 6.

No matter how it is measured, the size variation among new firms is quite substantial. Table 5.1 presents the total number of jobs (25,417), sales ($1,864 million), and out-of-region exports ($183 million) provided by the samples of new firms in Minnesota, Pennsylvania, and Wisconsin. In all states, the largest 10% of the firms provide half of the employment; the largest 10% provide almost 60% of the sales; and the largest 5% provide 90% of the "out-of-region" exports. Conversely, the smallest *half* are responsible for 10% of the jobs, 8% of the sales, and virtually no out-of-region exports. The same patterns are found across the three states and are widely reported in other studies of new firms (Birch, Haggerty, and Parsons, 1995; Storey, 1994).

There are several ways new firms can attain size: either they can start large, or they can grow large. Responding to this issue, analysis in this chapter, following a brief overview of the new firms, will be organized around differences associated with various growth trajectories. A number of technical and definitional issues associated with consolidating the three samples for analysis are presented in an appendix at the end of the chapter.

A number of issues are associated with the variation in size of new firms, those that complete the birth transition. What can be said about the individuals, alone or in teams, who implement new firms? What types of businesses are new firms? How does their implementation vary, based on retrospective accounts of those who established the new firms? How do they generally react to their context? What use do they make of the pro-

Table 5.1
Dispersion of New Firm Jobs, Sales, and Exports: By State

	Minnesota	Pennsylvania	Wisconsin	All
No. of new firms (1)	1,054	1,177	393	2,624
Total jobs (2)	9,325	13,520	2,572	25,417
Percentage provided by firm size				
00–24 percentile	1%	1%	2%	1%
25–49 percentile	11	7	16	9
50–74 percentile	19	12	20	15
75–89 percentile	30	23	18	25
90–100 percentile	39	58	45	50
Total	100%	101%	101%	100%
Total Sales ($millions) (3)	$629	$1,047	$188	$1,864
Percentage provided by firm size				
00–24 percentile	2%	1%	2%	2%
25–49 percentile	7	5	9	6
50–74 percentile	16	11	15	13
75–89 percentile	22	19	21	20
90–100 percentile	53	63	53	59
Total	100%	99%	100%	100%
Total out-of-region exports($millions) (4)	$82	$70	$31	$183
Percentage provided by firm size				
00–89 percentile	2%	2%	1%	2%
90–94 percentile	8	12	4	9
95–100 percentile	90	85	95	89
Total	100%	99%	100%	100%

Notes: (1) Firms with a sales history of 1–7 years; sample sizes may be reduced for some analyses.

(2) Interview year report, part-time jobs counted as one-half full-time job.

(3) Interview year report, all figures adjusted to 1992 dollar values; excludes one PA firm reporting sales, in 1992 dollars, of $160 million.

(4) Interview year report, all figures adjusted to 1992 dollar values, region defined as

grams and assistance available for new and small firms? In what ways might they differ, in terms of external financial support, management focus, or competitive emphasis?

The conclusion reviews some of the most salient differences and considers the implications for firm management and public policy.

OVERVIEW OF NEW FIRMS

An overview and comparison of the new firms from the three samples are provided in Table 5.2. The average and median number of years from the first sale to the interview are both about four, with the shortest time period among the Wisconsin sample of new firms. Based on the time over which sales have occurred, with a minimum of at least two years,[1] the compound annual growth rate averages about 44% per year, with a median of 25% for the combined samples. These growth rates, however, can be quite diverse, with a small proportion reporting negative growth rates, when first-year sales were greater than sales for the following years; a small number, with very low first-year sales, have compound annual growth rates exceeding 1,000%.

Sales, Jobs, and Exports. Initial-year sales, in 1992 dollars, averaged $330,000 for the combined samples, but half reported first-year sales of less than $83,000. Sales in the year of the interview averaged $935,000, but half reported sales of less than $260,000. The patterns for the samples from the three states are similar, with slightly smaller values for Wisconsin.

Computation of the average number of full-time job equivalents involved weighing each part-time job as one-half a full-time job. The average number of jobs reported in the interview was 10.5, but half reported fewer than 5 jobs. The largest firm was substantial, having grown to 300 employees in less than eight years. Again, all summary figures are slightly lower for Wisconsin.

The sales destinations are very similar across the three states, with 80% of sales in the year preceding the interview going inside the state and another 10% to adjacent states. The remaining 10% are largely delivered within the rest of the United States. Only 1% of sales, concentrated among a very few new firms, are to customers in Canada or other foreign countries.

Economic Sectors. The economic sectors of these new firms, presented in Table 5.2, reflect distributions that are similar to existing firms found in the respective states. This distribution is also similar to the distribution of existing U.S. firms provided in Table 3.8. Slightly more than half are in sectors emphasizing the local community, such as construction; retail; health, education, and social services; and consumer services. The remainder are sectors with a potential for export sales, such as agriculture, manufacturing, distributive services (which includes wholesale and transportation), and producer (or business) services. The initial survey, completed in Pennsylvania, omitted health, education, and social service firms from its sample. This does not appear, in any dramatic way, to affect the gross results. The three states have a full range of new firms in their samples.

Growth Topology. To develop a topology based on different growth trajectories, the entire sample was dichotomized on two dimensions. First, the new firms were divided into a high or low start-up group depending on whether

Table 5.2
Selected Characteristics of New Firms: By State

	MN	PA	WI	All
No. of cases (1)	1,054	1,177	393	2,624
Jobs, full-time equivalent, interview year				
Average (****) (2)	9.0	12.7	7.8	10.5
Median	5.0	6.0	4.0	5.0
Interview year sales (3) (1992 dollars, $1,000)				
Average (**)	694	916	573	784
Median	253	260	200	253
First year sales (1992 dollars, $1,000)				
Average (**)	206	440	346	332
Median	42	107	82	77
Age, sales years (4)				
Average (**)	4.3	3.7	3.3	3.9
Median	4.0	4.0	3.0	4.0
Compound annual growth rate				
Average (**)	57%	30%	82%	47%
Median	31	20	24	22
Sales destinations in interview year				
Within host state (*)	87%	84%	83%	86%
Adjacent states (****)	5	9	6	7
Rest of United States	7	6	8	6
International (**)	*	1	2	1
Total	99%	100%	99%	100%
Economic sector (****) (5)				
Agriculture	2%	1%	4%	2%
Mining (6)	*	*	*	*
Construction	10	16	12	13
Manufacturing	13	11	14	12
Distributive services	17	14	10	15
Producer services	16	19	23	18
Health, education, social services (7)	2	—	10	2
Retail	28	29	16	27
Consumer services	11	10	11	10
Total	99%	100%	99%	99%
Growth patterns (****)				
High-start, high-growth	5%	9%	7%	8%
High-start, low-growth	35	44	35	39
Low-start, high-growth	36	19	22	26
Low-start, low-growth	24	27	36	27
Total	100%	99%	100%	100%

Notes: (1) Due to missing data, sample sizes reduced for some analyses.
(2) One-way analysis of variance: *=0.05; **=0.01; ***=0.001; ****=0.0001 and beyond.
(3) Excludes one Pennsylvania firm with interview year sales in excess of $100 million.
(4) Firms with no sales or sales history for eight or more years excluded from the sample.
(5) Chi-square analysis: *=0.05; **=0.01; ***=0.001; ****=0.0001.
(6) * - less than 0.5 %.
(7) Not sampled in Pennsylvania.

first-year sales (adjusted to 1992 dollars) were above or below $100,000. Second, they were divided into high- or low-growth groups depending on whether their compound annual growth rate was above or below 40%. The result is four categories of firms, with 8% in the high-start, high-growth rate group; 39% in the high-start, low-growth rate group; 26% in the low-start, high-growth rate group; and 27% in the low-start, low-growth rate group. The distribution across states is similar, but Wisconsin has a slightly larger proportion of low-start, low- growth rate new firms, and Minnesota a slightly larger proportion of low-start, high-growth rate new firms.

Given the different time periods (1985, 1986, and 1993) in which the interviews were completed and the different sources of the samples, the similarities among the samples are more striking than the differences. If appropriate adjustments are made for differences in regional economic structures, these new firms are probably representative of new firms anywhere in the United States.

GROWTH AND CONTRIBUTIONS TO ECONOMIC WELL-BEING

There is considerable size variation among these new firms, as illustrated in Table 5.1. Half a dozen have annual sales in excess of $10 million and employment in the hundreds; one in four is a modest extension of self-employment. Does the pattern by which firms achieve their size make a difference? They can attain size by either starting large or growing to become large. The critical features of these patterns are presented in Table 5.3. There is, again, considerable diversity among the new firms and their growth trajectories.

The initial rows of Table 5.3 indicate that the classification reported earlier was appropriately implemented. Those identified as high-start new firms had, on the average, first-year sales twenty times larger than the low-start new firms. In a similar fashion, the growth rates among the high-growth firms were, on the average, seven to ten times higher than those of the low-growth firms.

Less obvious, however, are the age differences among these new firms. Age was not a criterion for the classification based on growth, so it can be considered an independent attribute. The high-start new firms seem to have been in place for a shorter period of time, particularly those in the high-start, high-growth category. This difference, which is statistically significant, suggests that these firms may have been implemented to exploit a "moving target" business opportunity. Similar results have been found in an analysis of the fastest growing 1% of new firms in Minnesota and Pennsylvania (Reynolds, 1993).

In terms of economic contributions, the faster growing firms appear to provide substantially more benefits. For example, the 8% of the high-start, high-growth firms are responsible for 15% of all jobs, 27% of all current sales, 40% of all out-of-state exports, and 46% of all out-of-region exports. In

Table 5.3
Growth Trajectories: Economic Contributions (Average Values)

First-Year Sales: Growth Rates	High High	High Low	Low High	Low Low	All Firms
No. of cases (1)	180	922	610	638	2,377
Percent of sample	8%	39%	26%	27%	100%
First-year sales (1992 dollars; $1,000)					
Average (****) (2)	592	707	28	45	342
Median	200	294	15	42	86
Compound annual growth rate					
Average (****)	142%	8%	119%	11%	48%
Median	59	8	81	14	23
Age, sales years (3)					
Average (****)	3.4	3.8	4.0	4.0	3.9
Median	3.0	4.0	4.0	4.0	4.0
Interview year sales (1992 dollars; $1,000)					
Average (****)	2,777	1,072	494	93	786
Median	1,301	456	247	68	260
Jobs, full-time equivalent, interview year					
Average (****)	20.9	14.2	9.2	3.7	10.6
Median	13.0	7.0	5.0	2.0	5.0
Sales destinations in interview year					
Within host state (****)	74%	85%	86%	90%	86%
Adjacent states (****)	11	8	6	5	7
Rest of U.S. (****)	14	7	7	5	6
International	2	1	1	*	1
Total	101%	100%	99%	100%	100%
Percentage of contributions					
Jobs	15%	53%	23%	9%	100%
Sales, year of interview	27	54	16	3	100%
Out-of-state exports	40	45	13	2	100%
Out-of-region exports	46	39	13	2	100%

Notes: (1) Due to missing data, sample sizes may be slightly reduced for some analyses.
(2) Statistical significance tested with one-way analysis of variance: * = 0.05; ** = 0.01; *** = 0.001; **** = 0.0001 or more.
(3) Firms that reported a sales history of up through seven years.

contrast, those 27% of the firms in the low-start, low-growth categories provide 9% of all jobs, 3% of all sales, and 2% of all out-of-state or out-of-region exports. The intermediate firms—high-growth, low-start and low-growth, high-start—have an intermediate level of contributions to economic well-being.

The strong relationship between size and contributions to jobs, sales, and exports and the growth trajectories is apparent from Table 5.4. In this presen-

Table 5.4
Growth Trajectories: Economic Contributions (Dispersion)

First-Year Sales: Growth Rates	High High	High Low	Low High	Low Low	All Firms
No. of cases (maximum) (1)	180	922	610	638	2,377
Percent of sample	8%	39%	26%	27%	100%
Interview year jobs, percent of total					
00–24 percentile	1%	21%	22%	55%	99%
25–49 percentile	3	30	26	40	99
50–74 percentile	6	44	31	19	100
75–89 percentile	14	51	26	8	99
90–100 percentile	21	59	18	2	100
$(r = 0.43;$ ****$)$ (2)					
Interview year sales, percent of total					
00–24 percentile	—%	8%	18	74%	100%
25–49 percentile	1	39	34	26	100
50–74 percentile	20	60	20	—	100
75–89 percentile	26	60	14	—	100
90–100 percentile	32	55	12	—	99
$(r = 0.67;$ ****$)$					
Out-of-region sales (3), percent of total					
00–89 percentile	6%	39%	26%	29%	100
90–94 percentile	14	42	32	12	100
95–100 percentile	33	44	22	1	100
$(r = 0.23;$ ****$)$					

Notes: (1) Due to missing data, sample sizes may be reduced for some analyses.
(2) Pearson product correlation computed from cross tabs; **** =statistical significance
0.0001 level or beyond.
(3) Sales outside home state or adjacent states.
(4) See also notes to Table 5.1.

tation, the percentage of firms in each size percentile is calculated in terms of their growth trajectories. So, for example, among the top 10% of the firms, those providing 50% of the jobs, 80% are "high-start" new firms; 21% fast-growth; and 59% slow-growth. Among the top 10% of the firms providing half of the sales, 87% are high-start; 32% fast-growth; and 55% slow-growth. Among the top 10% of the firms providing 90% of the out-of-region exports, 77% are high-start; 33% high-growth; and 44% low-growth. There is little question that the growth trajectories and size are highly related. It is a common finding among new firms (Storey, 1994) and leads directly to a major policy issue, whether to target public resources on high-growth new firms.

Because of the significant variation in contributions associated with firms with different growth trajectories, the remaining analysis emphasizes differences associated with these four types of firms.

START-UP TEAM AND FIRM GROWTH TRAJECTORIES

The start-up teams of the new firms are considered in terms of their size, family involvement, and team structure with regard to gender, ethnic background, educational attainment, age, work experience, and residential tenure. There are a number of systematic patterns related to the growth trajectories.

Size. If a start-up team is defined as persons who have or expect to have a partial ownership in the new firm, Table 5.5 shows that slightly more than half of all new firms are started by teams. One person initiates about two in five of all new firm start-ups, at least those that end up in the Dun and Bradstreet files or the Wisconsin state unemployment insurance files. Approximately one in six are implemented by teams involving three or more individuals. Firm start-ups that are basically self-employment, which may be half of all new businesses, are not included in this analysis.

Larger teams and fewer sole proprietorships are associated with firms with higher initial sales and higher growth trajectories, again indicated in Table 5.5. One of the more striking findings in an analysis of the largest 1% of Minnesota and Pennsylvania new firms was the substantially larger size of their start-up teams; fewer than 20% were owned by one person (Reynolds, 1993).

Table 5.5
Growth Trajectories: Start-up Team Size, Ownership Structure

First-Year Sales: Growth Rates	High High	High Low	Low High	Low Low	All Firms
No. of cases (maximum) (1)	160	852	569	595	2,176
Average team size (***) (2)	2.04	1.93	1.87	1.59	1.83
Team size: (***) (3)					
Sole proprietorship	35%	38%	42%	52%	43%
Two-person team	39	43	39	41	41
Three + team members	26	19	19	7	16
Total	100%	100%	100%	100%	100%
Family ownership: (**) (3)					
Wisconsin only: No. of cases	24	106	69	109	308
Sole proprietorship	41%	42%	37%	55%	45%
Family owned/family managed	36	25	33	30	29
Family owned/non-family managed	17	28	24	13	18
Non-family team ownership	6	15	6	2	8
Total	100%	100%	100%	100%	100%

Notes: (1) Due to missing data, may be reduced slightly for some analyses.
(2) Using one-way analysis of variance, statistical sign beyond 0.001.
(3) Using chi-square test stat sign: **=0.01; ***=0.001.

Family Firms. The data for Wisconsin allowed attention to the extent to which the start-up team was composed of family members. As indicated in Table 5.5, 29% of the Wisconsin new firms were implemented by a family or kin group that owned more than 50% of the firm and was at least half of the start-up team. Another 18% were owned by a family, but non-family members had a significant role on the start-up team. Finally, 8% of the start-ups were implemented by teams of unrelated individuals. In a more detailed analysis of the Wisconsin sample, firms not owned or managed by kin tended to have larger average sales, twice as many paid employees, and significantly more out-of-state exports when compared to sole proprietor-ships or family-owned new firms (Reynolds, 1995). For example, 98% of the low-start, low-growth firms were either sole proprietorships or family-dominated teams. In contrast, 15% of the high-start, low-growth firms were implemented by a non-family team.

Team Structure. The large proportion of team efforts complicates descrip-tions of those involved in newly founded firms. The interview procedure allowed one person to describe up to three additional team members, considered those who owned or expected to own part of the firm. By combining the data on all team members, it is possible to compute the percentage of individuals with different characteristics on the start-up teams. As shown in Table 5.5, the average number of start-up team members is almost two; this almost doubles the number of individuals included in the descriptions. Because of missing data, however, this tends to reduce the number of cases, although never by more than 20%.

Gender. One of the more complicated personal attributes to deal with is gender, as there are a number of possible combinations presented in Table 5.6, the variations depend on the team size. For example, it is clear that only one in six firms has an all-female start-up team, and four of five (81%) are solo efforts. In contrast, almost two-thirds of all start-ups teams are all male, and four of five (77%) are solo efforts. Twenty percent of all start-up teams are mixed gender, and 12% involve only two people. This would suggest that no more than 12% will be the infamous mom-and-pop businesses, although many solo operations may involve a spouse as an unpaid associ-ate, and a team larger than two may be organized around a married couple. Several four-person teams from the Wisconsin sample were composed of two married couples. Males are, in these analyses, more prevalent in larger firms, frequently due to a larger size at start-up.

Men were 75% and women 25% of nascent entrepreneurs reporting a successful new firm start-up, as presented in Table 4.4. This is, allowing for temporal and sample size differences, comparable to the patterns among new firms. The proportion of women on teams was somewhat higher for Wisconsin, 40%, than Pennsylvania, 35%, or Minnesota, 32%. The differ-ences between Pennsylvania and Minnesota disappear when the rate of involvement is controlled for age (there are more younger women in Pennsylvania; Reynolds and Miller, 1990). The higher proportion for Wis-

Table 5.6
Growth Trajectories: Start-up Team Composition

First-Year Sales: Growth Rates	High High	High Low	Low High	Low Low	All Firms
No. of cases (1)	172	879	590	597	2,238
Team Gender, percent (*, 2)**					
One male	48%	52%	44%	53%	50%
Two males	12	11	10	6	9
Three, four males	15	7	5	2	6
One female	4	8	15	20	13
Two females	1	2	1	2	2
Three, four females	1	1	1	*	1
Two mixed	11	9	16	12	12
Three, four mixed	9	10	8	5	8
	100%	100%	100%	100%	100%
Ethnic background, team percent:					
White	93%	90%	92%	91%	91%
Black	3	1	2	2	2
Hispanic	1	1	*	1	1
Asian (**, 3)	1	3	1	1	2
Other	2	6	5	5	4
	100%	100%	100%	100%	100%
Educational attainment, percent of team:					
Up to high school degree (**)	23%	28	23%	31%	27%
Post-high school experience (*)	26	28	34	31	30
College degree (*)	32	29	25	25	27
Post-college experience (*)	18	15	17	12	15
	99%	100%	99%	99%	99%
Age (at year of first sales), team percent:					
18–24 years old (****)	13%	23%	26%	29%	25%
25–34 years old (*)	44	38	41	34	38
35–44 years old	26	24	22	22	23
45–54 years old	15	12	10	13	12
55–64 years old	2	3	1	2	2
65 and up years old	—	*	*	—	*
	100%	100%	99%	99%	100%

Table 5.6 continued

First-Year Sales: Growth Rates	High High	High Low	Low High	Low Low	All Firms
Career status prior to start-up, team percent:					
Established organization (****)	75%	69%	64%	59%	66%
Other new firm	13	12	12	9	11
Unemployed	2	5	6	6	6
School	6	5	9	13	8
Other (****)	4	8	8	13	9
	100%	99%	99%	100%	100%
Experience in same industry, team percent:					
(Minnesota, Pennsylvania only: ***)	36%	47%	52%	59%	51%
0–5 years (****)	24	18	24	13	19
6–10 (****)	19	12	9	9	11
11–15 (***)	11	14	11	14	13
16–25	10	8	4	5	6
26–50 years (***)	100%	99%	100%	100%	100%
Prior experience with start-ups, team percent					
(Minnesota, Pennsylvania only: ***)	58%	60%	69%	70%	65%
None (****)	20	20	15	16	17
One (*)	8	12	8	7	9
Two (**)	13	8	8	7	8
Three or more	99%	100%	100%	100%	99%
Residential tenure, years in county:					
(Principal only, Wisconsin only) (**, 2)	12%	17%	24%	20%	20%
0–4 years	4	25	10	24	20
5–9.9 years	42	38	39	35	37
10–29.9 years	33	21	28	20	23
30 or more years	101%	101%	101%	99%	100%

Notes: (1) Due to missing data, sample size reduced for some analysis.

(2) Chi-square analysis: * = 0.05; ** = 0.01; *** = 0.001.

(3) One-way analysis of variance: * = 0.05; ** = 0.01; *** = 0.001; **** = 0.0001 and beyond.

consin may reflect a growing level of female participation in firm start-ups by the early 1990s.

Ethnic Background. The distribution by ethnic background in Table 5.6 emphasizes whites, which may be expected when half of the samples are from states (Minnesota and Wisconsin) where over 90% of the population is white. Asians are more likely to be associated with high-start, low-growth new firms. It is not, however, a statistically significant pattern.

Educational Attainment. Among the start-up teams there are slightly higher levels of educational attainment among the high-start, fast-growth firms, shown in Table 5.6. Almost 57% of the team members, across the three samples, have not completed college. This is sharply different from the preliminary analysis of those completing the start-up process, presented in Table 4.4, which indicated a much lower founding rate among those nascent entrepreneurs with college degrees and graduate program experience. Larger samples for the study of the start-up process itself would help resolve this issue.

Age. Team member age was obtained as of the date of the interview. As these firms were from one to seven years old, this was adjusted to obtain the age of each team member as of the year of first sales. This provides an age, in Table 5.6, that is more comparable to that of those studied in the start-up process. Among nascent entrepreneurs, as described in Table 4.3, 51% were from eighteen to thirty-four years old, while among the new firm start-up teams, 63% were from eighteen to thirty years old. Given the small samples of nascent entrepreneurs, this is a fairly good correspondence. The analysis of the new firm start-up teams suggests that the older members are often not the lead entrepreneurs but may be involved as a source of experience and perhaps funds, rather than energy. The larger new firms have a smaller proportion of team members eighteen to thirty-four years old.

Work Experience. The level of experience and background skills is reflected in three measures related to the start-up teams in Table 5.6: previous career status, years of experience in the same industry, and prior experience with starting new firms. The more substantial new firms are associated with a larger proportion of the start-up teams that left other established organizations or new firms, more years of industry experience, and more experience with new firm start-ups. It is to be noted, however, that two-thirds (65%) of all those involved in these new firms have never been involved in another start-up.

Residential Tenure. Much analysis of new firms involves attention to the extent to which the principals are well established in local social and business networks (Aldrich and Zimmer, 1986). This personal social embeddedness takes time, which would be reflected in the residential tenure of the start-up team. The last section of Table 5.6 indicates the years of residence in the county by the respondents in the Wisconsin study. One in five has lived in the county less than five years (fewer than one in ten has lived in the state less than ten years), and 60% report living in the county over ten years (three in four have lived in the state over ten years). There is some relationship to firm growth trajectory, as the principals associated with firms with higher initial sales and higher growth trajectories have lived longer in the host county.

In summary, then, start-ups are often a team project, usually involving a family-based effort. About 40% of those involved are women, frequently on teams with men. A broad range of ethnic backgrounds is involved, as is a broad range of educational attainments. Over 85% of those involved are between eighteen and forty-four at the time of the start-up. Over three in four move from one work context to the new firm; only about one in twenty (6%) is unemployed. About half of start-up team members have over five years' experience in the same industry, two-thirds have never started another new firm, and most have ample time to become established in the business and social communities.

Higher-growth new firms have more experienced teams, with an absence of very young adults, those with more industry and start-up experience, and principals well established in the community.

NEW BUSINESSES AND FIRM GROWTH TRAJECTORIES

As new businesses, these start-up firms are considered in terms of their economic sectors, emphasis on high technology, legal form, informal financing, start-up window, and start-up problems.

Economic Sector. While the sectoral distribution of new businesses is very much like that of existing businesses, there are some differences associated with alternative growth trajectories, as shown in Table 5.7. High-start, high-growth new firms are more likely to be associated with manufacturing or distributive services (wholesale, transportation) and producer (business) services; they are less likely to be in retail or consumer services. The sectors with an emphasis on high-start, high-growth new firms are also those most likely to have out-of-region exports. All sectors have a number of low-start, low-growth firms, although they are slightly more common among consumer services.

Technological Emphasis. The Wisconsin New Firm Survey included a series of questions about the extent to which the firm was emphasizing new or advanced technology. Four questions provided a reliable index related to high technology.[2] New firms where all the questions received a "Yes" were considered to have a strong emphasis on high technology. If half the questions were answered "Yes," the new firm went into the moderate emphasis. As shown in Table 5.7, seven in ten were found to have no technological emphasis, and only one in six had a strong emphasis. However, 50% of those reporting a strong emphasis are concentrated in the high-growth categories. Or, stated differently, more than twice the proportion of new firms in the high-growth categories report an emphasis on high technology.

Regional Context. In considering the regional context, presented in Table 5.7, the high-start, high-growth new firms are *not* more prevalent in major urban areas (the Milwaukee, Minneapolis-St.Paul, Philadelphia, or Pittsburgh areas in this analysis). The major differences are related to a higher prevalence of high-start, high-growth firms in regional centers and a reduced presence in rural areas. More about the regional context appears in the next section.

Legal Form. Table 5.7 indicates that, when initiated, about two in five new firms are sole proprietorships, and two in five are corporations, with the remainder partnerships. There is, after start-ups, a shift toward the corporate form, as half were corporations at the time of the interview. Larger new

Table 5.7
Growth Trajectories: Industry Sector, Context, and Legal Form

First-Year Sales: Growth Rates	High High	High Low	Low High	Low Low	All Firms
No. of cases (1)	180	922	610	638	2,350
Percent of sample	8%	39%	26%	27%	100%
Industry sector (****) (2)					
Agriculture	1%	1%	1%	3%	2%
Mining	*	*	*	*	*
Construction	13	16	10	12	13
Manufacturing	18	11	12	12	12
Distributive services	25	15	16	11	15
Producer (business) services	22	14	23	18	18
Health, education, and social services	1	1	3	3	2
Retail	16	32	23	27	27
Consumer services	4	10	11	13	10
Total	100%	100%	100%	100%	100%
High-tech emphasis (*) (Wisconsin only, n = 307)					
None	70%	75%	63%	72%	71%
Moderate	7	14	9	16	13
Strong	23	11	28	12	16
Total	100%	100%	100%	100%	100%
Regional context (***)					
Metropolitan area	59%	57%	60%	53%	57%
Regional center	32	26	25	26	26
Rural	9	17	15	21	17
Total	100%	100%	100%	100%	100%
Initial legal form (****)					
Sole proprietorships	18%	30%	42%	65%	42%
Partnerships (3)	11	15	16	18	16
Corporations (4)	71	55	42	17	42
Legal form as of interview (****)					
Sole proprietorships	8%	26%	33%	61%	31
Partnerships (3)	9	10	11	15	12
Corporations (4)	83	63	46	24	52

Notes: (1) Due to missing data, sample size reduced for some analysis.
       (2) Chi-square analysis: *=0.05; **=0.01; ***=0.001; ****=0.0001 and beyond.
       (3) Includes limited liability partnerships.
       (4) Includes Chapter S corporations.

firms are, however, more likely to be started as corporations or become corporations.

Initial, Internal Funding. Almost nothing attracts more attention than the financial needs of new firms. Table 5.8 presents information on the amount of initial funding provided for these new firms; defined as funding developed before the first formal loan or equity is provided from external sources. As before, all figures have been converted to 1992 dollars, using the reports of the month and year of first personal financial commitments

Table 5.8
Growth Trajectories: Initial Financial Support

First-Year Sales: Growth Rates	High High	High Low	Low High	Low Low	All Firms
No. of cases (1)	180	922	610	638	2,350
Percent of sample	8%	39%	26%	27%	100%
Initial financial support (1992 dollars, $1,000)					
All firms in sample, number	175	888	581	589	2,407
Average (****) (2)	$85	$64	$61	$29	$54
Median	10	3	10	3	3
Maximum	2,223	4,610	2,813	1,704	4,610
Firms with financial data, number	111	472	372	349	1,378
Average (****)	$138	$124	$99	$53	$98
Median	57	66	41	15	38
Maximum	2,223	4,610	2,813	1,704	4,609
Sources, percent of total					
Start-up team savings (*)	58%	49%	48%	52%	50%
Spouse, immediate family (**)	3	5	4	7	5
Other kin, relatives	6	7	7	10	8
Friends, business associates	3	4	3	3	3
Supplier credit (*)	9	8	7	7	7
Other (****)	21	26	31	20	26
Total	100%	99%	100%	99%	99%
Percent providing any financial support					
Start-up team savings (*)	88%	85%	89%	86%	87%
Spouse, immediate family (**)	6	14	13	18	14
Other kin, relatives	18	17	19	20	19
Friends, business associates	8	10	10	7	9
Supplier credit (*)	21	21	20	13	19
Other (****)	33	44	56	38	45

Notes: (1) Due to missing data, sample size reduced slightly for some analysis; total column may be larger that sum of columns.

(2) One-way analysis of variance: * = 0.05; ** = 0.01; *** = 0.001; **** = 0.0001 and beyond.

as the date informal funding began. This is complex to summarize, because such a large proportion reports little or no funding, and a small proportion has extremely high levels of funding. (In technical language, the distributions are highly skewed.) The absence of data is difficult to interpret, as it may mean there is no funding, the respondent does not know the answer, or the information is considered confidential.

The average funding for all new firms in these samples was $54,000, and the median was $3,000 (due to the large number of those with no reports on informal funding). But when restricted to those in the samples for which some informal funding is reported, the average is $98,000, and the median value is $38,000. If half a million new firms are implemented in the United States each year, then the total amount of funds assembled, mostly from within the team and informally, by firms completing the birth transition is from $12 to $29 billion each year. This would not include investments in start-up firms that do not complete the birth process.

There are clear differences associated with the firm growth trajectory, for the high-start firms report average initial financial support of $138,000 and $124,000; the low-start, high-growth firms an average of $99,000; and the low-start, low-growth firms, an average of $53,000. The median values follow the same pattern, suggesting this is true for all firms in each category. The maximum values, however, are in millions of dollars for all four groups.

Only one source of initial funds is almost universal. As shown in Table 5.8, 85% or more of the new firms in all categories report funds from the start-up team members. This is, generally speaking, about half of all initial funding provided and slightly higher for the high-start, high-growth new firms. Other sources—from a spouse or the immediate family, other kin or relatives, friends and business associates, or supplier credit— are reported on a regular basis, although seldom by more than one in five or as a source of more than 10% of the initial funding. "Other" is the other major source of initial funding, reported by almost half of the new firms, although least among the high-start, high-growth group and highest among the low-start, high-growth group. This suggests that the low-start, high-growth group is the most creative in locating diverse sources of financial support in the start-up phase.

Start-up Window. The new firm start-up window can be considered the time between the first and last of four major events—first personal commitment, first financial support, first sales, and first hiring—which may occur in any order (Reynolds and Miller, 1992). This window, as shown in Table 5.9, averages about a year, with a median value of six months. The relationship to the growth trajectories is, however, the reverse of what might be expected. The start-up window is shorter for firms reporting a high-start, high-growth trajectory and about two months longer for those with a low-start, low-growth trajectory. Fast-growth new firms, which require more initial funding, are put in place more quickly than the more modest

Table 5.9
Growth Trajectories: Start-up Window and Start-up Problems

First-Year Sales: Growth Rates	High High	High Low	Low High	Low Low	All Firms
No. of cases (1)	180	922	610	638	2,350
Percent of sample	8%	39%	26%	27%	100%
Start-up window (Minnesota, Pennsylvania only)					
Average, months (**) (2)	10.6	12.0	11.9	14.7	12.3
Median, months	6.0	5.0	6.4	7.0	6.0
Events in the first month					
Personal commitment	82%	84%	85%	83%	84%
Formal financial support	23	29	25	26	27
Sales income (**)	31	43	40	47	42
Hired employees (****)	32	36	24	18	28
Events in the last month					
Personal commitment (*)	16%	27%	23%	24%	24%
Formal financial support (**)	39	39	40	30	37
Sales income (**)	49	54	45	47	49
Hired employees (**)	45	54	52	44	50
Start-up problems					
Percent major	22%	21%	21%	18%	20%
Percent minor (**)	48	45	50	45	47
Percent did not occur (***)	30	34	29	37	33
Total	100%	100%	100%	100%	100%
Problem severity indices (Major = 3; Minor = 2; None = 1)					
Financial controls (**)	2.05	2.00	2.04	1.92	2.00
Financing (****)	2.12	2.01	2.03	1.84	1.98
Marketing	1.98	1.94	2.00	1.95	1.96
Regulations, insurance (**)	1.94	1.90	1.94	1.77	1.88
Planning, implement (***)	1.91	1.85	1.91	1.74	1.85
Personnel (****)	1.93	1.86	1.83	1.68	1.82
Site, location (*)	1.91	1.76	1.88	1.73	1.80
Physical infrastructure	1.43	1.42	1.39	1.33	1.39

Notes: (1) Due to missing data, sample size reduced slightly for some analysis; total column may be larger that sum of columns.
(2) One-way analysis of variance: * = 0.05; ** = 0.01; *** = 0.001; **** = 0.0001 and beyond.

endeavors—further evidence that they may be implemented to take advantage of a unique, perhaps temporary, opportunity.

The most frequent first event for the start-up window, as shown in Table 5.9, is a personal commitment, uniformly reported by over 80% for all firms regardless of their growth trajectory. This could, however, have been a financial or time commitment, so it is not strictly comparable to the analysis of nascent entrepreneurs in Chapter 4. On the other hand, firms that *do not* have a high-start, high-growth trajectory are more likely to have a personal commitment as a *last* event. This implies that those involved in high-start, high-growth firms become involved in firm management very quickly. High-start, low-growth firms appear to be more likely to start with sales and hiring of employees, and low-start, low-growth firms are more likely to have sales in the first month.

Start-up Problems. A standardized, forty-four item inventory of start-up problems was used in all three new firm surveys. Analysis of the prevalence of major start-up problems, reported in Table 5.9, indicates a clear pattern: the low-start, low-growth firms seem to have fewer problems. Starting large or growing fast was associated with more problems.

Analysis indicated that these forty-four items could be classified into eight dimensions, and scales were developed for each.[3] They are presented in Table 5.9 in the order of average severity. A major problem would have a value of "3," a minor problem "2," and no problem "1." "Financial controls" leads the list, followed closely by "obtaining financial support," as sources of major problems. Both reflect patterns related to the growth trajectories, with greater severity reported by the high-start, high-growth new firms and substantially less severity reported by low-start, low-growth new firms. Market and product development issues, including responding to the competition, are universally considered a major problem; there is no difference by growth trajectory. Dealing with regulations and insurance is considered less of a problem among the low-start, low-growth new firms. Planning and issues in implementation are considered more of a problem among the fast-growth firms, perhaps reflecting a continuous response to competitive changes. Personnel issues are not considered a problem among the low-start, low-growth firms, which have few employees, and are the greatest problem among the high-start, fast-growth firms which are constantly adding people. Site and location issues seem to be more of a problem among the high-growth firms. None reported a particular problem related to the local infrastructure.

In general, then, all report some start-up problems, but the best way to avoid them appears to be to start small and avoid growth. Growth seems to provide more problems, however, than starting large. The nature of the patterns among the start-up problems is consistent with an expectation that fast-growing new firms are challenged as they try to assemble and track resources (money, people, locations) to implement a competitive strategy.

REGIONAL CONTEXT, ASSISTANCE, AND GROWTH TRAJECTORIES

Most businesses are started where the start-up team lives. This suggests that if the local conditions are not considered appropriate for a new business, it will not emerge. Are there regional differences in the types of firms that appear? Is there variation among the different firms in terms of contextual factors considered important? A wide range of programs has been implemented to assist new firms. How much attention do these programs get from those starting new firms? Are they considered helpful?

Regional Context. There are four major metropolitan areas included within these three states (Milwaukee, Minneapolis-St. Paul, Philadelphia, and Pittsburgh); ten areas that could be considered regional centers; and the remaining sixteen were rural in character. As indicated in Table 5.10,

Table 5.10
New Firms and Geographic Context

Geographic Context	All	Metro (1)	Regional Center (2)	Rural (3)
No. of new firms (4)	2,350	1,334	611	405
Percentage of new firms	100%	57%	26%	17%
State				
Minnesota	100%	59%	19%	22%
Pennsylvania	100	62	28	10
Wisconsin	100	32	40	28
Sales growth patterns				
High-start, high-growth	8%	8%	9%	4%
High-start, low-growth	39	39	39	40
Low-start, high-growth	26	28	25	23
Low-start, low-growth	27	25	27	34
Total	100%	100%	100%	101%
Industry sector				
Agriculture	2%	1%	2%	3%
Mining	*	*	*	*
Construction	13	11	18	13
Manufacturing	12	12	14	10
Distributive services	15	15	14	16
Producer (business) services	18	23	14	10
Health, education, and social services	2	2	3	3
Retail	27	25	25	36
Consumer services	10	11	11	10
Total	99%	100%	101%	101%

Notes: (1) Milwaukee, Minneapolis-St. Paul, Pittsburgh; and Philadelphia metropolitan regions.

(2) Duluth, Rochester, and St. Cloud regions of MN; Allentown, Erie, Harrisburg, and Scranton regions of PA; Kenosha-Racine, Madison, and Fox Valley regions of WI.

(3) The remaining nine regions of MN; five regions of PA; and three regions of WI.

(4) Firms that reported a sales history of eight or more years were excluded from the sample. Sample sizes may be reduced slightly for some analyses.

half of the new firms in Minnesota and Pennsylvania emerged in the major urban centers; 70% of Wisconsin new firms emerged in the major urban center or the three adjacent regional centers. There are some systematic differences associated with the context. Rural areas tend to have a smaller proportion of the high-start, high-growth new firms and a larger proportion of low-start, low-growth new firms. The type of economic sector varies less than might be expected, although the proportion of manufacturing and construction new firms is highest in regional centers, producer and business service new firms are a higher proportion of new firms in the metropolitan regions, and retail businesses are most prevalent among new firms in rural areas.

Regional Context-Importance and Satisfaction. Those starting new firms in the three states were asked to rate a number of regional features on the basis of their importance and satisfaction. The overall level of satisfaction (average across all items) was almost identical for those starting new firms in Minnesota, Pennsylvania, and Wisconsin. A slightly different procedure was used for measuring importance in Wisconsin, and, perhaps as a result, the average level of importance for all items was lower among Wisconsin respondents. To compensate for this difference, ratings given by each respondent use that individual's average rating as the reference point.

Following an exploration of relative importance utilizing factor analysis and checking the reliability of alternative multi-item indexes, the twenty items were reduced to eight indexes, composed of from one to four items.[4] These represent eight dimensions of importance associated with the context and are found in Table 5.11 in rank order. The right column provides the

Table 5.11
Rankings of Contextual Features: Importance and Satisfaction

	Importance	Satisfaction
Quality of life	0.30	0.32
Access	0.28	0.16
Worker-related	0.06	0.06
Regulations, taxes	-.05	-.23
Physical infrastructure	-.09	0.13
Site, location	-.12	-.01
Intellectual infrastructure	-.43	-.14
Energy-related	-.67	-.28

Notes: Respondents use a three-point scale, rating from fifteen to twenty-six contextual features as "very," "somewhat," or "not," in terms of importance and current satisfaction. Number of cases for site, location ratings 1,298 or higher; for all other dimensions ranges from 2,000 to 2,946.

average satisfaction rating. In both cases, a positive value indicates that the factor is rated above average, and a negative value below the average for the individual respondents.

Quality of life tops the list as important and—this is the good news— also tops the list for satisfaction in Table 5.11. Access to customers, as well as inputs, suppliers and capital, is rated almost as important. The next four factors—worker-related, regulations and taxes, physical infrastructure, and site factors—are intermediate in importance. Two features are considered relatively unimportant—access to intellectual infrastructure and energy-related. There is, in general, a strong relationship between rated importance and satisfaction. The major exception is related to regulations and taxes, which are seen as typical in importance but relatively low in satisfaction.

There is, as shown in Table 5.12, no overall difference in importance among those starting a firm in different contexts. There are, however, some differences related to specific contextual features. Those in rural areas assign more importance to quality of life and aspects of the physical infrastructure. Those starting new firms in metropolitan areas assign more importance, compared to those in other contexts, to issues related to skilled workers and labor costs or energy costs and availability.

There is, however, a generally higher level of satisfaction with the context among those outside metropolitan regions. This is particularly true for quality of life, considered more important outside metropolitan regions and most satisfactory in a rural context. In addition, those outside a metropolitan area seem more satisfied with worker-related issues as well as site and location factors. Those in metropolitan contexts appear to be more satisfied with issues of access, the physical infrastructure, and access to intellectual resources. Those in regional centers seem least satisfied with energy-related issues. Those in all contexts are dissatisfied with regulations and taxes, although this appears greater in metropolitan areas.

Comparison by growth trajectories provides a major contrast, for there is considerable difference in importance given to most factors but almost no difference in levels of satisfaction. Those involved with larger firms tend to give more importance to everything. Those with a high-growth trajectory are more concerned about access to inputs and customers. The high-start, high-growth firms reflect substantially more concern about site and location issues. The low-start, low-growth new firms reflect more concern for quality of life, consistent with their image as lifestyle choices for their owners.

Remarkably, there are almost no differences related to satisfaction with contextual factors. One exception is "less dissatisfaction" among the low-start, low-growth new firms with regulations and taxes.

In general, then, the patterns have plausible interpretations, but major differences are probably associated with the specific situation of a specific new firm.

Competitive Context. An assessment of the competitive context was included in the Wisconsin survey. A series of questions asked about the

Table 5.12
Ratings of Contextual Features: By Context and Growth Trajectory

	Importance				Satisfaction			
Regional Context	Rural	Region Center	Metro	Sign (1)	Rural	Region Center	Metro	Sign (1)
No. of new firms (2)	503	770	1,597		501	768	1,593	
Overall measure	2.31	2.26	2.27		2.14	2.18	2.10	*****
Quality of life	0.37	0.34	0.26	***	0.39	0.30	0.30	***
Access	0.26	0.27	0.29		0.13	0.15	0.18	*
Worker-related	-.05	0.04	0.10	*****	0.04	-.03	0.00	*
Regulations, taxes	-.04	-.05	-.05		-.19	-.22	-.24	**
Physical infrastructure	-.03	-.12	-.09	**	0.09	0.18	0.12	**
Site, location	-.07	-.10	-.15	*	0.04	0.02	-.04	
Intellectual resources	-.47	-.44	-.41		-.24	-.19	-.08	*****
Energy-related	-.74	-.72	-.62	****	-.29	-.36	-.24	****

	Importance					Satisfaction				
Growth Trajectory	HI HI	HI LO	LO HI	LO LO	Sign (1)	HI HI	HI LO	LO HI	LO LO	Sign (1)
Start / Growth	HI	LO	HI	LO		HI	LO	HI	LO	
No. of new firms (2)	174	875	591	581		175	873	591	575	
Overall measure	2.32	2.34	2.26	2.20	*****	2.13	2.14	2.10	2.14	
Quality of life	0.20	0.26	0.31	0.37	**	0.30	0.35	0.38	0.33	
Access	0.30	0.26	0.30	0.31	*	0.17	0.17	0.12	0.14	
Worker-related	0.09	0.12	0.09	-.06	****	-.06	0.01	0.03	-.02	
Regulations, taxes	-.11	-.05	-.06	-.03		-.27	-.25	-.28	-.18	**
Physical infrastructure	-.04	-.07	-.09	-.08	**	0.15	0.14	0.17	0.12	
Site, location	0.07	-.12	-.13	-.14	*	0.03	-.01	-.03	0.01	
Intellectual resources	-.51	-.47	-.41	-.40	**	-.14	-.14	-.12	-.17	
Energy-related	-.65	-.70	-.60	-.61		-.30	-.28	-.23	-.33	

Notes: (1) Statistical sign from one-way analysis of variance: * - .05; ** .01; *** .001; **** 0.0001; ***** beyond 0.0000.
(2) Maximum number of cases, may be reduced slightly for some comparisons. See notes to Table 5.11 regarding sample sizes.

markets and competition confronted by the new firms. It turned out that these respondents appeared to consider their competitive context to have five independent features[5]: the rate at which products, production processes, and customer preferences changed; the level of competition, fair and unfair; the extent to which they were dependent on a few major suppliers and customers; geographic concentration of suppliers and customers; and situations where high level of demand and dependence on key personnel could exist.

New firms in Wisconsin with a high level of initial sales, particularly those with a high-growth trajectory, were more likely to consider their market and industry changed substantially faster than for the typical firm (statistically significant at the 0.05 level). There was no significant relationship to the other four market-competition dimensions. Those in distributive or producer service sectors were more likely to report rapid market and industry changes; those in manufacturing or distributive service were more likely to report dependence on a small number of customers or suppliers. There was no difference among firms in the rural, regional center, or metropolitan areas with regard to their judgments about the new firm's competitive context.

Knowledge, Use, Reaction to Assistance Programs. Government and nonprofit organizations have decided that providing assistance to entrepreneurs may promote firm creation and economic growth. As reported in the second chapter (see Table 2.8), 752 distinct offerings of assistance were identified within Wisconsin. These were classified into twenty-eight categories for this analysis. The Wisconsin new firm owners were asked questions about each of the twenty-eight types of assistance to determine whether the service was relevant; if it was, whether they knew it was available; and if they did, how much contact they had with each type. The results in terms of contact with the programs and knowledge of their existence are presented in Table 5.13.

First, as shown in Table 5.13, only two types of assistance were used by more than one-third of the new firm owners—information on laws and regulations and continuing education courses. About one-fifth of the new firm owners utilized assistance on accounting and general information on starting a business. Fewer than one in ten owners used the majority of categories of assistance. Ironically, some of the least-utilized types of programs—such as technology development and assistance, contacted by only 3%— are among the most glamorous and best publicized. Admittedly, the pool of interest for this form of assistance might be smaller than for other general business topics because it is aimed at manufacturers. Limited contacts with new business owners is a problem plaguing many of these assistance programs.

Part of the underuse problem is lack of knowledge about assistance among new business owners and nascent entrepreneurs. On average, just under two-thirds of the owners knew about the availability of specific

Table 5.13
Knowledge and Use of Assistance Programs

Category of Assistance	Percentage That:	
	Made Contact	*Did Not Know About*
Information on laws and regulations	42%	25%
Continuing education courses	34	18
Financing counseling	23	30
Information on financing resources	23	33
Accounting assistance	22	42
Business start-up or expansion	21	39
General business management	20	31
Networking/making contacts	20	34
Business plan development	17	39
Business advocacy groups	14	26
Venture capital	13	37
Information systems assistance	10	38
Marketing-demographic profiles	10	37
Business feasibility review	9	48
Marketing program assistance	9	42
Government procurement assistance (1)	8	36
Personnel management assistance	8	34
Minority business assistance	8	22
Business incubator	7	44
Marketing research assistance	7	39
Site location assistance	7	34
Retail/service business location	7	33
International trade assistance	6	26
Women's business assistance	6	25
Tourism business assistance	6	23
Manufacturing systems-technical	5	24
Patent and trademark assistance	5	23
Technology development assistance	3	29
Overall average	13%	34%

Note: (1) Provides assistance in selling to federal, state, and local governments.

services. The lack of knowledge about options ranged from a low of 19% for continuing education courses to a high of 47% for business feasibility review assistance. Obviously, there is a communications gap here. Ironically, many of the best-known forms of assistance are among those used the least.

Knowing that many Wisconsin new firm principals would have made contact with several programs (the average was over three), they were asked several questions about their most recent experience. The most common forms of recently received assistance were information on laws and regulations (36%), continuing education (31%), and accounting assistance (19%). They were also asked to indicate satisfaction with their most recent experience. The results, shown in Table 5.14, indicate a high level of satisfaction. In fact, over 80% considered the assistance somewhat helpful, very helpful, or extremely helpful. Only one in twenty said it was a waste of time; none said it was harmful. There may be many reasons not to seek assistance, but lack of effective services does not seem to be a major factor.

When the evaluation of the programs by firms with different growth trajectories is considered, those in the high-start, high-growth pattern are slightly more critical of the last assistance they received, but the difference is not statistically significant. There are, however, some differences in the utilization of these services related to the growth trajectory. The average number of responses across the 28 types of programs is provided in Table 5.15. This indicates, for example, that the typical Wisconsin respondent reported approaching 2.3 of the 28 types of programs for help and receiving something useful; considered an average of 8.6 not relevant to the business; and did not know about an average of 8.9 of these programs.

Two patterns associated with differences in growth trajectories are statistically significant. Most important, those reporting a high-start, high-growth trajectory also report helpful contact with substantially more forms of assistance, an average of 3.5, compared, for example, with those involved with

Table 5.14
Ratings of Program Assistance: Wisconsin New Firm Owners

Extremely helpful, critical to success	17%
Very helpful, contributed a lot	30
Somewhat helpful, gave us what we needed	36
Neutral, neither helpful nor harmful	12
Not helpful, not worth the time	5
Somewhat harmful, assistance hurt the firm	—
Very harmful, almost caused firm failure	—

Note: Weight adjusted n = 266; ratings by Wisconsin new firm principals of the value of the most recent help received.

Table 5.15
Growth Trajectories: Use of, and Reaction to, Assistance Programs

First-Year Sales: Growth Rates	High High	High Low	Low High	Low Low	All Firms
No of cases (maximum) (1)	24	106	69	109	308
Made contact and got help	3.5	2.7	1.4	2.4	2.3 **(2)
Made contact, but not helpful	1.3	0.8	1.2	1.1	1.0
No contact attempted, didn't think it would be helpful	3.7	5.8	2.6	5.6	4.9**
No contact attempted, not relevant to business	9.0	8.1	9.4	8.6	8.6
Could not find any help	1.0	1.2	1.7	0.7	1.1
Did not know help was available	8.8	8.5	9.6	8.7	8.9

Notes: (1) Due to missing data, sample size reduced slightly for some analysis; total column may be larger than sum of columns.
(2) One-way analysis of variance: * = 0.05; ** = 0.01; *** = 0.001; **** = 0.0001 and beyond.

low-start, high-growth businesses, who reported an average of 1.4 helpful contacts. It is not clear if the help contributed to the firm success or the people implementing the most successful firms were more likely to seek help.

There is also evidence that those with firms with low-growth patterns are more likely to avoid sources of assistance because they don't expect to benefit from the contact. As the number of contacts that were not helpful was low and uniform across firms with different growth trajectories, and there is strong evidence of a positive response to forms of assistance from new firm principals, it is not clear why these groups are avoiding contact with assistance programs.

BUSINESS OPERATIONS AND GROWTH TRAJECTORIES

Three features of operating businesses—new and established—get considerable attention: external financial support, the focus of management efforts, and their strategic or competitive strategy. All three can be reviewed with respect to the different growth trajectories of these new firms.

External Financing. The amounts and types of external financing provided to firms with different growth trajectories are of major significance for both the development of new businesses and public policy related to provision of financing. Firms in all three states provided summary data on the status of their financial support at the time of the interview. Adjusting all Minnesota and Pennsylvania responses to 1992 dollars facilitates analysis of the 3,000 new firms in this three-state sample.

The actual presence of external financial support, any sum reported over zero, is presented in Table 5.16, by the growth trajectories of the new firms. (This is the only analysis that includes firms with up to eight years of sales.) The top of the table provides information on specific types of external funding. The bottom of the table indicates the patterns associated with firm age—one to two, three to four, five to six, and seven to eight years old.

One-half (49%) of the firms one to eight years old report no external financial support. This "no support group" is lowest among the high-start, high-growth new firms, at 35%, and increases to 62% among the low-start, low-growth firms. When considered in relation to firm age, two distinct patterns are found. Among low-growth firms, the proportion reporting any financial support is larger among the older firms. If a firm is not growing, one way to increase return on the owners' investment is to borrow funds to support the capital requirements. Or, perhaps, those who were able to obtain outside funding were more likely to survive. The opposite pattern is found among the high-growth firms, with fewer of the older firms reporting external financial support. Perhaps growing firms are able to finance growth from internal sources, or growing firms with substantial external financing were less likely to survive.

Loans are the most common type of financial support: 49% report some type of debt, and 8% some type of equity financing. Only 2% report only equity financing; the other 6% with equity financing report some form of debt. As might be expected, high-start, high-growth firms are about twice as likely to report any type of debt as the low-start, low-growth firms, but the differences are matters of degree. Equity support is quite different, with the high-start, high-growth firms five times more likely to report external ownership than the low-start, low-growth new firms.

The most dominant form of external financial support, reported by 45% of the firms, is a traditional bank loan, usually backed by a physical asset. The widely discussed SBA guaranteed loan programs sponsor 2% of the firms. Among the total sample of 3,202 firms, fifty report a loan associated with the SBA. Fifty-three reported loans associated with some other government source.

The major source of external equity is private investors, followed by "other" sources of equity. This would include, for example, a bank or financial institution accepting ownership to complement a loan against a physical asset. Less than one-half of a percent report venture capital equity investments. There was a total of fifteen in the full sample of 3,202. Three of these reported amounts less than $25,000 (1992 dollars) suggesting they did not understand the meaning of "venture capital support" as they completed the questionnaire.

Characterizing the amounts associated with external financial support is complicated by two features of the diversity. First, as mentioned before, half don't report any financial support. Second, a very small proportion reports extremely high levels of external financial support. The largest

Table 5.16
Growth Trajectories: Sources of External Financial Support by Firm Age

First-Year Sales: Growth Rates	High High	High Low	Low High	Low Low	All Firms
No. of cases (maximum) (1)	180	924	611	643	2,359
Loans outside the start-up team					
Banks, financial institutions	56%	47%	50%	33%	45%
SBA-backed loans	3	2	2	*	2
Other government loans	5	2	2	1	2
Other loans or bonds	12	6	6	6	7
Equity outside the start-up team					
Private investors	10%	5%	5%	1%	4%
Public stock offerings	2	1	2	*	1
Venture capital	1	* (2)	*	*	*
Other forms of equity	5	8	4	2	3
Total external financial support					
Any loans in any form	63%	51%	54%	37%	49%
Any equity in any form	16	9	9	3	8
Any financial support in any form	65%	54%	56%	38%	51%
Any external loans					
1–2 years old	63%	47%	56%	30%	46%
3–4 years old	67	52	55	36	50
5–6 years old	54 (3)	51	51	40	48
7–8 years old	—	60	52	45	54
Any external equity					
1–2 years old	16%	12%	8%	3%	9%
3–4 years old	17	10	11	4	10
5–6 years old	13 (3)	10	8	3	6
7–8 years old	—	6	3	3	6
Any external financial support					
1–2 years old	64%	52%	57%	31%	49%
3–4 years old	71	55	57	37	53
5–6 years old	54 (3)	54	54	41	50
7–8 years old	—	61	52	45	50

Notes: (1) Includes data from all three states; all firms one to eight years old; all don't know
and refused responses, about 10% for each form of financial support, reset to zero
amounts. All values adjusted to 1992 dollars using the consumer price index (CPI).
Weighted to represent new firm population.
(2) * = less than 0.5%.
(3) Years five to six, n = 27, and seven to eight, n =12, combined.

external contribution in the sample is over $50 million. These features tend to make it difficult to provide a useful summary of the distribution with a single figure. Table 5.17 provides a summary in two ways. The top half presents the average amount of loans, equity, and total financing for the entire sample up to eight years old. The bottom half provides the same information but only for those new firms that report any financial support. As might be expected, the averages are somewhat larger if only those new firms with financial support are included, but the effect varies for those with different growth trajectories. For example, in the low-start, low-growth category, where two-thirds report no financial support, the average total support increases from $47,000 to $124,000 when the 62% with no support are excluded.

The amount of funding from the different sources and for each growth trajectory is presented in Table 5.18. The median amount of financing, that value above half the group but below the other half of the group, seems to provide a more useful summary measure. The amount of support appears to be inversely related to the prevalence of support. Many new firms receive small amounts from traditional sources; a few have very large amounts from distinctive sources. The rare venture capital or government loan is among the contributions most likely to be very large. The median bank loan, reported by almost half of all new firms, is about $59,000 (1992 dollars).

Overall external support does not seem, once corrected for inflation, to grow among these new firms. When compared to the prevalence in Table 5.16, it is clear that the growth in external support among low-start, low-

Table 5.17
Growth Trajectories: Average External Financial Support ($1,000s)

First-Year Sales: Growth Rates	High High	High Low	Low High	Low Low	All Firms
No. of cases (maximum) (1)	180	924	611	643	2,359
All cases in sample					
Total all loans in any form	$635	$171	$197	$41	$174
Total all equity in any form	45	69	27	6	40
Total all external financial support	680	240	224	47	211
All cases reporting any financial support					
Total all loans in any form	$1,013	$334	$366	$110	$370
Total all equity in any form	282	742	301	181	467
Total all external financial support	1,049	443	402	124	430

Note: (1) Includes data from all three states; all firms one to eight years old; all don't know and refused responses, about 10% for each form of financial support, reset to zero amounts. All values adjusted to 1992 dollars using CPI index. Weighted to represent new firm population.

Table 5.18
Growth Trajectories: Median Amounts of External Financial Support by Firm
Age ($1,000s)

First-Year Sales: Growth Rates	High High	High Low	Low High	Low Low	All Firms
No of cases (maximum) (1)	180	924	611	643	2,359
Loans outside the start-up team					
Banks, financial institutions	$130	$65	$57	$20	$59
SBA-backed loans	63	310	62	24	103
Other government loans	326	403	75	46	258
Other loans or bonds	119	53	30	19	36
Equity outside the start-up team					
Private investors	$99	$38	$25	$26	$32
Public stock offerings	22	180	38	24	33
Venture capital	1,220	313	# (2)	#	130
Other forms of equity	104	130	92	9	92
Any external loans					
1–2 years old	$130	$88	$41	$23	$65
3–4 years old	170	78	46	20	59
5–6 years old (3)	182	65	77	20	60
7–8 years old	#	101	70	27	65
All years (1–8 years old)	182	78	62	22	65
Any external equity					
1–2 years old	$45	$124	$39	$45	$54
3–4 years old	29	31	70	6	40
5–6 years old (3)	89	187	26	25	60
7–8 years old	#	13	117	101	60
All years (1–8 years old)	46	80	51	22	51
Any external financial support					
1–2 years old	$130	$90	$45	$25	$72
3–4 years old	169	78	54	20	61
5–6 years old	182	103	78	26	65
7–8 years old	#	112	70	28	65
All years (1–8 years old)	183	83	65	23	65

Notes: (1) Includes data from all three states; all firms one to eight years old; all don't know
and refused responses, about 10% for each form of financial support, reset to zero
amounts. All values adjusted to 1992 dollars using consumer price index (CPI).
Weighted to represent new firm population.
(2) # no cases in this cell.
(3) Years five to six, n = 27, and seven to eight, n = 12, combined for the first column.

growth firms is not accompanied by much of an increase in the median value. Median values tend to increase for loans in the other three groups, particularly among the high-growth categories—those where the prevalence is lower among older firms. Patterns associated with equity financing are particularly unstable, largely due to the very small number of firms reporting any equity support.

An important policy issue is associated with the total amounts of funds associated with new firms. The total amounts of funds generated internally from within the start-up team and from external loans and equity arrangements are presented in Table 5.19. For the total sample, in 1992 dollars, it is $667 millions. One-fifth is provided from within the start-up teams, two-thirds from loans, and the remainder (14%) from equity sources. Of this total, over half (54%) is provided from traditional banks or other lending institutions. The two sources with substantial media attention, SBA-backed loans and venture capital equity support, provide, respectively, 1% and 2% of the total funds.

This suggests that those starting new firms may expect to obtain most of their external funding from traditional sources, and only the exceptional new firm might be suitable for other forms of financial support and

Table 5.19

Aggregate Financial Support for New Firms: Internal and External Sources (Total Sample, $1,000s)

Pre-Start-up Funds			Total Funds	% of Total	
All sources (1)	$131,432	100%	$131,432	20%	20%
External loans (2)					
SBA-backed loans	$363,761	82%		54%	
Other government loans	9,469	2		1	
Other loans or bonds	33,267	8		5	
	36,049	8		5	
		100%	$442,546		66
External equity (2)					
Private investors	$46,339	49%		7%	
Public stock offerings	9,093	10		1	
Venture capital	12,715	14		2	
Other forms of equity	25,867	28		4	
		100%	$94,014		14
Total all sources			$667,992	100%	100%

Notes: (1) From Table 5.8; approximately 2,350 new firms, one to seven years old; adjusted to 1992 dollars using the consumer price index (CPI).

(2) All firms one to eight years old; all don't know and refused responses, about 10% for each form of financial support, reset to zero amounts. All values adjusted to 1992 dollars using the CPI. Weighted to represent new firm population. Approximately 2,640 firms.

other types of loans or equity financing. It is clear that even among equity sources, 86% of the equity funds are not provided through venture capital firms.

These estimates can be translated into aggregate national estimates by computing the average amount per new firm (one year old) and multiplying by annual number of U.S. start-ups. Assuming that half a million new firms are founded each year in the Unites States—and this is a low estimate, their total informal financing (in 1992 dollars) would require about $25 billion; they would generate a need for $84 billion in loans and about $18 billion in equity financing for a total of $127 billion, with slightly more than $100 billion from external sources. Additional funds are required after the first year for the growing new firms.

Based on the data from these surveys and focusing upon new firms reporting at least $25,000 in venture capital support, we would expect 0.22% of new firms to have such support, or 1,100 of 500,000 new firms, receiving a total of about $2.4 billion. In fact, over the 1982-92 period, venture capital firms provided an annual average of $2.9 billion in support to about 1,200 firms (U.S. Small Business Administration, 1994, Table 9.19). This suggests that the new firms in these samples are representative of those receiving venture capital support. It confirms the small, unique role played by this institutional sector.

Management Focus. Those managing new firms can do many things. The management focus may be related to the growth trajectory of the new firm. In the Minnesota and Pennsylvania surveys, the respondent was asked to characterize the emphasis of "company management, you and the other top executives" with regard to twenty-five different orientations and activities, such as "regularly use and update business plans" and "work together as a cohesive team." They responded on a five-point scale, ranging from "none" to "very much." These were organized, after explorations with factor analysis procedures and checking the reliability of alternative indexes, into seven dimensions that would characterize the firm management.[6]

These are presented in Table 5.20, rank-ordered in terms of overall emphasis. They appear to fall into four groups. The top group includes aspects that receive the most attention: industry experience and contacts, implementation of the marketing/sales plans, and high level of involvements by the principals in the business itself. Efforts devoted to coordination come next. Two items are third in overall emphasis, the focus on financial controls and the development of marketing strategies. Clearly receiving the least emphasis is work devoted to formal planning.

There is, however, considerable difference in emphasis among firms with different growth trajectories. Those larger high-start firms, particularly those with a high-growth trajectory, report more industry experience and contacts, higher levels of principal involvement, and more attention to financial controls, marketing strategies, and formal planning. These larger,

Table 5.20
Growth Trajectories: Management Emphasis

First-Year Sales: Growth Rates	High High	High Low	Low High	Low Low	All Firms
Management Emphasis					
No. of cases (maximum) (1, 2)	97	431	332	282	1,142
Industry experience/contacts (**) (3)	3.35	3.22	3.15	3.11	3.19
Marketing implementation	3.12	3.12	3.20	3.18	3.16
Principal involvement (***)	3.28	3.11	3.07	2.94	3.07
Coordination	2.84	2.73	2.79	2.87	2.79
Financial controls (***)	2.77	2.52	2.46	2.33	2.48
Marketing strategies (****)	2.73	2.44	2.37	2.10	2.37
Formal planning (***)	2.22	2.03	1.88	1.79	1.95

Notes: (1) This includes data from the Minnesota and Pennsylvania self-administered questionnaire only; answers were not obtained in follow-up phone interviews. Due to missing data, sample size reduced slightly for some analysis; total column may be larger that sum of columns.
(2) This includes data from all three states, both mail and phone interviews.
(3) One-way analysis of variance or chi-square significance: * = 0.05; ** = 0.01; *** = 0.001; **** = 0.0001 and beyond.

growing businesses report more attention given to the activities required in larger, growing businesses. For the five aspects on which the differences are statistically significant, the low-start, low-growth new firms provide the least emphasis. This suggests the greater number of start-up problems reported among the high-start, high-growth new firms require more managerial attention.

Competitive Strategy. Business success is generally considered to require an appropriate competitive strategy, a plan for attracting customers and clients who would, otherwise, buy from the competition. Respondents in all three states were asked to consider fourteen different business strategies—lower prices, better service, more choices, and so on—as critical, important, marginal, or insignificant to their strategic focus. After a factor analysis and consideration of the reliabilities of the indexes, these were used to develop six indexes.[7]

The six strategies are presented, ranked by emphasis, in the top of Table 5.21. One strategy dominates, customer service and quality. Three receive equivalent emphasis—lower prices, market responsiveness, and product diversity. Two receive the least emphasis—quality facilities and convenience and technologically advanced products and processes. These latter two probably receive the lower overall emphasis because they are specific

Table 5.21
Growth Trajectories: Competitive Strategy

First-Year Sales: Growth Rates	High High	High Low	Low High	Low Low	All Firms	
Strategic focus						
No. of cases (1)	176	866	586	596	2,224	
Customer service/quality	3.47	3.49	3.53	3.54	3.51	NS (3)
Lower prices	2.70	2.76	2.65	2.67	2.70	NS
Market responsiveness (**)	2.88	2.64	2.68	2.69	2.68	**
Product diversity	2.64	2.64	2.62	2.71	2.65	NS
Facilities and convenience (**)	2.26	2.47	2.33	2.34	2.38	**
High tech products/processes	2.34	2.34	2.35	2.22	2.31	NS
Strategy archetype (***) (2)						
Superachievers	28%	28%	25%	30%	28%	
Niche purveyors	10	22	17	15	18	
Price competitors	25	13	15	18	16	
Equivocators	13	15	16	16	15	
Quality proponent	18	14	16	11	14	
Technology values	7	9	11	10	9	
Total	101%	101%	100%	100%	100%	

Notes: (1) This includes data from all three states, both mail and phone interviews.
(2) This includes data from the Minnesota and Pennsylvania self-administered questionnaire only.
(3) One-way analysis of variance or chi-square significance: $* = 0.05$; $** = 0.01$; $*** = 0.001$; $**** = 0.0001$ and beyond.

to only certain industry sectors—facilities and customer convenience are more critical for firms in retail and consumer service. Only a small proportion of new firms is in sectors where technological advances are critical issues.

There are statistically significant differences, however, among the new firms on only two aspects of their strategic focus. The high-start, high-growth firms give substantially more attention to being responsive to the changing tastes and needs of their markets. The high-start, low-growth firms give more attention to facilities and convenience, consistent with the high proportion of these firms in the retail sector (Table 5.7).

A separate analysis has used these dimensions to classify the Minnesota and Pennsylvania new firms in terms of unique combinations of these seven dimensions (Carter et al., 1994). The result was six archetypes, presented at the bottom of Table 5.17. It is to be noted that more than two in five are either "superachievers"—trying to excel at everything—or "equivocators"—who have no emphasis in their strategic profile. Neither emphasis would seem optimal. There is also evidence that high-start, high-growth new firms are less likely to be serving a specific market niche or emphasizing technology, but give more attention to price competition or high-quality goods or services—but not both. In contrast, the high-start, low-growth new firms— concentrated in retail—tend to emphasize a special market niche and do not compete on price.

OVERVIEW AND IMPLICATIONS

Most regional and national economies are in constant turbulence and change. Existing firms shrink or disappear, and new firms emerge to replace these losses. This is usually in terms of replacements within, or expansions of, existing economic sectors. Occasionally, new firms may create a new sector. The results of these studies have confirmed much of what has been found in other research. First, new firms are one major source of economic growth: jobs, sales, and out-of-region exports. Second, a small proportion of new firms—those much larger than the typical new firm—accounts for the majority of these contributions.

The third major result may be unique. Whereas previous research, even that with the same data sets, has emphasized the importance of the growth of new firms, this analysis—which controlled for the effects of inflation— has found that the initial size of the firm was of greater significance in terms of firm size over the first seven years. The most significant contributions came from firms that were large in their first year of operation (sales in excess of $100,000 in 1992 dollars) and had annual compound growth of at least 40%. Only 8% of new firms meet this criterion, but they contributed 15% of all jobs, 27% of all sales, and 40% or more of all out-of-region exports. Firms that started large but had less growth were second in relative importance; those that started small but had high growth were third. The small start-up that stayed small had the smallest share of contributions to economic growth.

These high-starting, faster-growth firms were distinctive in a number of ways. While most new firms in all economic sectors tended to be modest endeavors, more of the larger new firms were in manufacturing, distributive services, and business services; retail and consumer service were underrepresented. Higher-potential new firms were more likely to be in regional centers than in metropolitan areas, least likely in rural areas. There was slightly greater emphasis on high technology among the high-growth new firms, although the differences were small.

All firms are started where the team members live. Assessment of their judgments about their context indicates that they were fairly satisfied with their current context, and they were more satisfied with those features considered more important. This satisfaction was somewhat greater for those with new firms outside the metropolitan areas and somewhat lower for issues regarding taxes and regulations. New firms with different growth trajectories had somewhat different rankings of importance—higher growth firms were more concerned with worker-related issues, lower-growth firms with quality of life—and there was no difference of consequence in terms of satisfaction with contextual features.

The start-up teams among higher-potential new firms had distinctive features. They had a higher proportion of men, slightly older team members, and those with more industry experience and more experience with starting new firms (although for two-thirds this was their first start-up). They tended to be working in established firms before the start-up and have lived in the region for decades. While about one-third of those involved in new firm start-ups were women, they tended to be a larger proportion of those associated with low-start firms.

The firms with more potential tended to get off the ground faster, an average of ten months, compared to over a year for the typical new firm. Firms with more potential reported more start-up problems of every kind and in the following order of decreasing significance: obtaining financing, managing money, dealing with regulations and insurance, planning and implementation, and personnel and site or location issues. This was reflected in reports of management emphasis, as high-potential new firms reported greater emphasis on all topics, but with particular emphasis on financial controls, marketing strategies, and formal planning. The competitive strategy of the high-start, high-growth firms emphasizes responsiveness to changes in customer tastes or competitor actions; that of the high-start, low-growth new firms—which have a high proportion in retail and consumer services—facilities and customer convenience. About two in five new firms, however, have no distinctive competitive strategy.

About half of all new firms reported no initial financing, from within the start-up team or elsewhere. Among those that do report initial, informal support, the higher-growth firms raised over twice as much as the lower-growth firms ($138,000 compared to $ 53,000 in 1992 dollars). Regardless of growth trajectory, over 80% get the majority of the funds from within the start-up team. Low-start, high-growth new firms were distinctive in the capacity to raise funds outside the team: friends, family, or business associates.

About half of these new firms reported no external financing of consequence at the time of the interview, although the average for all firms was about $211,000 in 1992 dollars. Among those that received any external financial support, it was $430,000 in 1992 dollars. The variation across the growth trajectories was substantial, as the average for the high-start, high-growth new firms was $1,049,000, eight times that of the low-start, low-growth firms, where it was $124,000 (both in 1992 dollars).

There was considerable difference in the sources, as only the higher-growth firms reported any equity financing of consequence. All firms reported that the single largest source of funding was banks and other financial institutions. Indeed, they provided 54% of all funds—internal and external—raised by the new firms. Two of the best-known sources, SBA loans and venture capital support, provided 1% and 2%, respectively, of the total funds assembled by these new firms.

The Wisconsin research provided an opportunity to determine the knowledge of, use of, and reaction to programs developed to assist new firms. The typical new firm had made contact with about three programs but was unaware of the presence of most of the twenty-eight forms of assistance provided by over 700 distinctive programs in over 400 agencies. New firm principals reported that when they did make contact, the assistance was almost always helpful, sometimes extremely valuable. Not one respondent had a major complaint. All evidence suggested that delivery of assistance was quite good but that a large proportion of potential clients was unaware of the programs. More coordination among programs, particularly cooperative marketing efforts, may do much to enhance the effectiveness of these programs in assisting new firms.

Implications for Starting a Business. There are many ways to start a business, and new firms can be implemented for many reasons. Clearly, modest efforts designed to provide one or two people with an acceptable living are quite common in all states, all types of regions, and—in addition—all economic sectors. Those who aspire to a substantial business seem to follow two courses of action. One is to identify a business opportunity that requires a firm of a particular size. The start-up effort seems to focus on putting the firm in place at this optimum size and then maintaining it. The alternative appears to emphasize a pattern of growth, either because the potential market is ambiguous or expanding or because resources are scarce at the start-up. In any case, the more significant endeavors clearly require larger, more experienced teams with substantial knowledge of both their region and markets. Regardless of the firm, one major source of financing will be banks and traditional lending institutions, even if other sources are approached. Equity financing is apparently associated only with a small proportion of growing firms. Venture capital funding is associated with about 1 in 400 new firms.

Public Policy Implications. If Wisconsin is a typical state with regard to helping programs, the delivery of programs is good, but awareness is low. This would suggest that the most effective way to improve "delivery of assistance" may be to significantly increase coordination among existing programs and develop joint promotional efforts. Such promotional efforts should be continuous, as new start-ups are initiated continually, and new firms are implemented continuously. The universally negative reaction to taxes and regulations may be resolved only through enhanced efforts to simplify requirements and reduce the burden of complying with regulations, which requires actions by hundreds of local, county, state, and federal agencies. Finally, public policies to improve the availability of funds to new firms will reach more new businesses—as well as all new firms with all growth trajectories—working through established banks and financial institutions. The amounts of funding for new businesses in their first year appear to be substantial, at least $100 billion a year in 1992 dollars, 80% in the form of loans.

CONCEPTIONS OF MODERN MARKET ECONOMIES

The three representative samples of new firms provide strong evidence related to most of the assumptions associated with the "perfectly competitive market" outlined in the introduction.

First, it is clear that new firms are neither rare nor unique. In fact, the high correspondence between the economic sectors of new and existing firms suggests that a continuous replacement process may be a fundamental feature of modern market economies. Separating the new firms that represent replacement of existing firms from those that represent a shift in the economic structure, perhaps due to technological or marketing innovations, is a major challenge.

Second, the majority of these new, operating firms are started and managed by teams, providing more evidence that assuming each firm is developed and guided by a solo entrepreneur may be a convenient fiction but is not the typical case. More important, the more significant new firms, those with higher-growth trajectories, the greater the likelihood that the start-up is a team effort. Decision making within a team may be more complex than for an individual focused on a single personal objective.

Third, the social background and experience of the owner/managers of new firms suggest they are, as with the nascent entrepreneurs, the more productive, experienced, and desirable members of the labor force. Very few are marginal participants with nothing better to do.

Fourth, there is further evidence on the time required to initiate new firms, which has a median of six months and an average of twelve months, with some variation associated with both growth rates and economic sector. New firms are not created overnight, although it may seem that way in growth regions.

Finally, about 90% of these new firms are either sole proprietorships or owned and managed by a family or kinship team. This suggests that many of the decisions for the firm may be influenced by family or social objectives, rather than a singular focus on maximizing financial gains.

APPENDIX: ISSUES IN NEW FIRM ANALYSIS

The following analysis of these issues relies on the data collected in surveys of Minnesota, Pennsylvania, and Wisconsin new firms. As discussed in Chapter 4, new firms are eventually incorporated in comprehensive business registries. Representative samples developed from such registries, the basis of the following analysis, are substantially less expensive than representative samples of nascent entrepreneurs based on human population surveys. Some aspects of the following analysis, therefore, are based on as many as 3,000 new firms, the combined total of representative samples for three states.

Two of these samples, Minnesota and Pennsylvania, were drawn from new entries in the Dun's Market Identifier (DMI) file, and the other, Wisconsin, from new listing in the state unemployment insurance file. The analysis in Chapter 4 (see Table 4.7) makes it clear that inclusion in unemployment insurance files occurs somewhat earlier than inclusion in the DMI file. Hence, new firms sampled from the DMI files, selected at a later point in the start-up process, can be expected to be somewhat larger. Firms that deactivate shortly after their first state unemployment insurance filing may not be included in the DMI file.

One way to avoid problems of "age incomparability" is to use a common birth date for all samples, not the date of first entry into the data registry. One such event that has been found to be the optimal solution is the year of first sales (Reynolds and Miller, 1992). Even with this adjustment, new firms in the Wisconsin sample are somewhat smaller than the new firms in the other two samples. This does not mean that Wisconsin is the land of business dwarfs, only that the Wisconsin sample is composed of younger and smaller new firms.

But this leads to two problems, standardizing the "sales history" of the new firms and taking the effects of inflation into account. Some firms had their first sales several years before entry into the respective registry. The analysis has been restricted, with one exception, to only those firms with their first sales within seven years of the interview, excluding the small proportion of "older" new firms with eight to ten years of sales. This reduces the total sample somewhat, to about 2,600 new firms with sales data. Some firms have no sales or sales for only one year. These are dropped when the growth trajectory is a focus of analysis.

Inflation is, however, a more serious problem. These three samples were collected at different time periods and involve sales reports over a fifteen-year period. The earliest sales figures for some Pennsylvania firms are for 1977, and in the Wisconsin survey, conducted in 1993, new firms reported sales for 1992. The "real" value of the U.S. dollar declined by more than half over the 1977–1992 period (U.S. Bureau of the Census, 1994, 487). For this reason, dollar figures for sales or financial support were adjusted, using the consumer price index, to the year—1992—the most recent annual sales figures were obtained for the Wisconsin sample.

Finally, in all three states there was systematic oversampling for some economic sectors (manufacturing, distributive services, producer services) and geographic regions (mostly rural). The values reported are adjusted to provide a representation of the total population that was the source of the sample.

NOTES

1. To minimize the production of truly extreme compound growth rates, all firms were allocated a first-year sales of at least $10,000.

2. These were (1) Is a high level of technical or scientific expertise critical to be an effective manager of this firm? (2) Is awareness of state-of-the-art developments in relevant scientific or technical areas critical to the firm's future? (3) Is your firm required to constantly make major technical changes in products or processes to be competitive? and (4) Would you consider the firm as hi-tech? (alpha reliability of 0.79.)

3. The following items are included in each index. *Financial controls*: five items- developing an accounting and control system; managing capital; managing cash flow; collecting accounts receivable; and selecting a lawyer or accountant (alpha reliability 0.74). *Financing*: four items—obtaining equity (ownership) investments; obtaining a long-term debt financing; establishing a banking relationship; and securing adequate short-term financing (alpha reliability 0.85). *Marketing*: eleven items—understanding market/industry trends; analyzing competition, competitors; finding competitive advantages; developing new; follow-on products/services; providing after-sale follow-up services; understanding/assessing customer needs; effective selling techniques; writing advertising copy/selecting media; providing customer service/follow-up; pricing products/services; and delivering on-time/within budget (alpha reliability 0.85). *Regulations, insurance*: two items—obtaining liability insurance and coping with government regulations (alpha reliability 0.47). *Planning, implementation*: six items—preparing a business plan; using/updating a business plan; setting goals/priorities for personnel; measuring performance against plans; clarifying goals/objectives; and implementing plans, strategy (alpha reliability 0.90). *Personnel*: six items—motivating/compensating personnel; coordinating tasks among personnel/units; finding qualified managers, executives; finding qualified technical/professional staff; finding qualified employees; and minimizing start-up team conflict (alpha reliability 0.84). *Site, Location*: two items—identifying/selecting suitable site(s) and locating suitable rental space (alpha reliability 0.87). *Physical infrastructure*: two items—appropriate transportation infrastructure and appropriate local infrastructure (alpha reliability 0.72).

4. Respondents use a three-point scale, rating from fifteen to twenty-six contextual features as "very," "somewhat," or "not," in terms of importance and current satisfaction. Scales were developed on the basis of importance ratings as follows. *Quality of life*: one item—quality of life. *Access*: three items related to access to customers, access to suppliers, and capital availability (alpha reliability 0.54). *Worker related*: two items related to availability of skilled workers and labor costs (alpha reliability 0.63). *Regulations, taxes*: four items related to local government regulations, land use and zoning, taxes, and government support for business (alpha reliability 0.71). *Physical infrastructure*: two items related to local physical infrastructure and transportation [highways, railroads] (alpha reliability 0.77). *Site, location*: four items related to building space availability, building space expenditures, land availability, and land purchase/rental costs (alpha reliability 0.80). *Intellectual infrastructure*: two items related to access to R&D facilities and education and training opportunities (alpha reliability 0.59). *Energy related*: two items related to the cost and availability and to the reliability of energy (alpha reliability 0.72).

5. Fourteen items each used a five-response scale: none; low; moderate; high; and extreme. First dimension composed of four items related to rate of change of methods used to market products/services; changes in methods used to produce products/services; changes in products/services in the market; and changes in customer preferences (alpha reliability 0.82). Second dimension composed of three items related to level of fair and normal competition; level of unfair and unethical competition; and the level of threat from industry conditions to survival of the firm (alpha reliability 0.72). Third dimension composed of three items related to dependence on a few critical suppliers, a few critical customers, and geographic concentration of most important suppliers (alpha reliability of 0.57). Fourth dimension composed of two items related to geographic concentration of important competi-

tors and customers (alpha reliability of 0.69). Fifth dimension consists of two items related to demand exceeding output and dependence on a few critical workers (alpha reliability of 0.52).

6. *Industry experience/contacts*: know industry, have technical experience in key areas, close customer contacts, clear market niche (four items; alpha reliability 0.71); *Marketing Implementation*: provide quality products-services; have product or service with clear competitive advantage; produce on time, within budget (three items; alpha reliability 0.68). *Principal involvement*: have enough business experience; willingness to take high levels of risk; high levels of motivation (three items; alpha reliability 0.60). *Coordination*: communicate goals-priorities, work as a cohesive team (two items; alpha reliability 0.74). *Financial controls*: have sound cash control system; generate enough cash from sales; accurately forecast cash flow needs; have sound cash flow position; have strong support from investment community; high certainty will survive the new few years (six items; alpha reliability 0.86). *Marketing strategies*: demonstrated ability to reach markets; aggressively sell products and services; active program of new product development (three items; alpha reliability 0.72). *Formal planning*: have written business plan; use and update business plan; set and follow-up on goals; accurate forecast results (four items; alpha reliability 0.87).

7. *Customer service/quality*: better service; quality products/services; customized product/service to clients (three items; alpha reliability 0.67). *Lower prices*: (single item). *Market responsiveness*: more effective marketing/advertising; fast response to changes in markets; serve those missed by others (three items; alpha reliability 0.59). *Product diversity*: more choices; distinctive goods/services; more contemporary/attractive products (three items; alpha reliability 0.62). *Facilities and convenience*: superior location/customer convenience; better, more attractive facilities (two items; alpha reliability 0.68). *Hi-tech products/processes*: utilize new/advanced technology; develop new/advanced technology (two items; alpha reliability 0.80).

Chapter 6

Fledgling New Firms: Persistence after Birth

Written with Mary Williams

A successful new firm "birth" is reflected in an operational business, one with sales or income, paying expenses and taxes, and, perhaps, with employees. If researchers are active about tracking down new firms, 90% appear to persist from year to year (Cooper, Dunkleberg, and Woo, 1988; Kirchhoff, 1994; Reynolds, 1987a). Current evidence suggests, however, that the tendency to persist increases somewhat after the initial period, the first five to six years. This increase may be considered another important transition, a transition from firm infancy, through firm youth, and into firm adolescence. Exploring the factors that may affect the successful completion of this transition is the central focus of this chapter. Simply put, which new firms survive infancy?

The metaphor for a business life course—and the study of business survival—is borrowed from assessments of biological life. Several critical features of this view of biological life are problematic when applied to business firms (Reynolds and Miller, 1992). First, a precise date—and even time of day—is attached to both human birth and death. In almost all societies considerable effort is devoted to creating an accurate record of such events: they are literally "chiseled in stone" on grave markers. As a consequence, the length of a human life is known with considerable precision, and very precise statements about average and expected life spans can be developed. Second, there is little confusion over which is a more desirable state of affairs—human life is universally considered better than human death.

Neither of these features is present with business firms. Both conceptually and in terms of available information, there are considerable problems in identifying a specific date for a business "birth" or "death." This makes it difficult to define firm age, particularly firm "age at death," with precision.

In addition, it is not always clear that the persistence of a business is more desirable than its discontinuance. A business may be marginal, profits may be low, and the owners may subsidize the entire effort with low or unpaid labor. It may be better for all concerned if the firm was shut down, and the resources—employees, facilities, equipment, capital, managerial talent— redeployed to other, perhaps more productive, uses. While some discontinuances may lead to social costs, not all discontinuances are, in the long run, an undesirable outcome. It may be better, then, to describe firms as persistent or discontinued, rather than "successful or failed" or "dead or alive."

There is, nonetheless, considerable merit to attempting to determine both the level of business mortality and those features associated with firm persistence and discontinuance. This chapter begins with a presentation of the data issues associated with determining persistence for these samples and discusses the impact of the timing of the initial interview on the subsequent patterns. This is followed by a review of a large number of factors that, when considered individually, appear to have a statistically significant impact on firm persistence. This review is followed by a multivariate analysis, where the effects of various combinations of factors, an exploration of joint effects, on firm persistence are considered. The final section considers the implications of these findings.

DATA ISSUES

Some headway on this issue—what is unique about firms that persist and complete the transition to adolescence?—is possible from the data assembled on new firms in Minnesota, Pennsylvania, and Wisconsin. For the following analysis, the year of first sales, as reported by the firm principal, is the primary source for establishing a "birth date" for each new firm. Where this is missing, the first year any sales were reported in the sales history is utilized as the birth year.

Current firm status (persistence or disappearance) is inferred from the two follow-up efforts, a phone contact with most Minnesota and Pennsylvania new firms completed in 1992 and a follow-up phone interview with the Wisconsin new firms completed in 1994. While the follow-up interviews provide good indicators that a firm may be in operation, they are less satisfactory with regard to discontinued firms. First, a significant percentage of the firms cannot be contacted, so it is not clear if these businesses have (1) discontinued, (2) been sold, (3) persisted with a change of location or owners, or (4) temporarily become dormant. Furthermore, among those firms that have discontinued, it is difficult to know when the firm ceased to exist if no contact with a principal is possible.

This is less of a problem with the Wisconsin follow-up, which occurred less than two years after the initial data collection and where detailed information was available on discontinued firms. For these firms, year of discontinuance was the last year sales or income was received. For the Minnesota and Pennsylvania follow-ups, completed five to six years after the initial data collection, firms were considered persistent if they (1) continued as independent businesses or (2) were bought and continued to operate under new ownership. Firms were considered discontinued if (1) there were reports of inactivity, permanent or temporary, or (2) no one to speak for the firm could be located after a number of serious tries. Since deactivation could have occurred at any time over a six-year period, they were assigned a "death date" of 1988, approximately one-half the time between the initial interview and the follow-up data collection.

This disadvantage, lack of full information on the status of the disappeared firms, is offset by the considerable amount of information on the firms obtained in the initial interview. The following analysis is not definitive but is a step forward.

PERSISTENCE AND EARLY LIFE COURSE STAGE

The new firms in the original sample were deliberately chosen to cover a range of "early ages." These samples included firms from one to six years old at the time of the first interview. Hence, those firms five to six years old at the time of the interview had been in operation for five to six years. They received the same interview as firms that were one to two years old. The lack of agreement over the form of the "hazard curve"—the proportion of firms deactivating at each age in the early life of new firms—is directly related to the patterns expected n the first few years of firm life. For this reason, a separate analysis is completed for firms receiving their first interview at different stages in their early life course.

This is explored, in Table 6.1, by considering the probability of "discontinuance"—one minus the probability of persistence—at different years following "firm birth," where firm birth is defined as the year of first sales. The first column of Table 6.1 indicates the proportion discontinuing at each age, which is relatively low in years 3 and 4 and rises to a uniform level for years 5 to 10. No firms are indicated as deactivating in their first two years. The total percentage that discontinued after the first interview, 26%, is indicated at the bottom of the first column. The remainder, 74%, are considered active businesses at the second interview.

The next three columns reflect the same patterns after these new firms are sorted into three categories based on the time between first sales and the initial interview (zero to one years; two to three years; and four to seven years).[1] It is clear that the proportion that persists and the distribution of the hazard rate are substantially affected by the relationship of the first interview to the new firm development stage. Among those firms in late infancy, completing the first interview within one year of first sales, 59% persisted; of those in youth, completing the first interview two or three years after first sales, 71% persisted; and of those completing the first

Table 6.1
New Firm Probability of Discontinuance: By Firm Life-Course Stage

	Total Sample	First Interview Completed During:		
		Late Infancy	Youth	Early Adolescence
First sale to first interview: years	0–7	0–1	2–3	4–7
Number of firms	2,766	627	894	1,245
Probability of discontinuance (1) Years after first sale				
0	— (2)	—	—	—
1	—	—	—	—
2	—	—	—	—
3	0.03	0.14	—	—
4	0.01	0.07	0.01	—
5	0.06	0.30	0.07	—
6	0.05	—	0.15	—
7	0.05	—	0.10	0.04
8	0.05	—	—	0.09
9	0.06	—	—	0.08
10	0.06	# (3)	—	0.07
11	—	#	#	—
12	—	#	#	—
Proportion				
Persisting (4)	74%	71%	72%	77% (****)
Discontinuing (5)	26	29	28	23 (6, 7)
By state (proportion persisting)				
Minnesota	70%	66%	68%	71% (****)
Pennsylvania	75	65	74	83 (****)
Wisconsin	80	79	86	— (****)
	(****)	(****)	(****)	(****)

Notes: (1) All computations completed by SPSS PC 5.01 survival analysis with weighted sample to adjust for sampling stratification (Norusis, 1992a).

(2) Probability of discontinuing is zero (0.00).

(3) # indicates truncated time period precludes estimates.

(4) These are new firms for which the ultimate disposition is unknown, technically referred to as left censored observations.

(5) These are new firms for which a date of discontinuance is known, technically referred to as uncensored observations.

(6) Statistical significance indicated within parentheses: NS = not significant; * = 0.05; ** = 0.01; *** = 0.001; **** = 0.0001.

(7) Comparisons across columns refer only to three on the right.

interview four to seven years after the first sale, 76% persisted. These differences are statistically highly significant. The later the timing of the first interview, the higher the proportion of the new firms that persist to the second interview.

For these analyses statistical significance is based on procedures that provide a way to compare the patterns of survival over time. They take into account that the "date of death" is unknown for the majority of the cases, referred to as "censored observations," and variation in length of time a given firm is tracked from "birth" to the end of the observation period may vary (the Wilcoxon [Gehan] test, Norusis, 1992a, 268). This statistical test is more conservative and appropriate than a simple Chi-square utilized with a two-way table.

The state from which the sample was drawn, as shown in Table 6.1, has a statistically significant effect, with the largest differences associated with Wisconsin. But the source of the sample was different for Wisconsin, and the time lag between the initial interview and the follow-up was much shorter. The differences between Minnesota and Pennsylvania, which are not statistically significant for the late infancy comparison, may reflect a more intense focus on locating Pennsylvania new firms in the follow-up effort. The follow-ups for both these states were conducted from Philadelphia. Given these substantial procedural differences and the wealth of comparisons indicating little difference between the states, it is not clear if there are "real" differences in new firm persistence between these states. For the following analysis, then, the state will be ignored, waiting for a definitive comparison with identical procedures in all the states.

These results cannot, unfortunately, help resolve the debate over the "true" form of the hazard curve, the changing probability of discontinuance over the early years in the firm life course. Some suggest that the hazard rate, the probability of a firm discontinuance, is highest at birth and then declines thereafter, captured in the phrase "liability of newness" (Stinchcombe, 1965; Carroll, 1983; Freeman, Carroll, and Hannan, 1983; Phillips and Kirchhoff, 1989). Others find that the initial probability of discontinuance is very low, followed by a sharp increase, followed by continued decline, captured by the phrase "liability of adolescence" (Ben-Ner, 1988; Bruderl and Schussler, 1990; Bruderl, Preisendorfer and Ziegler, 1992; Finchman and Levinthal, 1991; Preisendorfer and Voss, 1990; Reynolds and Miller, 1992; Wagner, 1994). There were no new firms in these data sets where (1) interviews were conducted during the "birth year" and (2) follow-ups were completed at short, frequent intervals, every six to twelve months. Hence, there is no information on firms in early infancy, the period where the debate over the form of this relationship hinges. If "late infancy" is redefined as "adolescence" for the purposes of this debate, then the patterns in Table 6.1 provide support for both hypotheses. A systematic follow-up of new firms identified in the gestation period would provide a resolution to this argument.

It is clear that exploration of the factors that would affect firm persistence should be separated for the three different subsamples identified in Table 6.1: late infancy, youth, and early adolescence. This is done in all the following analyses.

START-UP FACTORS AFFECTING NEW FIRM PERSISTENCE

A number of factors associated with the beginning of a new firm can be considered in relation to persistence. Because of the way the sample was drawn and the need to minimize ambiguity over causal relationships, the following analysis first focuses on those factors that may be considered initial conditions or features associated with the actual firm births. The second emphasis is on factors that occurred between the firm birth and the date of the interview. For all factors reviewed, the sample size and state of context may vary, and there is some variation in the number of firms with data suitable for the analysis. Reliance on statistical significance, using the conservative tests associated with the survival procedure, helps to minimize errors of inference. A final section provides a general overview of the results, by firm life-course stage.

Birth Period Factors. The effects of the community context, the economic sector, the amount of initial start-up funds, and the initial year sales on firm persistence are reported in Table 6.2. Three have a small, statistically significant impact for one of the comparisons. Community context seems to affect new firms only in late infancy, with a slightly higher persistence rate for those in regional centers and the lowest for those in metropolitan centers. The industry sector has little effect except for a slightly higher rate of persistence among firms in consumer service, particularly when compared to other new firms in the youth or early adolescence stages. The amount of funding assembled for the start-up, before formal funding was available, seems to have an unexpected effect, for firms reporting no such funding or high levels of funding are more likely to persist during the youth stage. This may reflect the refusal of some robust new firms to report on this early-stage funding.

The fourth factor reported in Table 6.2, initial-year sales, has a major effect on new firm persistence in all three stages. In general, new firms reporting higher first-year sales, adjusted for inflation to 1992 dollars, tended to persist for all three stages.

Almost all comparisons, save one, across the life-course stages were statistically significant. In most cases the statistical significance was extremely high. This pattern is present in the following analyses as well.

Comparisons based on the initial legal form, the percentage of start-up funds provided by the start-up team, or, for Wisconsin, the extent of emphasis on high technology, resulted in no statistically significant differences.

Table 6.2
New Firm Probability of Persistence: Selected Firm Birth Factors

	Total Sample	First Interview Completed During:		
		Late Infancy	Youth	Early Adolescence
First sale to first interview: years	0–7	0–1	2–3	4–7
Percentage surviving to end of period (1, 2, 3)				
Urbanicity				
Metro area	73%	67%	72%	76% (****)
Regional center	75	75	71	80 (****)
Nonmetro	75	71	76	77 (****)
	(NS)	(*)	(NS)	(NS)
Economic sector				
Agriculture, mining	74%	76%	47%	86% (**)
Construction	74	71	72	77 (****)
Manufacturing	75	71	73	79 (****)
Distributive services	74	71	71	77 (****)
Producer, business services	72	74	68	73 (****)
Health, educ., social services	82	84	73	88 (NS)
Retail	71	65	73	73 (****)
Consumer services	80 (4)	70	83 (4)	84 (4) (****)
	(NS)	(NS)	(NS)	(NS)
Start-up funding				
None reported	74%	66%	76%	76% (****)
$1–49,999	72	77	64	75 (****)
$50–5 million	75	69	75	78 (****)
	(***)	(NS)	(**)	(NS)
First-year sales				
$10–19,999	68%	71%	63%	69% (****)
$20–74,999	71	64	68	80 (****)
$75–249,999	75	75	77	73 (****)
$250,000–$30 million	80	76	76	86 (****)
	(****)	(**)	(**)	(****)

Notes: (1) All computations completed by SPSS PC 5.01 survival analysis with weighted sample to adjust for sampling stratification.

(2) Statistical significance indicated within parentheses: NS = not significant; * = 0.05; ** = 0.01; *** = 0.001; **** = 0.0001.

(3) Comparisons across columns refer only to three on the right.

(4) Differences between consumer service and from two to four other sectors is statistically significant with a pair-wise comparison.

Aspects of the start-up team are reviewed in Table 6.3, including age, gender, education, and two measures of work experience. The modal age of the start-up team members at the first sale has an effect for persistence only in the youth period, where older teams are associated with firm persistence. Gender is complicated by the comparison of teams of differing size and mix, but it is clear that if men are involved, the persistence is higher, particularly for late infancy and early adolescence. Firms started only by women are less likely to persist. Educational attainment of the start-up team has very little systematic effect; a slightly higher firm persistence among those started by teams with graduate education in late infancy is offset by a reduced firm persistence among those started by college graduates.

Prior experience in the new firm's industry and general work experience are reflected as significant in two variables. Firms started with teams with less than five years experience are less likely to persist than firms started with those with over five years of experience. Firms started by teams with individuals who have just left jobs with established organizations or new firms are more likely to persist when compared to those started by those previously unemployed, leaving school, retirement, or some other activity.

A number of other factors, such as the size of the start-up team, start-up team ethnic status, and prior experience with firm start-ups, had no impact on firm persistence. The impact of prior start-up experience was U-shaped. New firms with teams reporting some prior start-up experience had higher persistence than those with no prior experience or experience with two or more other start-ups.

As shown in Table 6.4, the effect of the length of the start-up window, the time between beginning the process and completion with the firm birth, was modest, as was the effect of the sequence of events. There is a hint that a start-up period of greater than a month may lead to greater persistence, but the effect is small. In addition, the evidence on the effect of timing of financial support is mixed. Financial support at the end of the start-up period seems to increase persistence in a firm's late infancy, but financial support early in the start-up process seems to increase persistence in a firm's youth.

On the other hand, placement of first sales, hiring, or major personal commitments by the start-up team to the firm in the start-up period had no statistically significant relationship to new firm persistence.

The problems that occurred during the start-up period, reported in Table 6.5, appear to have some relationship to firm persistence. A higher percentage of major problems seems to reduce persistence through the youth period; a higher percentage of minor problems seems to increase prevalence in early adolescence. Greater problems with external financial support seem to reduce persistence, as does a higher level of problems with systems of financial control. Those with more problems with the physical infrastructure have higher persistence in early adolescence, and those with more initial problems with regulations are more likely to persist.

Table 6.3
New Firm Probability of Persistence: Start-up Team Background

	Total Sample	First Interview Completed During:		
		Late Infancy	*Youth*	*Early Adolescence*
First sale to first interview: years	0–7	0–1	2–3	4–7
Percentage surviving to end of period (1, 2, 3)				
Modal team age at first sales				
18–24 years old	73%	69%	61%	78% (****)
25–34 years old	72	65	69	76 (****)
35–44 years old	74	64	75	77 (****)
55–75 years old	73	61	81	71 (****)
	(NS)	(NS)	(**)	(NS)
Team gender mix				
One male	75%	73%	72%	79% (****)
Two or more males	74	68	74	78 (****)
One or more females	68	58	75	68 (****)
Mixed gender	76	80	69	81 (****)
	(*)	(***)	(NS)	(**)
Team modal educational attainment				
High school	75%	74%	77%	75% (****)
Post-high school	72	73	69	74 (****)
College degree	73	62	69	80 (****)
Graduate degree	78	82	76	77 (**)
	(NS)	(*)	(NS)	(NS)
Team same industry experience				
0–5 years	70%	62%	69%	74% (****)
6–50 years	77	70	76	79 (****)
	(***)	(NS)	(NS)	(**)
Team prior work activity				
Organization/new firm	77%	75%	75%	80% (****)
Unemploy./school/other	67	63	65	70 (****)
	(****)	(NS)	(**)	(***)

Notes: (1) All computations completed by SPSS PC 5.01 survival analysis with weighted sample to adjust for sampling stratification.

(2) Statistical significance indicated within parentheses: NS= not significant; * = 0.05; ** = 0.01; *** = 0.001; **** = 0.0001.

(3) Comparisons across columns refer only to three on the right.

Table 6.4
New Firm Probability of Persistence: Start-up Period Features

	Total Sample	First Interview Completed During:		
		Late Infancy	Youth	Early Adolescence
First sale to first interview: years	0–7	0–1	2–3	4–7
Percentage surviving to end of period (1, 2, 3)				
Length of start-up window				
0–5 months	73%	63%	74%	77% (****)
6–11 months	72	72	73	71 (**)
12–35 months	75	66	69	83 (****)
36–140 months	77	90	71	77 (NS)
	(NS)	(NS)	(NS)	(*)
Start-up events: financing				
First month	79%	69%	80%	81% (***)
One-month window	68	46	66	73 (****)
Last month	73	77	64	77 (****)
	(NS)	(**)	(**)	(NS)

Notes: (1) All computations completed by SPSS PC 5.01 survival analysis with weighted sample to adjust for sampling stratification.
(2) Statistical significance indicated within parentheses: NS = not significant; * = 0.05; ** = 0.01; *** = 0.001; **** = 0.0001.
(3) Comparisons across columns refer only to three on the right.

Problems with marketing, personnel and hiring, planning, or the actual site where the new firm is located have no statistically significant relationship to firm persistence.

Post–Firm Birth Factors. A number of factors occurred during the firm birth process but prior to the initial interview. The impact of the firm's competitive strategy and emphasis of the management, as reported by the principal completing the interview, on firm persistence is presented in Table 6.6.

While the overall comparisons related to competitive strategy show little impact, perhaps because they are nominal categories and not scaled on an underlying dimension, they revealed some differences with pairwise comparisons. New firms whose only strategy focus is on low prices have a reduced tendency to persist, especially during the youth stage. Those pursing technological emphasis seem to have a reduced tendency to persist in the early stages but are more robust in the latter periods. The major differences occur in early adolescence, when equivocators seem to be less likely to persist, while niche purveyors or those promoting technology in some form are more likely to endure.

Table 6.5
New Firm Probability of Persistence: Start-up Problems

	Total Sample	First Interview Completed During:			
		Late Infancy	Youth	Early Adolescence	
First sale to first interview: years	0–7	0–1	2–3	4–7	
Percentage surviving to end of period (1, 2, 3)					
Start-up problems: percent major					
0–9	76%	79%	71%	79%	(****)
10–24	72	72	74	71	(****)
25–100	71	76	60	75	(****)
	(*)	(NS)	(**)	(NS)	
Start-up problems: percent minor					
0–34	70%	73%	68%	68%	(****)
35–54	72	74	67	76	(****)
55–100	78	81	72	81	(****)
	(NS)	(NS)	(NS)	(NS)	
Start-up problem index: financial support					
Low	73%	74%	70%	76%	(****)
Medium	76	77	73	78	(****)
High	70	74	60	75	(****)
	(**)	(NS)	(**)	(NS)	
Start-up problem index: financial control					
Low	72%	75%	74%	69%	(****)
Medium	78	77	72	83	(****)
High	71	75	64	74	(****)
	(*)	(NS)	(*)	(**)	
Start-up problem index: infrastructure					
Low	72%	70%	72%	72%	(****)
High	77	76	70	84	(****)
	(NS)	(NS)	(NS)	(**)	
Start-up problem index: regulations					
Low	69%	71%	67%	70%	(****)
Medium	74	77	70	77	(****)
High	77	78	70	81	(****)
	(*)	(NS)	(NS)	(NS)	

Notes: (1) All computations completed by SPSS PC 5.01 survival analysis with weighted sample to adjust for sampling stratification.

(2) Statistical significance indicated within parentheses: NS = not significant; * = 0.05; ** = 0.01; *** = 0.001; **** = 0.0001.

(3) Comparisons across columns refer only to three on the right.

Table 6.6
New Firm Probability of Persistence: Competitive Strategy

	Total Sample	First Interview Completed During:		
		Late Infancy	Youth	Early Adolescence
First sale to first interview: years	0–7	0–1	2–3	4–7
Percentage surviving to end of period (1, 2, 3)				
Strategy Archetypes				
Superachievers	74%	64%	77%	77% (****)
Price competitors	69 (4)	57	67 (5)	74 (****)
Equivocators	71	73	74	68 (5) (NS)
Technology value	74	63	67 (5)	86 (6) (****)
Niche purveyors	77	69	70	85 (7) (****)
Quality proponents	71	53	73	73 (****)
	(NS)	(NS)	(NS)	(**)
Management Emphasis				
Financial control				
Low	57%	49%	50%	67% (****)
Medium	76	77	76	76 (*)
High	83	81	85	83 (*)
	(****)	(***)	(****)	(**)
Formal planning				
Low	70%	63%	62%	77% (****)
Medium	69	61	64	75 (****)
High	79	74	78	81 (***)
	(***)	(NS)	(**)	(NS)
Organizational coordination				
Low	69%	55%	61%	79% (****)
Medium	76	76	74	79 (***)
High	72	66	71	75 (****)
	(*)	(NS)	(NS)	(NS)
Marketing strategy				
Low	73%	66%	63%	81% (****)
Medium	68	58	65	73 (****)
High	76	74	79	75 (**)
	(**)	(NS)	(*)	(NS)
Marketing implementation				
Low	68%	60%	65%	73% (****)
Medium	73	54	69	80 (****)
High	75	83	73	74 (*)
	(NS)	(**)	(NS)	(NS)
Principal involvement				
Low	67%	67%	62%	70% (****)
Medium	70	57	68	78 (****)
High	77	67	73	80 (****)
	(***)	(NS)	(NS)	(**)

Table 6.6 continued

	Total Sample	First Interview Completed During:		
		Late Infancy	Youth	Early Adolescence
Industry expertise				
Low	66%	62%	66%	68% (****)
Medium	70	62	68	75 (****)
High	77	72	72	82 (****)
	(***)	(NS)	(NS)	(**)

Notes: (1) All computations completed by SPSS PC 5.01 survival analysis with weighted sample to adjust for sampling stratification.

(2) Statistical significance indicated within parentheses: NS = not significant; * = 0.05; ** = 0.01; *** = 0.001; **** = 0.0001.

(3) Comparisons across columns refer only to three on the right.

(4) Lower than 1st or 5th, statistically significant.

(5) Lower than 1st, statistically significant.

(6) Higher than 2nd, 3rd, or 6th, statistically significant.

(7) Higher than 1st, 2nd, 3rd, or 6th, statistically significant.

Seven aspects of the management emphasis measured were related to persistence. These were all multi-item indicators and are described in Chapter 5. New firms with a greater emphasis on financial control and formal planning seem to have a greater persistence. A related emphasis on coordination presents a more mixed effect; it would appear that a moderate level of coordination is optimal for firm persistence. A greater emphasis on marketing strategy seems appropriate for firm persistence during late infancy and youth periods; an emphasis on marketing implementation during late infancy seems particularly related to persistence.

Higher levels of team members' involvement and commitment to the firm seem to be associated with persistence, especially during firm youth and early adolescence. This is consistent with the higher level of industry expertise and contacts, particularly important during early adolescence.

The impact on persistence of the ability to acquire formal financing for the new firm is presented in Table 6.7. Care should be taken in this analysis because those respondents who failed to report financial information, a small proportion, have been combined with those who have no financial information to report. Confidence in interpretations is greater when levels of financial support are compared. If the "none reported" categories are excluded, the results—in terms of statistical significance, are not changed.

It is clear that firms that raise more funds are more likely to persist, although this seems to indicate the presence of loans from banks and other institutions rather than equity funding. This may reflect the small proportion of new firms, less than 10%, that have reported any equity financing. The statistical significance reflects, primarily, the higher level of persistence among new firms with large amounts of financing, over $150,000 in loans

Table 6.7
New Firm Probability of Persistence: Financial Support

	Total Sample	First Interview Completed During:		
		Late Infancy	Youth	Early Adolescence
First sale to first interview: years	0–7	0–1	2–3	4–7
Percentage surviving to end of period (1, 2, 3)				
Total loans reported (1, 2, 3)				
None (4)	74%	68%	74%	78% (****)
$1–39,999	70	80	64	69 (****)
$40–149,999	70	68	69	72 (****)
$150,000 and up	80	72	81	83 (****)
	(***)	(NS)	(**)	(**)
Total equity reported				
None (4)	74%	70%	72%	76% (****)
$1–99,999	80	78	72	92 (***)
$100,000 and up	77	70	84	76 (*)
	(NS)	(NS)	(NS)	(NS)
Total financial support				
None (4)	74%	67%	74%	78% (****)
$1– 49,999	69	76	64	70 (****)
$50–199,999	72	69	70	74 (****)
$200,000 and up	82	78	81	85 (***)
	(****)	(NS)	(**)	(**)

Notes: (1) All computations completed by SPSS PC 5.01 survival analysis with weighted sample
to adjust for sampling stratification.
(2) Statistical significance indicated within parentheses: NS = not significant; * = 0.05;
** = 0.01; *** = 0.001; **** = 0.0001.
(3) Comparisons across columns refer only to three on the right.
(4) "None" includes a proportion that did not respond.

or over $200,000 total, rather than the slightly elevated persistence among those reporting no financing in some years.

Causality is, as always, an issue, for either financing contributes to persistence, or those firms that can attract financing are more likely to persist.

A final feature that developed between birth and the time of the first interview is related to the sales growth trajectory of the new firm. This is presented in Table 6.8 in two ways, as a single factor and then in relation to two broad industry sectors.

These sectors are, first, those with export potential and, second, those focusing on the local or regional customers. Out-of-region exports may occur in agriculture, mining, manufacturing, distributive services, and producer (or business) services sectors. All other economic sectors, where the customer is

Table 6.8
New Firm Probability of Persistence: Growth Trajectory and Sector

	Total Sample	First Interview Completed During:		
		Late Infancy	Youth	Early Adolescence
First sale to first interview: years	0–7	0–1	2–3	4–7
Percentage surviving to end of period (1, 2, 3)				
All economic sectors	68%	59%	71%	76% (****)
Hi Start-Hi Growth	78%	84%	75%	77% (NS)
Hi Start-Lo Growth	81	76	79	83 (****)
Lo Start-Hi Growth	73	75	70	76 (****)
Lo Start-Lo Growth	64	59	62	68 (****)
	(****)	(****)	(***)	(****)
Export potential sectors (3)	73%	72%	70%	77% (****)
Hi Start-Hi Growth	81%	91%	76%	81%
Hi Start-Lo Growth	77	75	76	80 (****)
Lo Start-Hi Growth	73	71	70	77 (***)
Lo Start-Lo Growth	69	63	68	73 (****)
	(*)	(**)	(NS)	(NS)
Local market sectors (4)	74%	69%	70%	77% (****)
Hi Start-Hi Growth	72%	73%	71%	71% (NS)
Hi Start-Lo Growth	82	75	81	86 (****)
Lo Start-Hi Growth	73	77	69	75 (**)
Lo Start-Lo Growth	60	54	57	64 (****)
	(****)	(**)	(***)	(****)

Notes: (1) All computations completed by SPSS PC 5.01 survival analysis with weighted sample to adjust for sampling stratification.

(2) Statistical significance indicated within parentheses: NS = not significant; * = 0.05; ** = 0.01; *** = 0.001; **** = 0.0001.

(3) Includes agriculture/mining; manufacturing; distributive services; and producer (or business) services.

(4) Includes construction; retail; health, education, and social services; and consumer services.

almost always in the immediate area, are placed in the local market sector, including construction, retail, consumer service, and health, education, and social services (Reynolds and Freeman, 1987; Reynolds and Miller, 1988).

Considered by itself, the growth trajectory of the new firms has a major impact at all stages of the process, with the low-start, low-growth firms least likely to persist beyond each firm life-course stage. High-start, high-growth new firms are more likely to persist beyond the earliest stage, late infancy, but not the later stages.

Considered by itself, there is no substantive or statistically significant difference between the new firms with export potential or oriented toward a local market. However, the interaction effects between economic sector and growth patterns are substantial. The range of persistence—the focus of attention—is considerably increased, from a high of 91% among high-start, high-growth, export-oriented new firms in late infancy to a low of 54% among low-start, low-growth, local market new firms in late infancy. Clearly, interaction among these different factors has a major effect on firm persistence.

Summary of Factors Affecting Prevalence. A summary of the major factors affecting prevalence of new firms, by period where the first interview is completed, is presented in Table 6.9. When the full sample is considered, statistically significant relationships to firm persistence are found for eighteen different factors, all measured from one to eight years before persistence is assessed for these new firms.

For example, persistence of firms in late infancy appears to be enhanced if they are in a regional center, have higher first-year sales, have males on the start-up team, have a team with more educational background, receive financial support toward the end of the start-up period, emphasize financial controls and marketing implementation, and have a high growth trajectory, particularly if they are in an export potential economic sector. There is no evidence that the number or severity of start-up problems or the presence of financial support has an effect at this stage.

Persistence of firms in youth appears to be facilitated by operating in the consumer services sector, greater levels of start-up financial support, higher first-year sales, older team members recently shifting from established organizations, financial support early in the start-up process, an absence of major start-up problems (particularly related to financial support), with a management emphasis on financial controls, planning marketing strategy, and with a heavy emphasis from the principals, with substantial financial support, with a high-growth trajectory, and operation in an export sector.

The persistence of firms in early adolescence is affected by the same factors affecting young firms, but with more emphasis on the work experience of the start-up team and the firm strategy and less with regard to their management emphasis.

Further, the number of statistically significant relationships seems to grow for firms initially assessed later in the firm life course, from nine factors for those assessed in late infancy to seventeen for those assessed during youth and sixteen for those assessed during early adolescence. This may reflect the large sample sizes available for the older new firms, or it may reflect a larger influence of other factors, not assessed in these studies, on the persistence of very young, or infant, new firms.

MULTIPLE FACTOR IMPACT AND NEW FIRM PERSISTENCE

Two strategies can be utilized to explore the joint impact of different combinations of factors on firm persistence. The first, discriminant analysis,

Table 6.9
New Firm Probability of Persistence: Summary of Major Factors (1, 2)

	Total Sample	First Interview Completed During:		
		Late Infancy	Youth	Early Adolescence
First sale to first interview: years	0–7	0–1	2–3	4–7
Birth period factors				
Regional center context		*		
Consumer services sector	*		*	*
Start-up funding	***		**	
First-year sales	****	**	**	****
Modal team age			**	
Males on start-up team	*	***		**
Team educational attainment		*		
Same industry work experience	***			**
Transition from organizational work to start-up	****		**	***
Length of start-up window				*
Financial support first			**	
Financial support last		**		
Absence of major start-up problems	*		**	
Presence of minor start-up problems				*
Absence: financial support problems	**		**	
Absence: financial control problems	*		*	**
Post-firm birth factors				
Strategy: not price focused	*			
Strategy: not equivocators				*
Strategy: tech or niche				*
Management emphasis:				
Financial control	****	***	****	**
Planning	***		**	
Marketing strategy	**		*	
Marketing implementation		**		
Principal's involvement	**		*	**
Total loans	***		**	**
Total financial support	****		**	**
Growth trajectory	****	****	***	****
Growth x economic sector	****	**	***	****

Notes: (1) All computations completed by SPSS PC 5.01 survival analysis with weighted sample to adjust for sampling stratification.

(2) Statistical significance indicated within parentheses: NS = not significant; * = 0.05; ** = 0.01; *** = 0.001; **** = 0.0001.

Source: Previous tables in chapter.

utilizes a specialized version of regression analysis designed to develop predictions of dichotomous outcomes. These results are supplemented by a procedure that locates critical interaction among factors associated with new firm persistence. This automatic interaction detection (AID or CHAID for SPSS; Magidson, 1992) procedure is the same technique employed in exploring factors associated with becoming a nascent entrepreneur in Chapter 3. The two analyses provide different information with regard to critical factors associated with firm persistence.

Linear Additive Regression Modeling. The procedure used, discriminant analysis (Norusis, 1992b), is designed for dichotomous dependent variables (such as firm discontinuance or persistence), continuous independent variables, and complete data for each case in the analysis. The basis for variables chosen to be included in this analysis was Table 6.9, but some were excluded because data were missing for a large number of new firms. Most important, data on management focus and the presence of start-up problems were unavailable for half of the sample. Most of the remaining factors were covered in one form or another, although the total number of new firms with data on all the variables selected for analysis was 1,402.[2]

The stepwise procedure employed to develop the linear models used the potential of each variable to improve the predictions (reduce unexplained variance) as the major criterion for inclusion. Even though 27% of the new firms were considered deactivated, the modeling procedure gave equal emphasis to predictions of discontinuance and persistence. As shown in Table 6.10, the predictions of the "best fit" models were correct for about six of ten cases, although predictive accuracy was lowest for new firms in their youth, compared to those in late infancy or early adolescence. The fit of all models to the data is statistically highly significant, although this does not preclude other models from having a statistically highly significant fit to the data.

The major results are presented in Table 6.10 for the total sample and those firms where the first interview occurred at different times in their life course. The percentage persisting increases from 63% to 72% to 76% for the three subgroups and 73% overall; accurate predictions are made for 65%, 59%, and 63% of the cases in these three subgroups and 59% for all cases combined. On the other hand, a prediction that all new firms persisted would be accurate in 73% of the cases.

Most of the variables retained in the models as predictions of persistence have a uniform impact across the new firm life course. (The correlations with persistence in Table 6.10 provide a convenient check on the direction of impact.) Those start-ups implemented outside urban areas are more likely to persist. Higher first-year sales lead to greater new firm persistence, as do higher amounts of loans for late infancy new firms. A competitive strategy that includes an emphasis on service and quality or low prices is associated with new firm persistence. New firms with males on the start-up team, individuals shifting from jobs in established organizations, implementation by older team members, and initiation by those with same-industry work experience are more likely to persist.

A number of factors have the opposite impact at different stages in the new firm life course. For example, higher compound growth rates are associated with reduced persistence for youthful new firms but increased persistence for those in early adolescence. A strategic focus on facilities and customer convenience is related to a reduced persistence in late infancy but an increased persistence in early adolescence. A focus on product diversity seems to increase persistence for youthful new firms but reduce persistence during late infancy or early adolescence. New firms implemented by teams with prior start-up experience are more likely to persist through late infancy but less likely to persist through new firm youth.

A number of factors included in the step wise modeling procedure were not chosen for inclusion in any of the models: strategic focus on identifying niche markets; a strategic focus on high technology; total cash provided to the new firm by the start-up team before formal financing acquired; whether or not the new firm was in an export potential or locally oriented economic sector; educational attainment of the start-up team; the total equity financing of the start-up; or the total of all formal financing (loans plus equity) provided to the start-up. This would suggest that these other factors were either not important, or their presence was highly correlated with the other variables.

Traditional multiple linear regression models, even when adapted for a dichotomous dependent variable, such as new firm persistence and discontinuance, assume that the effects of independent variables are additive. For example, it is assumed that the effect of first-year sales can be added to the impact of a rural location and the effect of a focus on low prices to develop the prediction of the outcome. The number of potential interaction effects—such as the joint effect of high initial sales with an urban location—is enormous; it is impossible to systematically consider the impact of all potential interactions. For this reason, a different analysis strategy is utilized to identify significant interactions.

Identifying Factor Interactions. Systematic assessment of possible interactions between factors involves a multistage procedure, CHAID (Magidson, 1992). It follows a strategy of identifying the single most significant factors associated with new firm persistence and then sorting all cases based on that factor. For this reason, each independent variable must be in the form of three to four discrete values. Each subgroup is then considered in terms of the remaining factors that may affect firm persistence. This procedure continues until the remaining factors no longer have any impact on new firm persistence, the impact is no longer statistically significant, or the group has fewer than fifty cases.[3]

The major results of the use of an automatic interaction detection procedure for the full sample, deleting only those new firms for which persistence cannot be determined, are presented in Table 6.11. The table should be read

Table 6.10
Linear Additive Discriminant Models Predicting Persistence (1, 2, 3, 4)

	Total Sample		First Interview Completed During:					
			Late Infancy		Youth		Early Adolescence	
Number of new firms	1,402		205		522		724	
Discontinued	27%		37%		28%		24%	
Persisting	73		63		72		76	
Percentage correct predictions								
Discontinued	55%		58%		60%		51%	
Persisting	60		70		58		66	
All cases	59%		65%		59%		63%	
Standardized coefficients and (correlations)	Coeff	(Corr)	Coeff	(Corr)	Coeff	(Corr)	Coeff	(Corr)
Independent variables (5)								
Proximity to urban area	-.21	(-.03)	-.29	(-.09)			-.24	(-.04)
First-year sales	0.47	(0.08)			0.29	(0.08)	0.47	(0.09)
Compound growth rate					-.24	(-.04)	0.26	(0.03)
Total loans all sources			0.49	(0.11)				
Strategic focus:								
Service and quality	0.56	(0.08)	0.58	(0.17)			0.63	(0.09)
Facilities and convenience	0.36	(0.06)	-.20	(-.01)			0.40	(0.07)
Product diversity	-.29	(-.00)	-.22	(-.12)	0.25	(0.06)	-.38	(-.01)
Low prices	0.17	(0.05)	0.31	(0.21)	0.24	(0.08)		
Start-up team:								
Males on team	0.50	(0.10)	0.41	(0.24)	0.34	(0.08)	0.59	(0.13)
Shift from established org	0.56	(0.07)			0.68	(0.14)		
Age at firm birth	0.17	(0.02)			-.57	(-.09)		
Prior start-up experience			0.27	(0.10)				
Same-industry work experience			0.22	(0.16)				

	Total Sample	First Interview Completed During:		
		Late Infancy	Youth	Early Adolescence
Measures of successful fit				
Wilks' Lambda	0.9663	0.8290	0.9417	0.9504
Chi-square	48.03	37.20	31.00	33.49
Statistical significance	0.0000	0.0000	0.0001	0.0000

Notes: (1) Analysis completed using SPSS PC 5.0 discriminant analysis with standardized defaults and stepwise selection of independent variables designed to minimize the unexplained variance (MINRESID) with equal emphasis on predictions of survival and discontinuance (Norusis, 1992b).
(2) Standardized discriminate coefficients provided in the body of the table are usually four times the standardized coefficients from multiple linear regression analysis.
(3) Correlation coefficients provide a check on the direction of influence of the independent variables.
(4) Weights adjusted to sum to the number of cases for each analysis.
(5) The following independent variables were not chosen for inclusion in any of the models: strategic focus on identifying niche markets; a strategic focus on high technology; total cash provided to the new firm by the start-up team before formal financing acquired; whether or not the new firm was in an export potential or locally oriented economic sector; educational attainment of the start-up team; the total equity financing of the start-up; or the total of all formal financing (loans and equity).

Table 6.11
New Firm Persistence, AID Analysis: All Firms

1st Level	2nd Level	3rd Level	4th Level	5th Level	Group ID*	Persistence
HiSt/HiGr; LoSt/HiGr;DK	Total financing None, $1–199K	S-U team education; High school degree	Non-metro		(1:n = 71)	89%
HiSt/HiGr; LoSt/HiGr;DK	Total financing None, $1–199K	S-U team education; High school degree	Regional center; Metro region	Superachievers; Price: equivalent	(2:n = 86)	60%
HiSt/HiGr; LoSt/HiGr;DK	Total financing None, $1–199K	S-U team education; High school degree	Regional center; Metro region	Tech; Niche; Quality	(3:n = 117)	85%
HiSt/HiGr; LoSt/HiGr;DK	Total financing None, $1–199K	S-U team education; Post-H.S., coll., grad.			(4:n = 1,009)	70%
HiSt/HiGr; LoSt/HiGr;DK	Total financing $200K and up	S-U team financing None reported			(5:n = 42)	65%
HiSt/HiGr; LoSt/HiGr;DK	Total financing $200K and up	S-U team financing $1K and up, DK	Regional center; Non-metro		(6:n = 44)	97%
HiSt/HiGr; LoSt/HiGr;DK	Total financing $200K and up	S-U team financing $1K and up, DK	Metro area		(7:n = 60)	81%
HiSt/LoGr	Total loans None reported	S-U team age 18–24; 35–75; DK	S-U team financing Up to $50K, DK	Ag;; DistS; ProdS; Hl, Ed, SoS; Retail	(8:n = 164)	86%
HiSt/LoGr	Total loans None reported	S-U team age 18–24; 35–75; DK	S-U team financing Up to $50K, DK	Const, Mfg.; ConsServ; DK	(9::n = 87)	100%
HiSt/LoGr	Total loans None reported	S-U team age 18–24; 35–75; DK	S-U team financing $50K and up		(10:n = 64)	78%
HiSt/LoGr	Total loans None reported	S-U team age 25–34 years			(11:n = 120)	77%

1st Level	2nd Level	3rd Level	4th Level	5th Level	Group ID*	Persistence
HiSt/LoGr	Total loans $1K and up	S-U team education; H.S., coll., grad.	Non-metro		(12:n = 64)	91%
HiSt/LoGr	Total loans $1K and up	S-U team education; H.S., coll., grad.	Regional center; Metro area	S-U window 0–12 months	(13:n = 158)	83%
HiSt/LoGr	Total loans $1K and up	S-U team education; H.S., coll., grad.	Regional center; Metro area	S-U window 12+ months; DK	(14:n = 90)	68%
HiSt/LoGr	Total loans $1K and up	S-U team education; Post-H.S.; DK			(15:n = 146)	68%
LoSt/LoGr	S-U team shift; From work, DK	1st year sales: Up to $75K, DK	Firm life stage Infant, youth; DK		(16:n = 206)	65%
LoSt/LoGr	S-U team shift; From work, DK	1st year sales: Up to $75K, DK	Firm life stage Early adolescence	S-U team ind. Exp: 0–5 years; DK	(17:n = 76)	74%
LoSt/LoGr	S-U team shift; From work, DK	1st year sales: Up to $75K, DK	Firm life stage Early adolescence	S-U team ind. Exp: 5+ years	(18:n = 56)	90%
LoSt/LoGr	S-U team shift; From work, DK	1st year sales: $75K and up			(19:n = 90)	54%
LoSt/LoGr	S-U team shift; From non-work	S-U team education; H.S. degree; grad.			(20:n = 66)	68%
LoSt/LoGr	S-U team shift; From non-work	S-U team education; Post-H.S., coll., DK			(21:n = 123)	44%

* First number identifies the group; the second, the number of cases in the group.

from left to right. Each row represents one unique group identified by the procedure; the final column provides the persistence rate for the group. The procedure was constrained to five levels of analysis, although the majority of the new firms were sorted in three or four levels.

The initial sort reflects the significance of the growth trajectory of the new firms, with all high-growth firms in one group, high-start, low-growth in a second group, and low-start, low-growth in a third. The second variable included in the first two groups related to the financial support assembled by the new firms; for the low-start, low-growth new firms the second major factor to enter the analysis was related to the shift in work careers among the start-up team; those firms started by principals shifting from a nonwork situation were less likely to persist. There is more diversity in the subsequent levels of analysis, although the start-up team education, informal financing by the start-up team, regional context, economic sector, competitive strategy, firm life-course stage, and start-up team work experience all enter into the analysis at some point.

One major benefit of this procedure is its ability to systematically identify categories of new firms with quite different levels of persistence. The twenty-one groups identified for the full sample are ranked by firm persistence in Table 6.12. There is considerable range, from 44% to 100% of the firms persisting. But when types of firms with similar patterns of persistence are identified, they are often quite different types of new firms.

For example, a group of eighty-seven new firms (group number 9) where all (100%) are persisting appears to have strong first-year sales but little growth; no loans; start-up team financing less than $50,000; a young or older start-up team; and operating in construction, manufacturing, or consumer service. The next group of forty-four (group number 6), where 97% are persisting, have high-growth trajectories; over $200,000 in total financing, with some contributed by the start-up teams; and location outside metropolitan areas.

This illustrates one side of the problem regarding predictions of new firm persistence. One group is of medium-sized, new firms that have little or no growth; established with funds from the start-up team and no formal financing; and operating in economic sectors well suited to such firms— manufacturing, construction, and consumer services. The second group of firms has a high-growth profile with more substantial firms that have substantial external financing, located outside urban areas—perhaps in an under-served, growing market. The high level of persistence among these two types of firms may be for quite different reasons. Other firms with similar profiles may also reflect high levels of persistence, but also for different reasons.

The two groups with the lowest levels of persistence may reflect quite different reasons for discontinuance. The lowest persistence (44% in group 21) is found among 123 new firms with low initial sales and a low-growth pattern; the start-up team shifted from a nonwork status (students, unemployed, homemaker) to begin the new firm; and most have a post-high school education or a college degree. They may have not had the skills or background to operate a new firm, despite the formal education, and were forced to close the firm when resources were exhausted. The firms with the next lowest persistence (54% in group 19) were firms with low growth, but first-year sales were in excess of $75,000, and the start-up team had experience in the world of work. These firms may have been closed when growth failed to reach expectations. While both interpretations are speculation, it is reasonable to assume that these firms are deactivated for different reasons. Not all new firm quits may be for the same reasons. Analysis based on the assumption that all firm deactivations reflect the same processes may have limited success, if there is substantial diversity in the reasons for a business to discontinue or if the reasons vary for different situations.

It should be noted that almost one-third of the new firms are in one group (number 4), which has a high-growth profile; from none to $200,000 in initial financing; and a start-up team that completed some education beyond high school. Seven in ten of these new firms were persisting in the follow-up interview. In a sense, these are the modal type of new firm, and their persistence is about the average for the entire group.

Additional analyses were completed for new firms in each of the three life-course phases, and the major results are presented in Appendices A, B, and C at the end of this chapter. Table 6.13 provides a summary of the analyses. The presentation provides those factors included at each level of the analysis, along with the minimum, maximum, and range of persistences for each analysis. The difference between groups of new firms with the highest and lowest proportion persisting is substantial, from 56% to 78%. Further, a wide range of factors is incorporated in the analyses at different stages, some related to context, growth trajectories, first-year sales, competitive strategy, characteristics of the start-up team, and so on.

This provides strong evidence that while some general factors may be associated with firm persistence, a number of distinctive situations may develop with unique combinations of context, business operations, and features of the start-up team that may affect firm persistence. There are, also, very different combinations of factors at different stages in the early life of new firms. It also provides evidence that systematic progress on this complex phenomenon may be possible, but it will require the careful development of extensive data on large, representative samples of new firms. Current evidence does not, for example, allow us to explore the impact of assistance programs or government programs on new firm persistence.

OVERVIEW: THE TRANSFORMATION TO AN ESTABLISHED FIRM

Most firms, even new firms, survive from year to year. Generally speaking, over 90% of new firms will persist for an additional twelve months.

Table 6.12
New Firm Persistence, AID Analysis: Groups Ranked by Persistence

1st Level	2nd Level	3rd Level	4th Level	5th Level	Group ID*	Persistence
HiSt/LoGr	Total loans None reported	S-U team age 18–24; 35–75; DK	S-U team financing Up to $50K, DK	Const., Mfg.; ConsServ; DK	(9:n = 87)	100%
HiSt/HiGr; LoSt/HiGr;DK	Total financing $200K and up	S-U team financing $1K and up, DK	Regional center; Non-metro		(6:n = 44)	97%
HiSt/LoGr	Total loans $1K and up	S-U team education; H.S., coll., grad.	Non-metro		(12:n = 64)	91%
LoSt/LoGr	S-U team shift; From work; DK	1st year sales; Up to $75K, DK	Firm life stage Early adolescence	S-U team ind. Exp: 5+ years	(18:n = 56)	90%
HiSt/HiGr; LoSt/HiGr;DK	Total financing None, $1–199K	S-U team education; H.S. degree	Non-metro		(1:n = 71)	89%
HiSt/LoGr	Total loans None reported	S-U team age 18–24; 35–75; DK	S-U team financing Up to $50K, DK	Ag.; DistS; ProdS; Hl, Ed, SoS; Retail	(8:n = 164)	86%
HiSt/HiGr; LoSt/HiGr;DK	Total financing None, $1–199K	S-U team education; H.S. degree	Regional center; Metro region	Tech; Niche; Quality	(3:n = 117)	85%
HiSt/LoGr	Total loans $1K and up	S-U team education; H.S., coll., grad.	Regional center; Metro area	S-U window 0–12 months	(13:n = 158)	83%
HiSt/HiGr; LoSt/HiGr;DK	Total financing $200K and up	S-U team financing $1K and up, DK	Metro area		(7:n = 60)	81%
HiSt/LoGr	Total loans None reported	S-U team age 18–24; 35–75; DK	S-U team financing $50K and up		(10:n = 64)	78%
HiSt/LoGr	Total loans None reported	S-U team age 25–34 years			(11:n = 120)	77%

1st Level	2nd Level	3rd Level	4th Level	5th Level	Group ID*	Persistence
LoSt/LoGr	S-U team shift; From work, DK	1st year sales; Up to $75K, DK	Firm life stage Early adolescence	S-U team ind. Exp: 0–5 years; DK	(17:n = 76)	74%
HiSt/HiGr; LoSt/HiGr;DK	Total financing None, $1–199K	S-U team education; Post-H.S., coll., grad.			(4:n = 1,009)	70%
HiSt/LoGr	Total loans $1K and up	S-U team education; H.S., coll., grad.	Regional center Metro area	S-U window 12+ months; DK	(14:n = 90)	68%
HiSt/LoGr	Total loans $1K and up	S-U team education; Post-H.S., DK			(15:n = 146)	68%
LoSt/LoGr	S-U team shift; From non-work	S-U team education; H.S. degree; grad.			(20:n = 66)	65%
HiSt/HiGr; LoSt/HiGr;DK	Total financing $200K and up	S-U team financing None reported			(5:n = 42)	65%
LoSt/LoGr	S-U team shift; From work; DK	1st year sales; Up to $75K, DK	Firm life state Infant, Youth; DK		(16:n = 206)	65%
HiSt/HiGr; LoSt/HiGr;DK	Total financing None, $1–199K	S-U team education; H.S. degree	Regional center Metro region	Superachievers; Price: equivalent	(2:n = 86)	60%
LoSt/LoGr	S-U team shift; From work, DK	1st year sales; $75K and up			(19:n = 90)	54%
LoSt/LoGr	S-U team shift; From non-work; DK	S-U team education; Post-H.S., coll.; DK			(21:n = 123)	44%

Table 6.13
New Firm Persistence, AID Analysis: Critical Variables by New Firm Life-Course Stage

Sort Level	Full Sample	Late Infancy	Youth	Early Adolescence
1st	Growth trajectory	Team education	First-year sales	First-year sales
2nd	Total financing Total loans Start-up team work shift	Growth trajectory Start-up window	Start-up funding Competitive strategy Start-up team gender	Formal loans Competitive strategy
3rd	Start-up team education First financing timing Start-up financing amount Start-up team age Start-up team education First-year sales	Start-up team age Start-up team gender	Urbanization Formal funding Economic sector Start-up team age	Start-up team gender Start-up window Start-up team age
4th	Urbanization Start-up team financing New firm stage	Urbanization Initial sales	Start-up team work background First financing timing Competitive strategy Start-up team gender	First financing timing Urbanization First-year sales Formal loans
5th	Competitive strategy Economic sector Start-up window Start-up team industry exp.		Competitive strategy	First financing timing
No. new firms	2,941	651	894	1,245
No. groups	21	8	16	20
Prevalence				
High	100%	84%	100%	98%
Low	44	25	22	40
Range	56%	59%	78%	58%

This is much higher than completion of the gestation or start-up period, where perhaps half or more of all efforts are abandoned—or fizzle out—during the first year. Despite substantial numbers of problems with the data on new firms, an exploratory analysis using conservative measures of significance provides some striking conclusions.

Persistence, the probability that a firm will be in operation for twelve more months, increases over time, from late infancy through firm youth and into early adolescence. No data were available on firm persistence in the first one to two years after first sales occurred. For this reason, it was not possible to provide evidence that would distinguish between the "liability of newness" or the "liability of adolescence" form of the hazard function for new firms.

Some factors, summarized in Tables 6.9 and 6.10, appeared in various analysis as statistically significant influences on firm persistence. This included factors such as high first-year sales, presence of men on the start-up teams, greater levels of financial support from the start-up team, higher levels of formal financial support, start-up teams with work or same-industry experience, strategic focus that includes an emphasis on service and quality or low prices, a management emphasis on financial controls, and perhaps operating in an arena with reduced competition, outside an urban area or underserved economic sectors. These factors may vary for different life-course stages of a new firm.

But the more important implications are two. First, unique combinations of factors seem to have a powerful effect on new firm persistence. There are substantial differences associated with different life-course stages and different growth trajectories. Second, firms may persist for quite different reasons—some stable new firms may provide an adequate work life for the owner/managers; other high-growth firms persist because the owners find their wealth-producing potential attractive. Conversely, firms may be discontinued for quite different reasons, some because the start-up team is inept, or competition is too severe, and deactivation may be the best outcome for all concerned. Other new firms may have a promising future, but the owners find other opportunities more attractive and shift emphasis to achieve better returns on their resources—time, skills, or money. Future research should clearly delineate the reasons for new firm persistence or deactivation.

If turbulence and change increase in market economies, more new firms with limited useful lives can be anticipated. Understanding the factors associated with new firm persistence and discontinuance will require a more complete treatment of the context, processes, and ownership objectives associated with both outcomes.

Appendix A: Late Infancy Firms—CHAID Analysis

1st Sort	2nd Sort	3rd Sort	4th Sort	Persistence
High school Post-high school Graduate experience	HiSt/HiGr HiSt/LoGr LoSt/HiGr			78% (1: n = 328)
High school Post-high school Graduate experience	LoSt/LoGr	18–24 years 35+ years		25% (2: n = 33)
High school Post-high school Graduate experience	LoSt/LoGr	25–34 years	Rural	53% (3: n = 27)
High school Post-high school Graduate experience	LoSt/LoGr	25–34 years	Regional center Metro regions	84% (4: n = 44)
College degree	0–12 months Start-up window	Gender Homogeneous	1st-year sales Less than $75K	37% (5: n = 75)
College degree	0–12 months Start-up window	Gender Homogeneous	1st-year sales $75K and up	62% (6: n = 67)
College degree	0–12 months Start-up window	Gender Mix on Start-up team		74% (7: n = 41)
College degree	13–140 months Start-up window			77% (8: n = 35)

Appendix B: Youth Firms—CHAID Analysis

1st Sort	2nd Sort	3rd Sort	4th Sort	5th Sort	Persistence
1st-year sales Up to $75K	No start-up funding	Regional center or Rural			85% (1:n = 77)
1st-year sales Up to $75	No start-up funding	Metro region			67% (2:n = 131)
1st-year sales Up to $75K	$1K and up	No formal funding	Start-up team was working		75% (3:n = 43)
1st-year sales Up to $75K	Start-up funds	No formal funding	Start-up team was not working		45% (4:n = 35)
1st-year sales Up to $75K	$1K and up, Start-up funds	$1–49K, Formal funds	Financing in 1st month		60% (5:n = 30)
1st-year sales Up to $75K	$1K and up Start-up funds	$1–49K Formal funds	Financing after 1st month		22% (6:n = 40)
1st-year sales Up to $75K	$1K and up Start-up funds	$50K and up Formal funds	No focus or Niche focus		89% (7:n = 34)
1st-year sales Up to $75K	$1K and up Start-up funds	$50K and up Formal funds	Price competitors, Quality, Tech focus		55% (8:n = 20)
1st-year sales $75K and up	Superachiever strategy	Not retail, Consumer services	High school or College degree		65% (9:n = 33)
1st-year sales $75K and up	Superachiever strategy	Not retail, Consumer services	Post-high school, Graduate experience		95% (10:n = 25)
1st-year sales $75K and up	Superachiever strategy	Retail or Consumer services			100% (11:n = 65)
1st-year sales $75K and up	Superachiever strategy	18–44 years old	One male, Mixed gender	Price competitors, Niche strategy	61% (12:n = 160)
1st-year sales $75K and up	Price competitors, Equivocators,Niche strategy	18–44 years old	Two males, All females		73% (13:n = 37)

159

Appendix B continued

1st Sort	2nd Sort	3rd Sort	4th Sort	5th Sort	Persistence
1st-year sales $75K and up	Price competitors, Equivocators,Niche strategy	18-44 years old	Two males, All females	Equivocators, No known straegy	96% (14:n = 29)
1st-year sales $75K and up	Price competitors, Equivocators,Niche strategy	45 and up years old			92% (15:n = 35)
1st-year sales $75K and up	Tech, Quality strategy				80% (16:n = 100)

Appendix C: Early Adolescence—CHAID Analysis

1st Sort	2nd Sort	3rd Sort	4th Sort	5th Sort	Persistence
1st-year sales $10–19K	Total loans $1–150K, None	One male, Mixed gender	Formal financing in 1st month, DK		75% (1:n = 75)
1st-year sales $10–19K	Total loans $1–150K, None	One male, Mixed gender	Formal financing after 1st month		43% (2:n = 34)
1st-year sales $10–19K	Total loans $1–150K, None	One male, Mixed gender	Rural region or regional center		98% (3:n = 40)
1st-year sales $10–19K	Total loans $1–150K, None	One male, Mixed gender	Metropolitan region		80% (4:n = 67)
1st-year sales $10–19K	Total loans $1–150K, None	All men or 1+ women	Formal financing in 1st month, DK		43% (5:n = 84)
1st-year sales $10–19K	Total loans $1–150K, None	All men or 1+ women	Formal financing after 1st month		72% (6:n = 46)
1st-year sales $10–19K	Total loans $1–150K and up				93% (7:n = 23)
1st-year sales $20–249K	Superachiever, Price, Niche Quality Strategy	0-6 months start-up window			74% (8:n = 251)

160

1st Sort	2nd Sort	3rd Sort	4th Sort	5th Sort	Persistence
1st-year sales $20–249K	Superachiever, Price, Niche Quality Strategy	6–12 months start-up window	Financing early in window, DK		97% (9:n = 60)
1st-year sales $20–249K	Superachiever, Price, Niche Quality Strategy	6–12 months start-up window	Financing last in window		65% (10:n = 26)
1st-year sales $20–249K	Superachiever, Price, Niche Quality Strategy	12+ months start-up window	1st-year sales $20–74K		87% (11:n = 25)
1st-year sales $20–249K	Superachiever, Price, Niche Quality Strategy	12+ months start-up window	1st-year sales $75–249K		67% (12:n = 47)
1st-year sales $20–249K	Equivacator strategy				58% (13:n = 52)
1st-year sales $20–249K	Technology value strategy				93% (14:n = 32)
1st-year sales $250K + up/Unknown	1+ males or 1+ females	18–24, 35–44 years old			90% (15:n = 195)
1st-year sales $250K + up/Unknown	1+ males or 1+ females	25–34, 45–75 years old	Total loans, None reported		91% (16:n = 49)
1st-year sales $250K + up/Unknown	1+ males or 1+ females	25–34, 45–75 years old	Total loans $1K and up		40% (17:n = 25)
1st-year sales $250K + up/Unknown	1+ males or 1+ females	25–34, 45–75 years old	Total loans $1K and up	Financing in 1st month, DK	86% (18:n = 33)
1st-year sales $250K + up/Unknown	Mixed gender start-up team			Financing after 1st month	98% (19:n = 49)
1st-year sales $250K + up/Unknown	Team gender unknown				67% (20:n = 30)

NOTES

The follow-up data collection effort for Minnesota and Pennsylvania was coordinated and supervised by Professor Mary Williams of Widener University and the University of Pennsylvania Snider Entrepreneurial Center. Resources were provided by the University of Minnesota Carlson Entrepreneurship Center and the University of Pennsylvania Snider Entrepreneurial Center. Substantial cooperation from the Dun and Bradstreet Corporation is appreciated.

1. The four to five and six to seven first sale-first interview groups were combined after SPSS PC 5.1 SURVIVAL analysis indicated no statistically significant difference in the probability of persistence.

2. Analysis using all firms on which persistence was known and replacing missing values with the median value produced very similar results.

3. If data are missing for an independent variable, treatment of the case will vary depending on the impact of that variable on persistence for the remaining cases under consideration.

Chapter 7

Entrepreneurial Processes and Outcomes: The Influence of Gender

Written by Nancy Carter

Women-owned businesses represent one of the fastest growing segments of the U.S. economy. A report of the U.S. House of Representatives (1988) Small Business Committee demonstrates that between 1970 and 1988 the number of women-owned businesses grew over sixfold from less than 5% of all U.S. businesses in 1970 to over 30% by 1988. Between 1987 and 1992 their numbers increased by 1.8 million or another 42%, and their receipts by $365 million, or 131% (Phillips, 1995).

Despite this growth rate, many argue that significant barriers still remain for women in establishing and growing businesses. These barriers may explain why businesses owned by women are smaller, with receipts substantially lower than those of men-owned businesses in comparable industries. Data from the Wisconsin surveys of nascent entrepreneurs and new firms can be used to contrast the experiences of women and men as they attempt to establish and grow new ventures. By isolating differences that might exist, distinctive challenges that women business owners face are revealed.

WOMEN'S INVOLVEMENT IN THE ENTREPRENEURIAL PROCESS

The Wisconsin survey[1] of typical adults identified two categories of entrepreneurs who were in the early stages of starting a new business (Reynolds and White, 1993a): (1) nascent entrepreneurs—those actively working to start the firm; and (2) discouraged entrepreneurs—those who had become discouraged with their start-up efforts and had given up. Within these two groups men outnumbered women almost two to one. Only 33% of the nascent entrepreneurs and just 39% of the discouraged entrepreneurs were identified as women. The gender disparity of women in the entrepreneurial process is particularly notable when considering that in 1990, 57% of all American women age sixteen and over were in the labor force (Reis and Stone, 1992). Thus, although more women than ever before are participating in the workforce, their numbers as business owners still lag considerably behind those of men.

Further examination of the gender distribution among the early-stage entrepreneurs in the sample reveals that the ratio of men to women participants is heavily influenced by the white majority in the sample. More than 62% of the entrepreneurs classified their ethnic status as white, and within this category, 63% are men, and 37% women. This ratio does not represent the prevalence pattern across other ethnic groups. Black and Asian women are about equally as likely to engage in entrepreneurial initiatives as black and Asian men. Hispanic women, conversely, appear to be less likely to engage in the entrepreneurial process. Only 19% of the Hispanic nascent entrepreneurs are women.

FACTORS THAT INFLUENCE THE CREATION OF NEW FIRMS

Conditions that have been viewed as stimulating the birth of new firms range from labor market conditions, industrial competition, literacy, and technological innovation, to personality characteristics of individuals. For entrepreneurs in the early stages of establishing their businesses, two sets of conditions seem especially critical: incubator influences, factors that encourage the "propensity to act," and facilitating factors, conditions that foster the gestation process once start-up has been initiated.

Incubator Influences

Incubator influences are factors that stimulate the "triggering" event or the propensity to select self-employment as a viable work alternative. Four influences that are thought to be particularly instrumental are (1) perceptions regarding favorableness of the environmental context, (2) life-stage position of potential entrepreneurs, (3) employment status, and (4) work values. The following discussion, and Table 7.1, examine whether the effect of these incubator influences varies by gender of the entrepreneur.

Entrepreneurial Climate. The extent to which potential entrepreneurs view the environmental context surrounding them as supportive of entrepreneurial efforts may influence whether they initiate start-up efforts. During the interview the respondents were asked a number of questions about how favorable they thought the local environmental context was for starting a new business. From these data a "climate" assessment was constructed, as discussed in Chapter 2. Overall, women were only slightly more positive in their judgments than men, and this was due to a more

Table 7.1
Selected Characteristics of Men and Women Entrepreneurs

	Men		Women	
	Nascent	*Discouraged*	*Nascent*	*Discouraged*
No. of cases	58	28	34	20
Participating entrepreneurs	67%	61%	33%	39%
Age (average years)	38	42	40	34
Marital status (married)	64%	72%	71%	74%
Children at home	1.3	1.4	1.2	1.3
Work status				
Full-time	57%	67%	48%	65%
Part-time	5	4	13	15
Self-employed	23	11	23	5
Entrepreneurial climate evaluation (1)	2.5	2.3 (*)	2.5	2.5
Work values				
Autonomy	3.4	3.4	3.5	3.4
Task interest	3.6	3.3 (**)	3.5	3.4
Wealth	3.2	2.7 (**)	2.8	3.0
Community-centered	3.0	3.0	3.0	3.0
Education				
High school degree or less	63%	16%	62%	31%
Some college	26	44	22	47
College degree	11	28	—	21
Graduate education	—	12	16	—
Household income (mean)	$41,688	$46,286	$34,885	$30,000
Industry (2)				
Upstream	35%		10%	
Downstream	65		90	
Expected start-up financing (3)				
Under $10,00	30%		68%	
Under $50,000	63		80	
Start-up financial sources				
Entrepreneur's money	33%		57%	
Informal money	12		8	
Formal money	47		26	
Team money	8		9	
Expected sales (3)				
First year (median)	35,000		20,000	
Fifth year (median)	100,000		40,000	
Business status at 2nd interview				
Continuing in gestation	31%		33%	
Hiatus	—		11	
Discourgaged	7		28	
Fledgling new firm	63		28	

Notes: (1) Statistical significance: * = 0.05; ** = 0.01.

(2) Upstream includes agricultural, mining, construction, manufacturing, distributive services. Downstream includes retail; restaurants; consumer services; business services; health, education, and social services.

(3) Downstream industries only.

negative assessment by men who were discouraged entrepreneurs. On three aspects of the environment, however, there were some notable differences: perceptions regarding government assistance, perceived level of social support, and favorableness of financial support.

Women nascent entrepreneurs were more negative in their assessment of government assistance than their male counterparts and saw assistance programs as more supportive of men than of women. A comparison of mean differences reveals that women nascent entrepreneurs viewed the support provided men by state and local government as significantly more positive than men viewed that support (mean value = 2.76 vs. 2.38). These women also felt more strongly that people would start new businesses if it were not so complicated to get help and approval from the government (mean value = 3.33 vs. 2.98).

Women entrepreneurs who had become discouraged and had given up efforts to start a business indicated feeling the least social support for their business initiatives. Discouraged women were significantly more likely to think that if a person's business fails, that person would never be respected again (mean = 2.40 vs. discouraged men entrepreneurs, 1.96; or nascent women entrepreneurs, 1.93). Similarly, these women were less likely than the other entrepreneurs to think they would repeat entrepreneurial initiatives once having tried and discontinued the process. These judgments may be an outcome of their negative perceptions regarding financial support. Discouraged women were least likely to think that bankers and investors want to help new businesses get started.

Overall, the entrepreneurs were positive in their perception that the environmental context supports entrepreneurship. There are, however, some important differences of opinion between women and men, and among these, women who had become discouraged and had given up their entrepreneurial efforts were most negative. These women associated the greatest stigma to failure, were most dissatisfied that financial institutions would help them start their businesses, and indicated they were least likely to try another entrepreneurial initiative.

Life Stage. The second set of incubator factors considered reflects the life stage of entrepreneurs when making the decision to initiate start-up activities. Life stage includes the entrepreneur's age when committing to establish the new business, marital status of the entrepreneur, and the number of children living at home. Of interest is whether the life stage of women establishing entrepreneurial ventures differs from that of men.

There is little difference in the ages of men and women nascent entrepreneurs. Both groups tend to be about thirty-nine years old. Discouraged women entrepreneurs, however, are significantly younger (mean age of 34 years) than discouraged men (mean age of 42 years), and they tend to be about five years younger than the nascent entrepreneurs. There is no significant difference in the marital status of the entrepreneurs. Approximately 70% of both nascent and discouraged entrepreneurs are married.

Similarly, there is no significant difference in the number of children living at home. Whereas previous research has suggested that life-cycle stage affects the growth of established new ventures, the Wisconsin survey reveals few differences in the life stage of women and men as they embark on initiating new businesses.

Employment Status. Discussions regarding whether people are pushed into starting new businesses because of unemployment or pulled by opportunities in the environment raise the question of whether the stimulus differs for men and women. The data reveal little support for the supposition that unemployment leads to creating new firms. Approximately 60% of the entrepreneurs indicated they were currently working full-time for someone else. Only about 5% of the entrepreneurs reported they were looking for work prior to attempting to start the current business. There are, however, significant gender differences among the work patterns of the entrepreneurs, with women nascent entrepreneurs least likely to be working full-time (48%). They are more likely than men to be working part-time (13% vs. 5%), and they are more likely than discouraged women entrepreneurs to be self-employed (23% vs. 5%). Women's higher rate of part-time employment may indicate that these women are underemployed relative to men and, having fewer work alternatives, may turn to self-employment.

The most striking difference in employment status existed not between gender categories but between the nascent and discouraged groups. Discouraged entrepreneurs are more likely than nascent entrepreneurs to be working full-time. More than 65% of the discouraged entrepreneurs reported working full-time, which may indicate that the security of a "day job" made it easier for them to abandon start-up initiatives.

Work Values. Previous studies have suggested that the reasons for selecting self-employment or entrepreneurship as a career alternative may differ by gender. Men have been seen as establishing new businesses out of a desire to be entrepreneurs, or to not work for someone else. Women, on the other hand, have been viewed as wanting to create new ventures where they can balance work and family (Brush, 1992). Respondents to the survey were asked a series of questions about their work interests or values. A factor analysis of these items revealed four distinct dimensions: autonomy or independence, task interest, wealth or income, and a desire to stay in the community. A comparison of the work values by gender provides mixed support for previous research findings. As expected, the nascent men entrepreneurs placed a higher value on wealth and prestige than did nascent women entrepreneurs. There is no statistically significant difference by gender among the discouraged entrepreneurs. Both men and women seemed to place their highest value on autonomy and independence or pursuing challenging, interesting work. Women placed, relative to wealth, a higher value on staying in their community.

Overall, the findings support previous contentions that women seek to create new ventures that integrate their desire to own a business with family, societal, and personal relationships. Women in this sample indicated they want to provide wealth or build an estate for their families, but they want to do this while remaining in the area where they presently reside. Presumably, the relationships they have established in the local environment are as important to them as wealth creation.

Facilitating Factors

Once potential entrepreneurs have made the decision to initiate the start-up process, they enter what many have referred to as the gestation stage of the firm's life cycle. Studies on how preorganizations or organizations-in-creation become fledgling new businesses have sought to identify factors that facilitate the transition as well as systematic barriers or obstacles that may hinder the emergence of new ventures. Some have speculated that certain subpopulations of emerging ventures may be especially vulnerable during this early developmental stage. Women may represent one such group. Research on established, women-owned businesses suggests three reasons nascent women entrepreneurs may experience early difficulties. Women have been found to have (1) fewer human capital resources to bring to the firm creation (Bates, 1985); (2) fewer financial resources (Cromie and Birley, 1991); and (3) different intentions for their businesses (Brush, 1992). Additionally, (4) women may not utilize assistance programs offered entrepreneurs by government or private sources as readily as do men.

Human Capital Resources. Human capital derives from investments individuals make in themselves, often through education and training. Women have been viewed as having lower levels of human capital as a result of cultural stereotyping. Data from the survey reveal few gender differences among the nascent entrepreneurs in their level of human capital, as measured by educational attainment. Women nascent entrepreneurs tend to have somewhat higher educational attainment than men, but the difference is not significant. Approximately 38% of nascent women entrepreneurs have some post-high school education in comparison to 37% of their male counterparts, but more than 16% of nascent women entrepreneurs have some graduate educational experience.

The most striking difference in educational attainment is between the nascent and discouraged entrepreneurs. Both discouraged men and discouraged women have substantially higher levels of education than the nascent entrepreneurs. More than 70% of the discouraged men entrepreneurs reported having post-high school education, and 12% postcollege. More than 68% of discouraged women entrepreneurs report education at the technical college level or above. This difference may suggest that discouraged entrepreneurs may have more flexibility to discontinue activities related to creation of their new ventures since their education makes alternative career options viable. More of the discouraged entrepreneurs are, after all, working full-time.

Financial Resources. Both systemic barriers and overt discrimination have been viewed as restricting women's access to resources for starting new businesses. Access to financial resources has been regarded as one of the most important factors denied women. When considering financial resources, two issues are salient: how much money will be sought and where the money will be acquired.

The survey asked specific questions regarding the entrepreneurs' expectations about the amount of money they would need to establish their ventures and how they intended to fund the initiative.[2] More than 65% of the women reported they intended to start their businesses with less than $10,000, and 80% of them said they would start with less than $50,000. One reason these amounts may be so low is that 90% of the women indicated they were attempting to establish firms in "downstream" industries, where fewer financial resources are required get a business up and running (e.g., retail, restaurants, consumer services, business services). But even when considering only these industries, men report seeking higher levels of resources. Only 30% of the men entrepreneurs in "downstream" industries reported expecting to start with less than $10,000, and 63% with less than $50,000. The median amount women in these industries expect to apply toward start-up was $2,000, in comparison to men's expecting to start with $29,000.

One reason men may report intending to start with more financial resources is that they have larger personal resource bases upon which to draw. Savings and household income are two indicators of personal financial wherewithal. Data from the study revealed that 65% of the men expect to support their households during the start-up of their business by using personal savings. Only 43% of women indicated they would use savings. This difference is consistent with differences in household income reported by the two groups. Approximately 45% of the men respondents reported income of less than $40,000; more than 60% of the women fell below that level. A comparison of the average household income across all four groups of entrepreneurs further supports this gender difference. The highest amount was reported by discouraged men ($46,286) and the lowest by discouraged women ($30,000).

In addition to scale differences, the men and women anticipated having different sources of financing. Four sources of funding were examined: (1) loans and equity the entrepreneurs intended to contribute from personal sources; (2) equity and loans secured from family and friends; (3) equity and loans from banks and private investors; and (4) money other start-up team members would contribute. The data reveal that men anticipated having considerably greater access to formal sources of money (banks and private investors). Men expect that almost half (47%) of their financing will come from outside formal sources in comparison to women's expecting this type of funding to represent only about a quarter (26%) of their total resource base. In contrast, women report that personal financial sources will make up more than half of the total financial base they will have available at start-up. Men expect only one-third of their total will come from personal equity and loans to the business. Neither women nor men anticipated relying much on family and friends or other start-up team members as sources of financing. Only about 10% will be contributed by each of these sources.

When asked about their overall satisfaction with access to financial resources, discouraged entrepreneurs expressed the most dissatisfaction. Over 55% of discouraged women and over 40% of discouraged men indicated they were not satisfied with their access to bank loans. Similarly, of the four categories, discouraged women were least likely to be satisfied with capital availability.

In general, men anticipate having substantially more money at the start-up stage than do women, men are more likely to rely on formal sources of financing, and men have more personal resources in the form of savings and household income. These findings are consistent with previous studies of established businesses. However, the finding that women do not see family and friends as viable sources of financial support differs from findings of previous studies (Hisrich and Brush, 1987). The anomaly may have to do with differences in the lifestage being studied. Previous research has focused on established businesses. It may be that women who succeed in getting their businesses up and running can do so only with the assistance of family and friends. At the nascent stage of development, however, it may be that women do not yet view these as viable sources. It may be that only when all other financing options are exhausted, do they turn to family and friends.

Intentions/Aspirations. In addition to human capital and financial resources shaping differences in the business initiatives of women and men, personal aspirations and intentions are thought to play a key role. It has been found that the men nascent entrepreneurs placed a high value on wealth and prestige.

Data are also available on the entrepreneurs' expectations for both the size and growth plans of their new businesses. Specifically, the respondents were asked, "If the business is launched, what sales would you expect at the end of the first year? At the end of the fifth year?" Comparison of the median expected sales reveals only slight differences in what the entrepreneurs anticipate achieving by the end of the first year. Men reported they expected to have approximately $35,000 in sales, in comparison to women's expectation of $20,000. But by the end of the fifth year of operation, men expected average sales to reach $100,000, in comparison to women's expectation of $40,000. In other words, men anticipate almost tripling the initial year's sales by the fifth year of operation. Clearly, the vision men and women have about the future size of their businesses differs. As vision represents intentions, the size differential in women- and men-owned businesses seems to be "set at the start," as argued by

Birley (1986). Women appear to anticipate having smaller businesses over time than men.

Assistance Programs. The extent to which entrepreneurs successfully take their businesses through the gestation process may relate to the types of assistance they seek and receive along the way. The survey asked the respondents about twenty-eight different categories of services provided by government agencies or private sources. In addition to questions about general awareness of the programs, the entrepreneurs were asked whether they actually sought and obtained help. Of interest in this chapter are differences between the experiences of women and men.

Of the four categories of entrepreneurs considered, discouraged women were almost three times less likely to have sought and obtained help than the other groups. The areas in which this difference were most striking were in their use of continuing education courses and making use of programs designed to provide a network of contacts. Only 2% of discouraged women got help from continuing education programs. In contrast, 20% of discouraged men sought and obtained help from these courses, and over 35% of nascent entrepreneurs (both women and men) took advantage of this resource. Only 18% of discouraged women obtained assistance from networking programs, in comparison to 39% of nascent women.

Nascent women entrepreneurs were substantially more likely than the other three groups to obtain general business management assistance (31%, in comparison to approximately 10% for the other groups), accounting assistance (31% vs. approximately 25%), and information systems assistance (16% vs. approximately 9%) and to seek information on laws and regulations (50% vs. approximately 35%).

Among the types of assistance sought by all the entrepreneurs (both women and men), the two most frequently taken advantage of were accounting assistance and information sources on laws and regulations.

One of the most curious findings was women's low reliance on programs especially designed for them. None of the discouraged women entrepreneurs reported getting help from women's business assistance programs, and only 7% of the nascent women used such assistance. Further analysis of the data suggests this was not due to a lack of awareness. For each of the types of assistance programs, respondents were asked to indicate whether they "couldn't find help" or "didn't know about help." Both groups of women seem to be informed about the availability of women's assistance programs. Only 7% of each group indicated they didn't know about such programs, and none indicated that they couldn't find the help when they sought it. Thus, to increase the utilization rate of these assistance programs, those responsible for the programs may need to illustrate and communicate more effectively how and why the services will benefit women.

In general, there appear to be differences in the pattern of program utilization by women and men and by whether entrepreneurs became discouraged and gave up. Nascent women entrepreneurs were most successful in getting the help they sought. Discouraged women entrepreneurs sought and got the least help.

Preceding sections have illustrated how factors that stimulate the propensity to select self-employment and how the process of creating the firm differ by gender of the founding entrepreneur. The findings reveal that women are less likely than men to engage in entrepreneurial initiatives. But for those who do, women appear to have somewhat more positive judgments about the entrepreneurial climate, they were more likely to have worked part-time or to have been underemployed prior to embarking on creating the new business, and they appear to be creating businesses that integrate their desire to create wealth for their families with their preference to remain in their local community.

Factors that facilitate or influence the process of creating businesses also appear to differentially influence the experiences of women and men. Women reported expecting both the scale and sources of financing to differ from those of their male counterparts. They indicated that they will need fewer financial resources to start their business and that they will rely more heavily on personal financial resources rather than loans from banks or other outside formal sources.

Outcomes of Incubator and Facilitating Influences

The implicit assumption made in examining the influences of incubator and facilitating factors is that the founding of new firms is a process of activity rather than an identifiable event. This time period of activity from when entrepreneurs first take action to start the new venture and when the firm becomes a viable economic entity has been termed the gestation period. From the findings discussed earlier in this chapter women were found to be less likely than men to engage in entrepreneurial initiatives. But for the women who do, does the rate of their success in making the transition from the nascent stage to fledgling new firm status differ from that of men? Data collected during a follow-up with the nascent entrepreneurs provide insight on this question. Erosion in the sample between the two data collection periods requires caution in interpreting the findings, but, though tentative, the findings are instructive.

Of the nascent entrepreneurs interviewed during a second data collection, only 28% of the women reported that their business was up and running. Of the men, 63% reported the status of their firm as a new fledgling business. Just over 30% of the entrepreneurs indicated they were still continuing efforts to establish the business. Women were much more likely than men to have put their efforts on hold for the time being (a hiatus) or to have become discouraged and given up the process. Thus, it appears that not only do fewer women select self-employment as a career objective, but those who do have more difficulty in getting the firm through the gestation process than their male counterparts. Future research will be needed to verify the extent to which these findings are a reflection of the regional context. Data from the midwestern state represented in this sample will need to be compared with those of other geographic regions.

CHARACTERISTICS OF NEW FIRMS: DOES GENDER MATTER?

The survey of Wisconsin new firms provides a sample of entrepreneurs who have successfully made the transition from the gestation stage of the organization's life cycle to that of fledgling new firm, or adolescence. Data on firms in this stage of development can be used to examine the influence of gender on the structure and strategy that businesses adopt as they attempt to establish a market presence.

Because new firms are often started by a team rather than an individual, the conceptualization of gender for comparisons at this developmental stage must be broadened to accommodate mixed-gender groups. The start-up teams of the new firms responding to the survey were classified into one of five categories: (1) sole proprietorship started by a woman; (2) sole proprietorship started by a man; (3) an "all- women firm" (team comprising women only); (4) an "all-men firm" (team comprising men only); and (5) a "mixed-gender firm" (both women and men on the team, the majority of these are husband-and-wife teams).

The data reveal that almost three times as many of the businesses were started as sole proprietorships by men as women. Only 13% of the businesses qualify as "one woman" firms, in comparison to 35% "one man" businesses. The gender difference is even greater in businesses started by teams. Just 4% of the businesses were started by women-dominated teams; 21% were started by teams of men. Approximately one- fourth of the firms were started by teams of men and women.

Initial Capital Resources

A major advantage of starting the business with a team, rather than alone, is that partnering would presumably yield a larger resource base to help the business weather the difficult start-up period, when they may be most vulnerable. The previous analysis of nascent entrepreneurs revealed that women both lowered expectations for the size and growth of their ventures and anticipated having access to fewer financial resources. The question is whether women can compensate for deficiencies in their resource base by teaming up with others. Most of women-owned businesses are in downstream industries close to the final consumer. Comparing business in only retail, restaurants, and services reveals that the disparity in financial resources found during the nascent stage also exists among the established new businesses.

Businesses that had the lowest level of financial resources at start-up were those of sole proprietorships started by women ($15,000 median total equity and debt). The second lowest level was for businesses that had a women-dominated team (median = $23,000). In comparison, 50% of the sole proprietorships started by men report beginning with approximately $36,000, and businesses begun by men-dominated start-up teams had the highest level of financial resources (median = $65,000). Even mixed-gender teams had greater financial resources (median = $52,000) than those started by only women. The discrepancy is most obvious in access to debt financing. Whereas 50% of the businesses started by men-dominated teams reported having $40,000 in debt financing, the median amount reported by firms with women-dominated teams was less than $1,000. Women were substantially more likely to rely on equity than debt financing. Thus, even within industries where women have traditionally begun businesses, the amount and sources of financing new businesses vary greatly for women and men.

Founding Strategies

One way that women may be able to compensate for deficiencies in financial resources is through the strategy they adopt for the business. The initial or founding strategy imprints future operations of the business and reflects distinctive choices made by the entrepreneur. Women, constrained by limited financial resources, may be more likely to choose narrow specialization strategies that take advantage of their desire to integrate family and work. Such strategies would rely on targeting a narrow segment of the market (and local community) and emphasizing quality, service, and responsiveness to the varying needs of diverse customers.

Respondents to the new firm survey were asked to indicate the important aspects of their competitive strategy by rating twenty different actions they might take on a four-point scale ranging from critical (4) to insignificant (1). Using only the responses from firms "downstream" where women's businesses are more prevalent, a strategic profile was created for each business. The profile was compiled by performing a factor analysis of the twenty competitive action items and then creating reliable scales for each of five factors.[3] The five factors, or basic facets of new firm competitive strategy, are (1) price, (2) emphasis on developing and using new technology, (3) responsiveness to customers in the marketplace, (4) aspects of the location and facilities, and (5) emphasizing quality and service. Virtually 80% of the new firms indicated that focusing on quality and service was important or critical to their competitive strategy. Because this dimension did not discriminate among the various groups of entrepreneurs, this factor was eliminated in creating the strategic profiles.

The findings reveal that firms with different gender composition on the start-up team have different strategic profiles. Table 7.2 displays the extent

Table 7.2
Start-up Team Gender Profiles and Competitive Strategy

Start-up Team Gender Profile	Relative Emphasis			
	Price	New Technology	Customer Response	Site/Facility Convenience
One woman	-.05	0.06	0.56	0.40
One man	0.29	0.03	0.16	0.22
Mixed-gender team	-.14	0.11	-.06	-.05
All-women team	0.42	0.15	0.13	0.27
All-men team	-.19	-.12	-.12	-.21

to which each of the start-up team types varies in emphasizing the strategy dimensions. The values displayed are the differences between the mean z-score for each start-up team type and the average for all new firms.

Only businesses started as sole proprietorships by women appear to conform to the expectation that women's founding strategy will choose narrow specializations' strategies and differentially emphasize service and responsiveness to varying customer needs. Relative to the other profiles, the competitive strategy of businesses owned by one woman is most likely to emphasize customer responsiveness and convenience of location. In contrast, businesses started by all-women teams or sole proprietorships started by men were most apt to emphasize multiple-strategy foci simultaneously, the hallmark of broad-based, general strategies. Within this broad strategy mix, the emphasis on pricing appears to supersede the stress placed on customer responsiveness.

Relative to the other profiles, businesses started by men-dominated teams emphasize none of the strategy dimensions. Recall that these businesses had the greatest level of financial resources at start-up. This finding may indicate that whereas women might attempt to overcome their limited access to financial resources through strategic positioning, men may rely more on their financial resource base for early success.

OVERVIEW AND IMPLICATIONS

The orientations and experiences of women and men, as they attempt to establish and grow new ventures, appear to differ. Both women and men nascent entrepreneurs in the sample tended to be white, married or living with a partner, and about thirty-nine years of age and have approximately one child living at home. Two sets of factors thought to explain why the experiences of women starting new businesses may differ from those of men were explored. Incubator influences were examined to see if they differentially stimulate the "triggering" event for self-employment. Facilitating factors thought to differentially affect the start-up process once the initial entrepreneurial decision was made were also studied. Among the differences isolated in the analyses are the following:

- The ratio of participation in the entrepreneurial process varies by gender and ethnic status. Men are almost twice as likely to be working to establish new businesses as women.
- Women entrepreneurs tend to have more positive judgments about the entrepreneurial climate than men but thought even more people would start new businesses if it were not so complicated to get help from the government.
- Few life-stage differences exist between men and women entrepreneurs in the early stages of creating their new business.
- Women entrepreneurs are more likely to have been working part-time just prior to initiating start-up activities. Their work status may indicate that they are underemployed relative to men, and self-employment may represent the most attractive alternative to part-time employment.
- Like men, women seek to create businesses that provide wealth for their families. Unlike men, however, women value remaining in their local community as just as important as wealth and prestige.
- Ninety percent of women nascent entrepreneurs intend to establish their new firms "downstream," where they will sell customers finished goods or services; only 65% of men intend to establish businesses in these industries.
- Women entrepreneurs tend to come from households where the level of income is as much as 20% less than household income of men.
- Men entrepreneurs expect to have considerably more financial resources at start-up than women, especially from outside loans.
- Men tend to have much higher expectations for the growth of their businesses than women do. Men expect to triple sales between the first and fifth year of operations.
- Despite the availability, women entrepreneurs do not seek or get help from women's assistance programs.
- Women are less likely to put together start-up teams of the same gender than men. Sole proprietorship and mixed-gender teams are favored as start-up team composition.
- The strategic profiles of women-dominated firms and men-dominated firms vary markedly.

In summary, the comparisons between women and men engaging in entrepreneurial activities suggest that they share many of the problems encountered in establishing new ventures. There are, however, some areas where experiences differ. In particular, financing may be a more significant issue for women. Women appear to have fewer financial resources available at start-up. They tend to come from households with lower income levels, and they register intentions to start the firm with considerably less financial support, particularly debt. These findings may suggest that women are not as aware of the magnitude of resources required to establish a business and/or that they have less access to financial resources.

Data from the follow-up interview reveal that the chances of women's and men's making the transition from nascent entrepreneur to new firm owner vary substantially. Only 28% of the women nascent entrepreneurs succeeded in getting their firms through gestation to fledgling new firm by the time of the second interview. Thus, not only is women's rate of participation in the entrepreneurial process as nascent entrepreneurs less than that of men, but women appear to have a greater attrition rate during the process.

The small sample size, particularly the fewer number of women who made the transition to ownership, demands caution in generalizing the findings. Further studies with larger samples in different regions are needed to verify and elaborate the results. For example, barriers previously thought to inhibit women's chances of making the transition—like more children living at home or lower levels of human capital—received marginal support here. It may be that these factors are more discriminating among established new firms than at early stages of the gestation process. In other words, these factors may have greater influence on whether women successfully get through the gestation process than on whether women choose to initiate entrepreneurial efforts in the first place.

The formulation of useful public policy to assist the efforts of nascent women entrepreneurs will require careful exploration of these issues. More attention needs to be given to whether the entrepreneurial process has the same significance for men or women, as women may see it as a route to self-employment and men an opportunity to create growth organizations.

NOTES

Prepared by Nancy M. Carter, Endowed Chair in Entrepreneurship, Graduate School of Business, St. Thomas University (St. Paul, MN).

1. All data analysis in this chapter is based on data assembled from the Wisconsin Entrepreneurial Climate Study (Reynolds and White, 1993b).

2. Since 90% of the women respondents indicated they were attempting to establish firms "downstream" in the economic sector supply chain, we limit gender comparison to entrepreneurs in this category. Downstream industries include businesses in financial, retail, restaurant, consumer services, and health, education, and business services.

3. Factor analysis of the strategy aspects yielded five factors that explained over 60% of the variance. The items within each factor were summed and divided by the number of items in the scale. The scales were converted to z-scores for standardization and to facilitate creating the strategic profiles. Chronbach's alpha, an internal measure of reliability, was computed for each of the five scales and is as follows: price (.63), technology (.91), market responsiveness (.66), site (.63), and quality (.77).

Chapter 8

Entrepreneurial Processes and Outcomes: The Influence of Ethnicity

Two different discussions link ethnic differences with entrepreneurship. One emphasizes a greater propensity to entrepreneur among some ethnic groups, particularly if they are recent immigrants. This is reflected in case analyses of specific ethnic subcultures and immigrant enclave economies (Aldrich and Waldinger, 1990; Bonacich, 1973; Light and Bonacich, 1988; Portes, Castells, and Benton, 1989; Waldinger, Aldrich, and Ward, 1990). The interpretations emphasize the problems immigrants have establishing traditional careers in unfamiliar host cultures, suggesting that founding new firms reflects desperate efforts to establish a role in the economy. The most dramatic examples of this process occur in South America (de Soto, 1989). The second discussion emphasizes the under- or overparticipation of some groups in entrepreneurial or small-business activity (Fratoe, 1986), frequently leading to proposals for public policy that will "even the playing field" and facilitate minority participation in self-employment or new firm start-ups equivalent to that of the majority.

The population survey completed in Wisconsin was designed to develop representative samples of the four major ethnic groups (American Indians, Asians, blacks, and Hispanics), even though 91% of the Wisconsin population is white. It can be used to address the second question, Is there a difference among ethnic groups in participation in the entrepreneurial process? If ethnic groups are underrepresented, what government policies might enhance their involvement? Wisconsin has not been, since the German and Scandinavian immigrants arrived in the last century, the primary destination for a significant number of new arrivals to the United States. No analysis is possible, therefore, with regard to "immigrant entrepreneurship" among ethnic groups in Wisconsin.

Members of all ethnic groups, including the majority, must complete the same entrepreneurial processes to implement a new firm. Comparisons related to ethnic background, therefore, will follow the different stages of the process: the nature of those who become involved in the start-up process, the differences of perspectives and behaviors associated with the start-up itself, and the differences associated with new firms. Because a special effort was made to develop representative samples of ethnic groups (see the chapter Appendix for details), the analysis of the early stages can focus on comparisons among different ethnic groups with substantial samples (in excess of 100) for each. Analysis of those actively involved in start-ups or as new firm owners are somewhat smaller, and the inferences are more speculative.

SOCIODEMOGRAPHIC COMPARISONS OF ETHNIC GROUPS

A portrayal of the Wisconsin population as well as each of the five ethnic groups is presented in Table 8.1. Survey data are based on the adult chosen at random from households chosen at random. White respondents tend to have higher household incomes and the largest proportion working full- or part-time.

Each of the four other ethnic groups has a distinctive set of characteristics, although the significance of some differences is difficult to ascertain. American Indian respondents are more frequently women, older, and more likely to be retired, have longer tenures in the state, and larger social networks; half live outside metropolitan or regional centers. Asians tend to be younger, have shorter residential tenures and smaller social networks, more likely to have children in the household, and have the highest levels of educational attainment. Survey data on Asian educational attainment were compared with 1990 U.S. Census data, and the survey findings were confirmed: a very high proportion of Wisconsin Asians have completed graduate programs. This would suggest that many live around university campuses, accounting for their dispersion across the state. Blacks are very similar to whites in many ways, except that four in five live in Milwaukee, the major urban area of Wisconsin. Hispanics tend to be younger, married, have children in the household, have not completed high school, and live in metropolitan areas or regional centers.

There is some variation in the nature of the social networks reported by the respondents. The largest networks are reported by those with longer tenure in the state, particularly American Indians, followed by whites. The smallest are reported by Asians; black and Hispanic networks are intermediate. Those with larger networks report more persons who are likely to be a good source of help, as well as more persons who are likely "not" to be such a good source of help. The number of persons in these social networks with some entrepreneurial experience varies considerably, with the highest level reported by whites and the lowest by Asians; American Indians, blacks, and Hispanics are intermediate in this regard.

There is little question that the differences among the ethnic groups are just as striking as their differences from the white majority.

INVOLVEMENT IN THE ENTREPRENEURIAL PROCESS

The tendency of individuals in each ethnic group to participate in the entrepreneurial process is presented in Table 8.2. There are no statistically significant differences among the five ethnic groups on any of these five aspects of entrepreneurial activity. This may, however, be due to the small samples, for some substantive differences are substantial. For example, American Indian and Hispanic respondents are less likely to report participation in new firm start-ups as nascent entrepreneurs. Asian and Hispanic respondents are less likely to report they are new firm owners.

Despite the small sample, the unique nature of these data justifies exploration of factors that may account for the substantive differences among the ethnic groups.

Inhibiting Factors. Much has been written about factors facilitating participation in the entrepreneurial process. Less attention has been given to inhibiting factors, those features that—if absent—may eliminate a person from active participation in starting a new firm. Three such factors related to Wisconsin are presented in Chapter 3 and illustrated in Table 3.3. Apparently, Wisconsin adults with less than a high school education, living in a household with an annual income below $10,000, and having lived in their county for less than five years are very unlikely to implement a new firm when compared to those who have completed high school (or gone beyond high school), live in a household with an annual income above $10,000 per year, or have lived in their county for more than five years. In these surveys, the social network was defined as the total number of work colleagues, adult siblings, adult children, parents, or spouse/partners (average = 12.00; median = 11.00; range 2–69). Other analyses (Denison, Swaminathan, and Rothbard, 1994) of the Wisconsin survey data have indicated that a small network of friends and family is also a major constraint, consistent with other research on the impact of social networks (Aldrich and Zimmer, 1986).

To explore the impact of these four factors on the propensity to pursue a new firm start-up, they were dichotomized to create a "minimal threshold." For three of the factors, as shown in Table 8.3, no one below the threshold reports efforts to start new firms, and for the fourth (years of residence in the county), those below the threshold are less than half as likely to initiate a new firm as those above the threshold. The far right column indicates the effect of having one or more impediments upon initiating a new firm. While it would seem reasonable to expect the same individuals to reflect several inhibitors, the joint occurrence is actually low. That is, there is little intercorrelation regarding the presence of these inhibi-

Table 8.1
Comparisons of Wisconsin Ethnic Groups

	Wisconsin Population (2)	White (3)	American Indian (3)	Asian (3)	Black (3)	Hispanic (3)	(4)
Number of respondents (1)	689	226	108	127	107	121	
Percent males	53.3	44.5	34.8	54.2	43.3	46.0	(NS)
Average age (years)	41.6	41.7	46.4	34.0	42.3	33.4	(****)
Average years lived in Wisconsin	32.4	33.1	42.9	7.6	28.4	17.4	(****)
Average years lived in county	24.4	24.5	30.6	6.6	27.6	15.0	(****)
Average household income ($1,000)	42.7	43.9	25.9	28.1	30.1	26.0	(***)
Household income: % less than $10,000	9.8	8.3	27.0	22.7	29.4	21.9	
Household income: % $10,000–$50,000	62.4	62.4	67.4	66.2	56.2	69.8	
Household income: % greater than $50,000	27.8	29.4	5.6	11.1	14.5	8.4	(****)
Not finished high school: %	8.5	7.3	16.7	13.6	19.9	27.0	
High school degree: %	36.2	37.2	25.7	16.0	23.1	32.4	
More than high school, not college degree: %	25.4	24.5	48.6	21.1	40.4	27.2	
College degree or more: %	29.9	31.0	9.1	49.4	16.7	13.5	(****)
Working full-time: %	57.2	57.9	50.1	38.3	50.9	50.8	
Working part-time: %	9.9	9.9	2.9	11.1	7.7	19.4	
Self-employed: %	5.2	5.3	3.8	5.1	5.8	8.7	
Unemployed: %	4.2	4.0	3.8	5.1	5.8	8.7	
Homemaker: %	5.6	5.5	3.1	10.8	5.9	6.3	
Retired: %	2.5	12.4	18.9	—	11.6	2.7	
In school: %	2.5	2.1	3.2	30.8	2.0	5.6	
Other: %	3.4	3.0	13.5	1.5	9.9	2.6	
Married/living with partner: %	65.2	66.6	43.2	68.5	42.0	65.3	(****)
Children younger than 19 at home: %	42.0	42.4	41.4	48.2	27.5	56.5	(***)

	Wisconsin Population (2)	White (3)	American Indian (3)	Asian (3)	Black (3)	Hispanic (3)	(4)
Size of social networks (average number of persons)							
Work colleagues	6.7	6.9	5.8	4.2	4.7	5.8	(**)
Family	5.2	5.2	8.0	2.6	4.3	4.8	(****)
Total social network	11.9	12.1	13.8	6.7	9.1	10.5	(****)
Average number of persons							
Very good help	2.4	2.5	2.4	1.2	2.1	2.3	(***)
Good help	3.5	3.6	4.1	2.3	2.8	4.1	(****)
Not a good help source	1.8	1.8	3.0	1.3	1.3	1.6	(****)
Net members with entre experience							
None	39%	38%	37%	66%	44%	43%	
1–2	33	33	42	23	36	35	
3 or more	28	29	21	11	20	22	(****)
Residential context (5)							
Metropolitan region	29%	26%	20%	35%	81%	55%	
Regional center	42	43	30	43	18	38	
Nonmetropolitan region	29	31	50	22	1	7	
Total	100%	100%	100%	100%	100%	100%	
Total number (1,000s)	4,892	4,462	39	54	245	93	
Percentage	100.0%	91.2%	0.8%	1.1%	5.0%	1.9%	

Notes: (1) Maximum number of cases, reduced for some comparisons due to missing data.
(2) Weighted to represent Wisconsin population, 92% white.
(3) Weighted to provide maximum precision for each ethnic group.
(4) Statistical significance refers only to comparisons for the five ethnic columns: NS = not significant; * = 0.05; ** = 0.01; *** = 0.001; **** = 0.0001.
(5) U.S. Census of the Population, 1990: Metropolitan region is the four-county greater Milwaukee Area; Regional Centers are the counties around Madison, Kenosha, and Racine and through the Fox River Valley; remaining counties classified as nonmetropolitan.

Table 8.2
Involvement in the Entrepreneurial Process: By Ethnic Group

	No.	Nascent Entre's	Discouraged Entre's	New Firm Owners (1)	Discontinued Firm Owner	Any Type
Wisconsin population (2)	689	4.2%	9.4%	2.9%	8.4%	17.2%
Ethnic background (3)						
White	226	4.3	9.5	3.1	8.6	17.5
American Indian	108	1.8	9.5	2.6	5.8	14.6
Asian	127	4.7	2.4	0.5	1.6	7.5
Black	107	5.0	8.2	2.0	9.0	14.8
Hispanic (Stat sign, 4)	121	2.7 (NS)	11.2 (NS)	0.0 (NS)	6.0 (NS)	16.3 (NS)

Notes: (1) First sales in previous ten years.
(2) Weighted to represent Wisconsin population, 92% white.
(3) Weighted to provide maximum precision for each ethnic group.
(4) Statistical significance: NS = not significant; * = 0.05; ** = 0.01; *** = 0.001; **** = 0.0001.

Source: From Reynolds and White, 1993, Table 5.1.

Table 8.3
Inhibiting Factors and Impact on Entrepreneurial Activity

	Years Lived inCounty 6 or More		Educational Attainment H. S. Degree		Household Income $10,000/yr		Social Network 6 or More		Inhibitors Present	
	No	Yes	No	Yes	No	Yes	No	Yes	1–4	None
No. 574	122	452	44	530	56	518	122	452	276	298
Wisconsin population (1)	21%	79%	8%	92%	10%	90%	21%	79%	48%	52%
Nascent entrepreneur	2%	5%	0%	5%	0%	5%	0%	5%**	1%	7%*** (2)
Any participation (3)	12	17	7	17	5	17*	13	17	12	19 *

Notes: (1) Only cases with data on all four variables included; weighted to represent total Wisconsin population, which is 91% white.
(2) Statistical significance: * = - 0.05; ** = - 0.01; *** = - 0.001; **** = - 0.0001.
(3) A person that reports current business ownership, past business ownership, current efforts to start a new firm, or recent but discontinued efforts to start a new firm.

tors, particularly between length of residence in the country and the size of the social network. This suggests it is appropriate to identify a person reflecting any inhibitor as "disadvantaged."

Among those with one to four inhibitors, shown in Table 8.3, only 1% are involved in a new firm start-up, compared to 7% among those with none of these four inhibitors. This is both statistically and substantively signifi-cant. The same pattern is present for any participation in the entrepreneurial process, although the significance of the patterns is less.

While about half of the Wisconsin respondents report at least one inhib-iting factor, a major question is related to differences among ethnic groups. This is presented in Table 8.4, which shows the percentages of the five major ethnic groups that are above and below each threshold and reporting at least one inhibiting factor.

The results vary by factor and ethnic group. For example, nine of ten black and American Indian respondents had lived in their county for six or more years, compared to eight in ten whites, seven in ten Hispanics, and five in ten Asians. In contrast, 93% of the whites had completed high school, closely followed by Asians (89%), blacks (84%) and American Indians (84%), with 73% of Hispanics completing high school. Whites were most likely (93%) to report an annual household income over $10,000. The other four groups were quite close together, with 71–78% reporting they were above this threshold. American Indians were most likely (94%) to have a social network greater than five, with similar results (80%) reported by whites, blacks, and Hispanics; Asians, however, were the lowest, as only 44% reported social networks of more than five.

The proportion of each group with one or more inhibiting factors is substantial, as shown in the right column of Table 8.4. The proportion

Table 8.4
Inhibiting Factors: By Ethnic Group

	Years Lived in County 6 or More		Educational Attainment H. S. Degree		Household Income $10,000/yr		Social Network 6 or More		Inhibitors Present	
	No	Yes	No	Yes	No	Yes	No	Yes	1–4	None
White (1)	22%	78%	7%	93%	8%	92%	21%	79%	36%	64%
American Indian	11	89	16	84	26	74	6	94	50	50
Asian	49	51	11	89	23	77	56	44	62	38
Black	7	93	16	84	29	71	20	80	43	57
Hispanic	31	69	27	73	22	78	21	79	77	23
(Stat sign, 2)		(NS)		(***)		(***)		(***)		(****)

Notes: (1) Weights adjusted to give maximum precision for each ethnic group.
(2) Statistical significance: * = - 0.05; ** = - 0.01; *** = - 0.001; **** = - 0.0001.

among whites is 36%, closely followed by blacks at 43%. The highest are Hispanics with 77%, with American Indians and Asians intermediate at 50% and 62%, respectively.

Impact of Inhibiting Factors. The effect of the presence of inhibitors on participation in the entrepreneurial process for the five ethnic groups is presented in Table 8.5. While few differences are statistically significant, the substantive differences are quite striking. The absence of inhibitors is associated with a somewhat greater participation in any aspect of the entrepreneurial process and dramatically higher levels of participation in new firm start-ups.

Most striking is the uniformity among the different groups for those who report an inhibiting factor, particularly with regard to assisting in a new firm start-up as a nascent entrepreneur. The lack of involvement is uniform among all ethnic groups. Except for the American Indians, the absence of inhibiting factors has a dramatic impact. Table 8.5 indicates that participation as a nascent entrepreneur increases by four to eight times among those without inhibiting factors. Blacks and Asians are higher than whites, and Hispanics are equivalent to whites. While American Indians are similar to all other groups in terms of the measure of any entrepreneurial participation, with higher measures among those not inhibited, the results are reversed for participation as nascent entrepreneurs. However, the level of American Indian activity as nascent entrepreneurs is so low, and the samples are so small, that these two categories, with and without inhibitors, should be considered equivalent.

There are distinctive results associated with two ethnic groups. First, the very high level among Asians is over twice that of typical Wisconsin adults, and, second, the very low level for American Indians is about one-third that of typical Wisconsin adults. The American Indian sample, however, has a higher proportion of older women than the other samples, and in general population samples, older women seldom report trying to start new firms. With larger samples the impact of other factors, such as age and gender could be considered in terms of these comparisons. It is also possible these differences are related to a "cultural factor" associated with American Indians and Asians. But with the heterogeneity within these two groups—in these samples American Indian respondents are from twelve different tribes, and Asian immigrants are from eighteen different countries—these other demographic factors deserve careful attention.

ENTREPRENEURS: NASCENT AND DISCOURAGED

A more precise comparison of those who had made recent efforts to start a new firm is made by examining information from ninety-two nascent and forty-eight discouraged entrepreneurs, those who had recently given up trying to start a new firm. This includes data from eighty-two white and from eleven to eighteen representatives of various ethnic groups. The

Table 8.5
Inhibitors and Participation in the Entrepreneurial Process: By Ethnic Group

	WI Pop. (1)	White (2)	Am-Ind (2)	Asian (2)	Black (2)	Hispanic (2)	Stat Sign (3)
No inhibitors	52%	64%	57%	23%	50%	38%	(****)
1–4 inhibitors	48	36	43	77	50	62	
Any entre participation (4)							
Total sample	16%	16%	9%	7%	14%	14%	(NS)
No inhibitors	19	19	13	21	23	26	(NS)
1–4 inhibitors	12	13	6	3	5	8	(NS)
Ratio (none/any)	1.54	1.42	2.26	6.94	4.34	3.32	
(Stat sign) (5)	(*)	(NS)	(NS)	(**)	(*)	(**)	
Nascent entre							
Total sample	4%	4%	2%	6%	6%	3%	(NS)
No inhibitors	7	7	1	17	10	6	(NS)
1–4 inhibitors	1	1	2	2	3	2	(NS)
Ratio (none/any)	7.66	8.33	0.47	7.32	3.67	3.98	
(Stat sign) (5)	(***)	(*)	(NS)	(**)	(NS)	(NS)	

Notes: (1) Weighted to represent Wisconsin population, 91% white.

(2) Weighted to provide maximum precision for each ethnic group.

(3) Statistical significance for comparisons of ethnic groups only: * = - 0.05; ** = -0.01; *** = -0.001; **** = -0.0001.

(4) A person who reports current business ownership, past business ownership, current efforts to start a new firm, or recent but discontinued efforts to start a new firm.

(5) Comparison of no inhibitors with those with one to four inhibitors.

entrepreneurs in each ethnic group are compared to the general population of their ethnic peers on fifteen attributes in Table 8.6. As there is a marginally statistically significant difference between the nascent and discouraged entrepreneurs on only two of these fifteen attributes, they are combined for this analysis of ethnic differences.

In general, the same differences between the adult population and the entrepreneurs are found for all five ethnic groups. The entrepreneurs are usually men in their middle years (thirty to forty-nine years old) who have completed high school, are from households with more than $10,000 per year in income, have lived in Wisconsin and their county for more than five years, are more likely to be married, and have children under nineteen in the home. Their judgments about the entrepreneurial climate in Wisconsin are similar to those of their ethnic peers who have not tried to start new businesses. Entrepreneurs generally show more interest in all aspects of work, particularly autonomy, task interest, and wealth.

If there is a distinctive pattern among the nonwhite entrepreneurs, it is the tendency for a slightly greater percentage to have full-time jobs and, compared to white entrepreneurs, a smaller percentage to report self-em-

Table 8.6
Adult Population and Entrepreneurs by Selected Characteristics: By Ethnic Group

	White		American Indian		Asian		Black		Hispanic	
	Adult Pop.	N & D Entre	Adult Pop.	N & D Entre	Adult Pop.	N & D Entre	Adult Pop.	N & D Entre	Adult Pop.	N & D Entre
Number of cases (1)	695	82	145	12	138	11	166	17	149	18
Gender										
Men	44%	62%	44%	50%	55%	46%	40%	53%	48%	83%
Women	56	38	56	50	45	54	60	47	52	17
		(**) (2)		(NS)		(NS)		(NS)		(**)
Age										
18–29 years old	20%	17%	20%	—	47%	36%	29%	24%	42%	22%
30–49 years old	49	62	51	75%	39	64	37	53	49	78
50 and up	31	21	29	25	14	—	34	23	9	—
		(*)		(NS)		(NS)		(NS)		(*)
Educational attainment (3)										
Up to high school	8%	5%	20%	25%	14%	—	22%	12%	28%	—%
High school degree	41	43	30	42	16	27	33	12	34	22
Post-high school	25	29	36	25	22	18	32	47	24	50
College degree, grad.	26	23	15	8	48	55	14	9	14	28
		(NS)		(NS)		(NS)		(NS)		(***)
Household income										
Up to $10K per year	10%	7%	22%	—	23%	—	29%	—	20%	6%
$10–49K per year	63	65	73	100%	66	64	61	69	70	72
$50K and up per year	27	29	5	—	11	36	10	31	9	22
		(NS)		(NS)		(*)		(**)		(NS)
County tenure										
0–5 years	18%	17%	16%	17%	52%	30%	7%	—	28%	20%
6–30 years	45	49	52	42	48	60	54	75%	59	60
31 years and up	38	34	32	42	—	10	39	25	13	20
		(NS)		(NS)		(***)		(NS)		(NS)
State tenure										
0–5 years	6%	7%	3%	8%	48%	30%	8%	—	20%	7%
6–30 years	36	34	37	17	50	60	53	69%	65	73
31 years and up	58	59	59	75	2	10	39	31	14	20
		(NS)		(NS)		(NS)		(NS)		(NS)

		White		American Indian		Asian		Black		Hispanic	
		Adult Pop.	N & D Entre	Adult Pop.	N & D Entre	Adult Pop.	N & D Entre	Adult Pop.	N & D Entre	Adult Pop.	N & D Entre
Type of region	Urban	26%	22%	19%	8%	35%	64%	81%	77%	55%	61%
	Regional center	43	46	28	33	42	18	19	23	38	33
	Rural	31	32	53	58	22	18	—	—	7	6
			(NS)		(NS)		(NS)		(NS)		(NS)
Labor force activity (3)	Full-time job	52%	50%	60%	50%	38%	73%	48%	77%	49%	72%
	Part-time job	10	7	6	25	11	9	9	—	18	11
	Self-employed	9	27	6	8	3	—	5	—	5	6
	Unemployed	3	5	3	8	5	18	7	—	9	—
	Homemaker	7	1	6	—	10	—	7	6	9	—
	Retired	16	6	11	8	—	—	13	6	3	—
	Student	3	1	4	—	31	—	4	—	5	11
	Other	2	2	5	—	1	—	7	12	2	—
			(NS)		(NS)		(NS)		(NS)		(NS)
Marital status	Alone	35%	30%	45%	—	32%	20%	61%	47%	36%	31%
	Spouse/partner	65	70	55	100%	68	80	39	53	64	69
			(NS)		(**)		(NS)		(NS)		(NS)
Children younger than 19 at home	None	72%	61%	54%	25%	52%	54%	73%	53%	51%	44%
	1–2	20	32	32	33	29	18	20	47	35	33
	3 or more	8	7	14	42	18	27	7	—	14	22
			(*)		(*)		(NS)		(*)		(NS)
Entrepreneurial climate index		2.48	2.50	2.42	2.24	2.64	2.51	2.40	2.20 (*)	2.55	2.50
Work values (3)	Autonomy	3.15	3.42 (****)	3.26	3.56 (***)	3.09	3.27	3.15	3.53 (***)	3.12	3.24
	Task interest	3.20	3.49 (****)	3.31	3.67 (*)	3.17	3.41	3.12	3.66 (***)	3.14	3.26
	Wealth	2.79	3.91	2.97	3.19	3.03	3.15	3.01	3.25	3.03	2.84
	Homebody	2.87	2.96	3.00	3.21	2.91	3.05	2.81	3.03	2.87	2.91

Notes: (1) Maximum number of cases; missing data may reduce total cases for some comparisons. Population weighted to precision of ethnic measures. All nascent and discouraged entrepreneurs given a weight of 1.

(2) Statistical comparisons utilized chi-square or one-way analysis of variance. Statistical sign: * = 0.05; ** = 0.01; *** = 0.001; **** = 0.0001.

(3) There are statistically significant differences (below 0.05) between nascent and discouraged entrepreneurs on educational attainment and work values: task interest. Marginally significant differences (below 0.10; above 0.05) on labor force activity and work values: wealth.

ployment as their primary labor force activity. This would suggest that a larger proportion of white entrepreneurs are starting a second business, while many nonwhites may be developing a second, perhaps part-time, work activity.

Starting the Business. Several features of the start-up effort can be compared across these different ethnic groups, even though the samples are small. This includes the character of the proposed business, the resources brought to bear for the start-up, and how the start-up was conducted.

The economic sector in which the new firm may be located and the emphasis on high technology are presented in Table 8.7. Given the low number of start-ups in the sample, there is little difference associated with economic sector that is statistically significant. There are, however, few nonwhite start-ups in agricultural, construction, or manufacturing, perhaps reflecting a lack of experience in these areas and the fact that the largest ethnic groups, blacks and Hispanics, do not live in the rural parts of Wisconsin. The differences in technological emphasis, using the same scale presented in Table 5.7, indicate no major differences, although there is a suggestion that Asians consider their proposed firms more technically sophisticated and that blacks may consider theirs less technically sophisticated.

Aspirations for the proposed firms show no statistically significant variation related to ethnic background. The anticipated future size of the start-up is presented in terms of expected annual sales in the first, fifth, and tenth years in Table 8.7. The patterns for the projected number of employees are similar. Regardless of ethnic background, a substantial proportion was not able to answer the question, rising from about one in five regarding the first year to half in the tenth year.

Most consider their involvement in the new firm relatively permanent, as over two-thirds, shown in the bottom of Table 8.7, say they never expect to sell the business itself. This long-term commitment appears to be greater among nonwhites.

Resources brought to bear on the new effort, such as social network connections, start-up team experience, start-up team time, and money, are presented in Table 8.8. There is no statistically significant difference related to the size of the principal's social network, although it is slightly larger for American Indians and slightly smaller for Asians. There is no statistically significant difference associated with prior experience with start-ups; some in each ethnic group—except Asians—report some past experience with start-ups. There is, however, a statistically significant difference associated with prior work experience, perhaps reflecting the very low level reported by Asians who are younger than other entrepreneurs.

Because of the very small number of cases in this sample, it is only possible to make a comparison between whites and nonwhites with regard to funds assembled from the start-up team for the new business or time devoted to the start-up. There is no difference on the first and a

Table 8.7
Start-up Firm Characteristics: By Ethnic Group

	White	American Indian	Asian	Black	Hispanic	
Number of firms	82	12	11	17	17	
Industry sector						
Agriculture	4%	—	—	—	—	
Construction	10	8%	9%	—	—	
Manufacturing	11	—	—	—	—	
Distributive services	8	17	9	12	—	
FIRE (1)/business services	9	8	18	29	12	
Health, educ., social services	6	—	—	12	—	
Retail and restaurants	29	33	36	41	41	
Consumer services	13	17	18	6	35	(2)
Other	12	17	9	—	12	(NS)
High-tech. emphasis						
Low	68%	58%	27%	75%	47%	
Medium	23	25	45	19	40	
High	10	17	27	6	13	(NS)
Sales expected: first year						
No answer	25%	18%	44%	18%	—	
$1 million and up	15	9	11	18	33	
$0–9,999	42	45	22	36	33	
$10–49,999	15	9	22	18	33	
$50,000–999,999	2	18	—	9	—	(NS)
Sales expected: fifth year						
No answer	30%	45%	56%	36%	—	
$1 million and up	8	9	11	18	33	
$0–9,999	20	27	—	9	33	
$10–49,999	32	18	22	36	33	
$50,000–999,999	10	—	10	—	—	(NS)
Sales expected: tenth year						
No answer	50%	36%	56%	46%	33	
$0–9,999	5	9	11	9	33	
$10–49,999	5	27	—	9	—	
$50,000–999,999	35	27	22	27	33	
$1 million and up	5	—	11	9	—	(NS)
Expect to sell business						
No	69%	80%	88%	67%	100%	
Yes	31	20	12	33	0	(NS)

Notes: (1) Fire, insurance, and real estate sectors.
       (2) NS = not statistically significant.

statistically significant difference on the second: whites report the start-up team spending more time on the new business. This would be consistent with a larger proportion of nonwhites developing a new firm as a "second job" rather than a potential replacement for a primary career focus.

Table 8.8
Start-up Resources Assembled: By Ethnic Group

	White	American Indian	Asian	Black	Hispanic
Number of firms	82	12	11	17	17
Friends network					
0–4	35%	27%	60%	33%	38%
5–7	31	45	20	40	38
8 and up	35	27	20	27	25
Family and relatives network					
0–4	35%	9%	33%	41%	50%
5–7	32	27	33	24	31
8 and up	33	64	33	35	19 (NS)
Total social network					
0–9	35%	18%	50%	41%	38%
10–14	37	36	20	24	38
15 and up	28	46	30	36	25 (NS)
Start-up firm experience					
Yes	35%	50%	—	38%	33%
No	65	50	100%	62	67 (NS)
Work experience (average)	19.0	17.7	7.8	17.6	16.3
0–9 years	22%	33%	80%	19%	36%
10–19 years	32	17	10	44	21
20–50 years	46	50	10	38	43 (NS)
Start-up team size					
1	38%	46%	33%	42%	60%
2	48	36	33	25	40
3 or more	13	18	33	33	— (NS)
Expected financial needs (total loans plus equity)					
None	53%	33%	36%	44%	80%
$1–10,000	16	17	9	12	13
$11–50,000	18	8	18	25	7
$51,000 and up	13	42	36	19	— (NS)

	White	Nonwhite	
Total time on start-up (hours/week: total team)			
1–9	10%	64%	
10–34	43	29	
35 and up	47	7	(***)
Total team investment			
Up to $9,999	69%	73%	
$10–49,999	23	18	
$50,000 and up	8	9	(NS)

Note: Statistical significance: NS = not significant; * = 0.05; ** = 0.01; *** = 0.001; **** = 0.0001.

Several features of the way the majority and minorities have gone about starting a new firm are explored in Table 8.9. The length of time devoted to the start-up, from the first to last activity reported in the interview, shows no relationship to ethnic background, although Hispanics may be a little faster and American Indians a little slower in moving through the start-up process.

The total number of activities does not vary much among different ethnic groups, and all complete several early activities in the start-up effort. The actual activities completed are presented at the bottom of Table 8.9, ranked by frequency of reporting among the white respondents. There are statistically significant differences among the ethnic groups for only two of the twenty-two activities. Whites were more likely to have purchased equipment or filed a federal tax return. Whites were also slightly more likely to be starting a new construction or manufacturing firm—where equipment may be important. A slightly larger proportion of whites seemed to be developing a new firm as a major work focus, which would be consistent with filing federal tax returns.

Use of Assistance. One of the primary mechanisms that society has to encourage the formation of new businesses is the transfer of useful information to those who are taking steps to start a new business. Chapter 2 discussed the 750 services provided from 452 different public and nonprofit programs found in Wisconsin. To assess the knowledge and utilization of such services, respondents were asked a series of questions on these services. They were asked whether they knew if each type of help was available, if they could locate each type of help, whether such help was relevant to their specific business, whether they attempted a contact, and, for those who made contact, whether it was helpful.

The overall results are presented in Table 8.10, which indicates some variations associated with ethnic background. For example, the average number of total responses for Asians was somewhat lower than for other groups. An average response of 19.8 suggests that for eight of twenty-eight forms of assistance, Asians were not able to provide a response, perhaps because they were not familiar with some forms of assistance. There are statistically significant differences related to several patterns: blacks were more likely to say they couldn't find help; blacks and Hispanics were less likely to say the help was not relevant; and Asians were more likely to respond that a form of assistance would not be helpful.

There is no difference, however, in those who considered the assistance received as helpful, either as a general response to experiences or an evaluation of their most recent encounter with a helping agency. Only a small proportion, less than 5% for any ethnic group, reports that visits to a helping program were not worthwhile.

Table 8.9
Start-up Gestation Features: By Ethnic Group

	White	American Indian	Asian	Black	Hispanic	
Number of cases	53	12	9	13	14	
Start window						
(average/month)	18.1	32.7	10.8	10.9	5.1	(NS)
0–1 month	36%	33%	22%	15%	57%	
2–12 months	32	25	44	46	29	
13 or more months	32	42	33	39	14	(NS)
Start-up activities						
Count						
Months 0–1	2.5	1.8	1.5	2.4	2.7	(NS)
Months 2–12	1.6	2.0	0.9	1.2	1.9	(NS)
Months 13 and later	1.9	0.6	1.4	1.5	0.4	(NS)
Total reported	5.9	4.3	3.8	5.1	5.0	(NS)
Percent						
Months 0–1	53%	51%	52%	52%	68%	
Months 2–12	22	30	25	23	24	
Months 13 and later	25	19	23	25	7	(NS)
Activity reported						
Serious thought	65%	50%	73%	65%	72%	(NS)
Look for equipment	57	50	54	58	50	(NS)
Invest own money	56	33	18	59	50	(NS)
Buy equipment	50	25	18	12	33	(**)
Sales or income	48	42	27	18	50	(NS)
Positive cash flow	17	8	18	—	17	(NS)
Assemble team	41	25	45	53	61	(NS)
Save to invest	35	42	54	41	28	(NS)
Patent, trademark	35	17	27	35	39	(NS)
Business plans	34	33	36	65	44	(NS)
Full-time commitment	32	17	—	12	17	(NS)
Ask for funding	29	25	54	29	17	(NS)
Other actions	28	25	27	12	33	(NS)
Got funding	24	8	18	23	11	(NS)
Rent equipment	21	17	9	29	11	(NS)
Hire employees	20	17	—	12	6	(NS)
Create legal form	16	17	9	23	11	(NS)
Model or prototypes	16	25	—	6	11	(NS)
Federal tax return	24	8	9	—	5	(*)
FICA payments	16	—	—	—	11	(NS)
Unemployment insurance	12	—	9	6	6	(NS)
D&B listing	5	8	—	18	6	(NS)

Note: Statistical significance: NS = not significant; * = 0.05; ** = 0.01; *** = 0.001; **** = 0.0001.

Table 8.10
Utilization of Assistance Programs: By Ethnic Group

	White	American Indian	Asian	Black	Hispanic	
Number of cases	61	12	10	15	15	
Average number of total responses	26.0	23.6	19.8	24.7	24.5	(**)
No contact:						
Didn't know available	29%	34%	25%	46%	40%	(NS)
Could not find help	2	3	*	7	1	(*)
Not relevant	47	40	45	25	31	(*)
Wouldn't be helpful	7	7	16	10	4	(*)
Contact made:						
Not helpful	4	1	2	4	4	(NS)
Helpful	11	15	11	9	19	(NS)
Reaction to most recent help						
No. of responses	40	7	6	7	5	
Extremely helpful	35%	29%	17%	—	80%	
Very helpful	38	57	33	43	20	
Somewhat helpful	15	14	33	43	—	
Neutral	13	—	—	—	—	
Not helpful	—	—	17	14	—	
Somewhat harmful	—	—	—	—	—	
Very harmful	—	—	—	—	—	(NS)

Note: Statistical significance: NS = not significant; * = 0.05; ** = 0.01; *** = 0.001; **** = 0.0001.

Respondent assessment of whether particular types of service were relevant varied by race as well as subject. The business assistance forms deemed most relevant are listed below for white and nonwhite respondents.

White Respondents		**Nonwhite Respondents**	
1. Info on laws and regulations	78%	Business advocacy groups	90%
2. Business feasibility review	76%	Minority business assistance	88%
3. Financial counseling	72%	Business incubator	87%
4. Network: making contacts	72%	Business feasibility review	84%

By subject, nonwhites thought that business advocacy groups were the most relevant (90% agreeing) and patent and trademark assistance were the least relevant forms of assistance (36% saying this was relevant). Whites agreed with them on the low end (27%) but thought that information on laws and regulations was the most relevant (78%), followed closely by business feasibility review (76%). Reviewing the relative need for the various types of advice, it seems that nonwhites thought that almost all forms of advice were more relevant than did whites. This would suggest that it is important to deliver such advice to this population if it is to have a better chance of succeeding as entrepreneurs.

The inadequacy of current attempts to inform the nonwhite community of the availability of these information services is shown by comparing the percentage of respondents who thought that each service was relevant with the percentage that knew that each service was available. Between one-quarter and two-thirds of all nonwhite respondents did not know that certain forms of assistance were available. Again, with a few exceptions, nonwhites consistently have less knowledge of the available options than whites. When one sees that 84% of the respondents think that assistance on business feasibility review is relevant but that 61% of nonwhite respondents did not know that such information was available, or that 90% thought that business advisory groups were relevant but that 55% did not know of them, it is clear that a large gap exists in the service delivery system. Nonwhites have not generally been as well informed as whites of the assistance options available.

Possibly a reason for the lack of knowledge of the options by so many nonwhites is that their counterparts have not received help and, as a result, have not told others about the services they received. But when one examines who has used these services, the lack of information does not come from any greater underutilization of the existing services. Nonwhites generally have taken as much advantage of these services as whites. Why a disproportionate number of nonwhites do not know of such services does not appear to be due to their exclusion from receiving these services.

A further possible explanation is that those nascent and discouraged entrepreneurs who have used the services did not find them particularly useful. But when queried as to how useful the most recent form of assistance they received was, nonwhite respondents were quite positive, as shown in Table 8.10. Only two of twenty-five reported their most recent experience was not helpful. Whites and nonwhites report, on the average, more than two contacts with assistance sources that were helpful. The relatively high ranking of the program quality suggests that the lower level of knowledge of the options is not due to the refusal to spread the word because of poor service. It must be due to other factors such as poor marketing of the availability of such services, poor location of such services relative to the population, or lack of need for the programs currently offered.

NEW FIRMS

It is possible to compare new business owners from different ethnic groups. These are the individuals who have gone through the preparatory stages and emerged as new business owners. The percentage of new firms included in the Wisconsin new firm sample owned and operated by different ethnic groups was approximately the same as the proportion of ethnic groups in the population. The maximum number of nonwhite respondents was forty-two, although this is slightly reduced for some analyses due to missing data and the effects of weighting the sample to represent all geographic areas in Wisconsin.

The following comparisons are developed with one central objective: to determine if there are significant differences among the new firms associated with the ethnic background of the owners. This exploration begins with characteristics of the individual responding for the new firm, continues with the character of the start-up team that expects to share in the ownership of the new firm, and then reviews selected features of the new firm itself. The ethnic background of the primary respondent is used to characterize the new firm ownership. There is, as it turns out, a high degree of ethnic homogeneity among these new firms (see Table 8.12), so this provides a very accurate method for characterizing the ethnic ownership of these new firms.

Selected characteristics of the principal, outlined in Table 8.11, cover gender, age, number of children in the household, residential tenure, annual household income, orientations toward the state's entrepreneurial climate, work values, and how much time is devoted to the new firm. The only difference related to ethnic background is related to duration of residence in the county and Wisconsin. As with the nascent entrepreneurs, American Indians have a long tenure, two to three decades, and Asians have a relatively short residential tenure, averaging less than ten years.

The attitudes of the owners toward the entrepreneurial climate in Wisconsin or their general work orientations, shown in Table 8.11, reflect little difference, with one exception, based on ethnic identification. The one exception is a stronger interest in wealth and prestige among all nonwhite new firm owners, a difference that was statistically significant. The weekly work effort, with the majority of the respondents reporting over forty hours per week devoted to the new firm, does not vary by ethnic identification.

The characteristics of the start-up teams of the new firms are presented in Table 8.12. There is no statistically significant difference in the average size of the start-up teams, although it would appear that American Indian and Hispanic start-up teams may be slightly smaller. The start-up teams are clearly very homogeneous. There is a striking absence of diversity for all five ethnic groups. The family nature of the new firms has no statistically significant variation related to ethnic background, and the large majority are either sole proprietorships or family-owned. The gender structures of the start-up teams do not vary by ethnic background. Educational attainment of the start-up team members does not vary much by ethnic background, although the levels reported reflect the population distributions reported in Table 8.1. The highest levels of educational attainment are reported by Asians. Only with regard to recent career shifts is there a statistically significant difference, and this is related to the higher percentage of Asians and slightly higher percentage of blacks who appear to join a new firm start-up team soon after completing an educational degree program.

A wide range of new firm characteristics is explored in terms of potential differences based on the ethnic background of the start-up team in Table

Table 8.11
New Firm Principal's Selected Characteristics: By Ethnic Group

	White	American Indian	Asian	Black	Hispanic	
Number of cases	364	10	7	14	7	
Principal's gender						
Men	73%	60%	82%	53%	81%	
Women	27	40	18	47	19	(NS)
Principal's age						
18–24 years	2%	10%	15%	7%	—	
25–34 years	26	20	30	7	29	
35–44 years	39	40	41	41	71	
45–54 years	23	20	15	17	—	
55 years and up	10	10	—	29	—	(NS)
Principal household: children under 18						
None	22%	14%	22%	36%	17%	
1–2	59	71	78	64	33	
3–6	18	14	—	—	50	(NS)
Principal's residential tenure						
Same county (avg. years)	19.7	25.4	7.9	25.7	13.0	(*)
Same state (avg. years)	27.8	32.6	8.7	26.6	17.6	(**)
Principal's annual income 1991 average ($1,000)	65.1	40.8	52.1	60.5	30.5	(NS)
Principal's orientations						
Entrepreneurial climate	2.3	2.5	2.5	2.2	2.3	(NS)
Work value: autonomy	3.4	3.4	3.1	3.6	3.4	(NS)
Work value: task	3.4	3.5	3.2	3.4	3.6	(NS)
Work value: wealth	2.8	3.1	3.1	3.1	3.4	(**)
Work value: homebody	2.8	2.9	2.7	3.1	2.5	(NS)
Principal work effort						
0–20 hours/week	11%	40%	—	10%	13%	
21–40 hours/week	17	30	—	8	13	
41–60 hours/week	50	20	67%	64	46	
61 and more hours/week	21	10	33	18	27	(NS)

Note: Statistical significance: NS = not significant; * = 0.05; ** = 0.01; *** = 0.001; **** = 0.0001.

8.13. Firms started by American Indians tend not to be in urban areas, while those started by blacks and Hispanics tend to be started in urban areas or regional centers. In both cases, this reflects current residential patterns. There are no statistically significant differences associated with the economic sector of the new firm or the extent to which it has a technical emphasis, although a subset of Asian firms may be emphasizing technology. In terms of the legal form of the firm, it would appear that white-owned new firms are much more likely to utilize a Subchapter S corporate form, a statistically and substantive difference.

Table 8.12
New Firm Start-up Team Characteristics: By Ethnic Group

	White	American Indian	Asian	Black	Hispanic	
Number of firms	333	9	8	14	7	
Size of start-up team						
1	49%	50%	48%	54%	67%	
2	35	50	33	29	27	
3	10	—	13	—	6	
4 or more	6	—	6	17	—	(NS)
Average size	1.8	1.5	1.8	1.9	1.4	(NS)
Ethnic composition of team						
White %	99%	—	9%	7%	—	(****)
American Indian %	*	100%	—	—	—	(****)
Asian %	*	—	91	—	—	(****)
Black %	*	—	—	93	—	(****)
Hispanic %	*	—	—	—	100%	(****)
Family structure						
Sole proprietorship	46%	50%	48%	46%	67%	
Kin-owned/kin-managed	29	20	19	45	13	
Kin-owned/others managed	18	20	13	10	—	
Not kin-owned	7	10	20	—	19	(NS)
Start-up team genders						
1 male	35%	20%	36%	28%	54%	
1 female	12	30	12	20	13	
2 males	15	40	—	—	—	
2 females	4	10	—	7	—	
2 mixed	17	—	13	29	27	
3–4 males	8	—	33	—	—	
3–4 females	1	—	6	—	—	
3–4 mixed	10	—	—	17	6	(NS)
Team educational attainment						
Up to high school degree	31%	50%	7%	31%	58%	(NS)
High school degree	31	39	21	52	29	(NS)
College degree	23	11	48	7	13	(NS)
Graduate experience	15	—	23	10	—	(NS)
Team career shift						
School—new firm	5%	—	27%	10%	—	(*)
Estab. org.—new firm	66	75%	49	47	53%	(NS)
New firm—new firm	17	10	24	38	23	(NS)
Unemploy.—new firm	3	10	—	—	16	(NS)

Note: Statistical significance: NS = not significant; * = 0.05; ** = 0.01; *** = 0.001; **** = 0.0001.

Table 8.13
New Firm Characteristics: By Ethnic Group

	White	American Indian	Asian	Black	Hispanic	
Number of firms	333	9	8	14	7	(2)
Context						
Urban area	30%	—	38%	70%	40%	
Regional center	40	90%	49	21	60	
Nonurban area	30	10	13	9	—	(**)
Industry sector						
Agriculture	4%	11%	13%	—	—	
Construction	11	11	13	—	27%	
Manufacturing	12	11	33	—	13	
Distributive services	10	22	—	20	—	
FIRE (1)/business serv.	24	22	17	32	—	
Health, educ., social serv.	9	—	—	26	—	
Retail and restaurants	17	11	24	16	33	
Consumer services	13	11	—	7	27	(NS)
High-tech emphasis						
Low	71%	90%	54%	60%	87%	
Medium	14	—	—	20	13	
High	15	10	46	20	—	(NS)
Legal form: 1992						
Sole proprietorship	36%	—	36%	48%	67%	
Partnership	8	38%	6	9	—	
Corporation	29	38	58	43	13	
Corporation S	25	—	—	—	6	
Other	2	25	—	—	13	(****)
Jobs in 1992 (avg. full-time)	6.7	2.1	8.3	5.7	1.9	
0–25 percentile	26%	60%	26%	48%	81%	
26–50 percentile	38	20	35	16	—	
51–75 percentile	23	20	6	29	6	
76–90 percentile	9	—	33	—	13	
91–95 percentile	3	—	—	—	—	
96–100 percentile	2	—	—	7	—	(*)
Sales: 1st year (avg., $1,000)	350	201	775	197	26	(NS)
Sales in 1992 (avg., $1,000)	495	113	1,211	117	39	(NS)
0–25 percentile	24%	40%	—	18%	60%	
26–50 percentile	30	40	48	69	40	
51–75 percentile	24	20	14	—	—	
76–90 percentile	13	—	—	13	—	
91–95 percentile	6	—	15	—	—	
96–100 percentile	3	—	23	—	—	
Growth trajectory						
Hi Start-Hi Growth	8%	—	15%	—	—	
Hi Start-Lo Growth	34	60%	58	27%	—	
Lo Start-Hi Growth	23	—	—	17	20%	
Lo Start-Lo Growth	35	40	27	56	80	(NS)

Table 8.13 continued

	White	American Indian	Asian	Black	Hispanic	
Financial support:						
percentage reporting						
Any loans	43%	50%	24%	22%	27%	(NS)
Any equity	20	20	13	20	—	(NS)
Any financial support	49	50	24	22	27	(NS)
Financial support:						
1992 totals						
None	51%	50%	75%	78%	73%	
$0–25,000	17	20	6	20	27	
$26–100,00	18	30	5	2	—	
$101–500,000	13	—	13	—	—	
$501,000 and up	2	—	—	—	—	(NS)
Knowledge, use of						
assistance programs						
Reaction (avg. no.)	26.8	25.5	27.8	27.3	26.2	(NS)
Contact: got help	9%	15%	12%	18%	6%	(NS)
Contact: not helpful	4	7	6	9	*	(NS)
Didn't expect help	19	8	12	21	14	(NS)
Not relevant	31	39	17	22	48	(NS)
Couldn't find help	3	6	7	2	—	(NS)
Didn't know available	32	25	45	28	32	(NS)
Strategic focus						
Lower prices	2.5	2.6	3.1	3.1	2.7	(NS)
Market responsiveness	2.7	3.4	2.8	3.4	3.7	(***)
Product diversity	2.6	2.6	2.8	2.5	3.4	(NS)
Customer serv./quality	3.6	3.3	3.3	3.8	3.4	(NS)
Facilities, convenience	2.3	2.4	3.0	2.6	2.9	(NS)
High tech	2.1	2.4	2.9	2.7	2.3	(*)
Future plans for business						
Enhancement	29%	—	32%	11%	6%	(NS)
Contraction, quit	7	—	—	—	2	(NS)

Notes: (1) Fire, insurance, and real estate sectors.

(2) Statistical significance: NS = not significant; * = 0.05; ** = 0.01; *** = 0.001; **** = 0.0001.

The size or scope of these new firms varies slightly, with modestly smaller numbers of full-time jobs and lower sales reported by American Indian and Hispanic new firms. Although there is no statistically significant difference in the growth trajectories reported by these firms, only white- or Asian-initiated new firms are in the high-growth categories. Asian new firms tend to have higher sales in the first year.

Patterns reported in Table 8.13 suggest little difference in terms of presence or level of external financial support, perhaps because more than half, regardless of ethnic identification, report no loans or equity investments in their firm.

Reaction to programs and activities that provide assistance to new firms reflects no difference by ethnic background. The patterns are similar to those found among nascent and discouraged entrepreneurs, with the largest proportion unable to find help or uninformed about the existence of programs. In general, for every three who made contact with a program, two considered it helpful.

The strategic focus or competitive strategy of these new firms reflects few differences related to the owner's ethnic background: nonwhites appear to give more emphasis to market responsiveness and high technology than white new firm owners.

When future plans for the business are considered, most of those who respond are planning an enhancement; very few are planning a contraction or disengagement from the new firm. There is no difference related to ethnic background.

In summary, then, if there is a major difference in the new firms initiated by Wisconsin residents from the five ethnic groups, it has not appeared in this analysis. It seems reasonable to consider that the opportunities pursued, the strategies employed, and the support from the host context are pretty much the same regardless of the ethnic background of the start-up team.

OVERVIEW AND IMPLICATIONS

Most states and regions will prosper when all population segments, all ethnic groups, have an opportunity to fully participate in the entrepreneurial process. In this chapter analytical attention was given to ethnic comparisons related to three stages of the entrepreneurial process: those entering the process to start new firms, those actively involved in the start-up process, and those who had successfully implemented new firms. Major differences among five ethnic groups were found only for the first stage of the process.

But the first stage is rather critical. Specifically, when five major ethnic groups were considered in terms of the presence of inhibiting factors—the proportion of the adult population that had not completed high school, was from households with annual income under $10,000, had lived in their county for less than six years, or had fewer than six people in their social networks—there were major differences. From 36% to 77% of the adult populations were found to have at least one inhibitor.

However, among adults in four of five ethnic groups that did not have an inhibiting factor, there was no evidence that nonwhites were either at a disadvantage in the entrepreneurial process or pursued new firm start-ups in a distinctive manner. The one exception was American Indians, who were less likely to participate in the entrepreneurial process than the other four ethnic groups. In contrast, Asians without inhibiting factors were the most active in the entrepreneurial process. Both American Indians and Asians, however, are very diverse groups, suggesting that more careful attention to differences within these groups may be required to develop a more complete understanding of their entrepreneurial activity.

There is considerable evidence that members of ethnic groups are not well informed about the existence and nature of current programs of assistance for new and small firms. In this regard, however, there is little difference between white and nonwhite entrepreneurs and new firm owners. The patterns presented in this analysis are very similar to those provided in Chapter 3, related to business start-ups, and Chapter 5, related to new firms. Analysis based on ethnic identification adds little to the portrayal of this problem—a large proportion of Wisconsin entrepreneurs and new firm owners is uninformed about sources of help.

There are two major arenas available for public policy regarding the participation of ethnic groups in the entrepreneurial process: first, reducing the proportion of the ethnic groups that are inhibited from full participation in the entrepreneurial process and second, expanding efforts to inform ethnic groups about the availability of forms of assistance.

The first is the greater challenge, for at least two of the inhibiting factors—short duration of residence in the county and a relatively small set of friends or relatives—do not seem amenable to government influence. The other two—lack of a basic education and a shortage of money—do seem more suited to government programs. Programs that increase the proportion of all adult citizens, whites and nonwhites, who have the equivalent of a high school education would have benefits for all workforce activity, regular employment as well as participation in the entrepreneurial process. An expansion of sources of financial support for those from low-income households may also encourage more start-ups, although some care may be required to ensure other inhibitors are not present, such as an inadequate educational background.

Expanding efforts to inform minorities about assistance programs, however, is consistent with one of the major policy implications related to the entire entrepreneurial process. Lack of awareness of assistance programs is endemic among all those involved in implementing or managing new firms. The difference is only one of degree. The proportion of those involved in the entrepreneurial process that is uninformed about programs of assistance, white or nonwhite, is too large. As new programs would not be required, reducing this "information gap" would seem a very cost-effective way of promoting the involvement of ethnic groups in the entrepreneurial process.

CONCEPTIONS OF MODERN MARKET ECONOMIES

One of the pervasive assumptions reviewed in Chapter 1 was that most of those participating in new firm start-ups are marginal to the labor force. The analysis of the effect of inhibitors on participation in start-ups provides dramatic evidence that those with any one of the inhibiting factors—lack of education, lack of funds, lack of an established social network, lack of experience in a community—are unlikely to implement the start-up of a new firm. Only individuals who had passed a minimum threshold on all four of these dimensions were active in the start-up process. The assumption, then, that those starting new firms are marginal to the labor force and economic activity is clearly inappropriate; nascent entrepreneurs are among the most fully integrated members of their communities.

APPENDIX: ETHNIC SAMPLE DEVELOPMENT

In 1992, the data file of all those holding Wisconsin automobile driver licenses was, technically speaking, a public document. A machine-readable data file on all Wisconsin drivers was obtained. A separate file was created for each ethnic group (ethnic identification appears in the data files but not on the physical license). Each of the four files was then sorted by residential address. As a result, the records for two or more persons in the same ethnic group with the same address would be adjacent, identifying a "minority household." Charles Palit, Associate Director of the University of Wisconsin Survey Research Laboratory, was responsible for the development of this procedure.

These households, then, were the source of a representative sample for each ethnic group. In about 80% of the cases, the individuals interviewed in these households identified themselves as belonging to the target ethnic groups. The sample of whites, 91% of the Wisconsin population, was drawn through traditional random digit-dial selection of household phone numbers. A small proportion of the nonwhite respondents was part of this sample.

Chapter 9

Overview: The Entrepreneurial Engine and Implications

A lot of people in the United States are spending a lot of time and resources trying to start a lot of businesses. At any given time, 7 million persons may be trying to start over 3 million new firms. Most who try to start new businesses are between twenty-five and forty years old, have finished high school, are in households above the poverty level, have lived in their communities for a substantial period of time, have well-developed social networks, and are well established in the world of work. Over half start with a team, usually with a relative or family member. Within a year after they start working on the new firm, from one-third to one-half will have a new, operating business in place. One in six will abandon his or her efforts, and a substantial minority, about a third, may take considerably longer—some up to five years—to reach closure on their start-up efforts.

Three in four of the new firms will be operating five years after their first sales. There is some growth for the average firm, which may have two owner/managers and four employees in its first year. By the fifth year the typical firm will provide ten or more jobs. However, a small proportion, less than one in five, of new firms may account for half to three-quarters of all new firm jobs in any given cohort.

Knowing the general outlines of the process, we can consider the implications for the conceptualizations of modern market economies, public policy, and those considering entrepreneurial career options. The assumptions about the role of new firms and entrepreneurship associated with "perfect competitive markets" are clearly inappropriate and may have misled many to underemphasize their importance.

Policymakers are generally concerned with economic growth. It is possible to consider the process whereby new firms develop jobs and contribute to overall economic growth. Government policy can be directed toward different stages of the entrepreneurial process. It is possible to speculate on the most efficient policy strategies for maximizing job contributions from new firms.

It is also possible to present an outline—for those considering a new firm start-up—of what they might expect. Data from those who have "taken the plunge" and worked on firm start-ups provide descriptions of these people, their experiences, and the outcomes. This may be useful for others considering an entrepreneurial career move.

CONCEPTUALIZATION OF MODERN MARKET ECONOMIES

As has been mentioned, the dominant paradigm for interpreting modern market economies includes a range of assumptions about the prevalence and nature of new firms and the start-up process. Data relevant to at least seven of the assumptions associated with this conceptual scheme were covered in the preceding analysis.

Included among these assumptions are the views that (1) the entrepreneurial process leading to a firm birth is a unique and distinct event, not widespread in modern economies, (2) new and small firms have a minor role in economic growth and adaptation, (3) new firms are created by "solo entrepreneurs" acting on their own and solely for their own benefit, (4) new firms are initiated by people who are not well integrated in the modern economy, as better-trained, more competent workers pursue long-term jobs in established firms, (5) new firms appear almost instantaneously in response to new opportunities and trends, (6) there is little or no social cost to the start-up process, only riches for successful entrepreneurs, and (7) the typical new business is solely oriented toward maximizing profits or return on equity.

First, it is clear that it is neither rare nor unique for a U.S. adult to become involved in a new firm start-up at the end of the twentieth century. With one in twenty-five adults and one in eight men twenty-five to thirty-four years old starting new firms and two in five heads of households reporting self-employment over their work careers, it would seem that participation in the entrepreneurial process is very widespread. Each year more adults are involved in firm start-up efforts than in a marriage or childbearing. A recently established time series of new firm births based on household samples suggests a similar level of involvement (Dennis, 1997). In short, in the United States of today, becoming involved in the creation of a new business entity is a very common activity.

Second, there is strong evidence that in all advanced market economies, at least since the 1960s, new and small firms have become a major source of economic growth and adaptation. While established large firms continue to have an important role to play, they now share the stage with new and small firms. Neither new and small or large and established firms can be considered the *only* source of economic well-being.

Third, it is clear that the majority of new firms are implemented by teams: over half of the start-up efforts and the new firms involved two or more people who expected to own part of the business; about 15% involved three or more individuals. The more substantial the new firms—the larger the firm or the higher the growth rate—the less likely that it was a one-person effort. While the new firm samples in this study were drawn from populations of established firms and were likely to omit the self-employed, the nascent entrepreneur samples made no such distinction, and the typical start-up firm had two or more on the team. It may be theoretically convenient to anthropomorphize a start-up as an economically "rational" decision-maker attempting to optimize the current value of an income stream, but this perspective does not lead to an accurate conception of how new firms are brought into existence.

Fourth, there is the image that those pursing entrepreneurship are "misfits cast off from wage work" (Evans and Leighton, 1989) or that "the entrepreneur may lead a parasitical existence that is damaging to the economy" (Baumol, 1990). There is little question that the vast majority of those involved in new firm start-ups are among the most stable and respected participants in the labor force. They are clearly mainstream, midcareer adults seeking new options. They typically have substantial experience and are moving from established organizations to a new firm. They usually make this shift after it is clear that the new enterprise is a viable option. They reflect a rational set of motives and do not appear to be "risk-oriented," as some have suggested. While it could be argued that much of the start-up process is a replication of existing business activity—and does not, therefore, represent a dramatic shift in the market structure associated with "true entrepreneurship"—this does suggest that most efforts to move away from wage work are oriented toward a productive contribution within the existing rules. Of course, the United States has had several centuries of experience in developing rules that will ensure that most entrepreneurship is productive—a contribution to the greater good.

The fifth assumption, that new firms appear instantaneously in response to shifts in economic structure or market opportunities, may be appropriate if time is measured in decades or centuries. Some firms are implemented in a few months, and the average time for a start-up is one year, both relatively short compared to the history of mankind or the development of the modern world. On the other hand, from the perspective of those who are implementing the firm, the time required to implement a firm may be a substantial part of one's work life. Start-ups are not instantaneous, and much can happen to affect the outcome.

There is, in relation to the sixth assumption, a substantial social cost in the start-up process. Each viable firm birth may require three start-up efforts, two of which don't make it. The major social cost of each successful firm birth may be borne by the teams—and the families of the teams—of the start-ups that were abandoned. The direct benefits, however, are achieved by those whose start-ups are successful and lead to new firms. While the aggregate net benefits may outweigh the aggregate net costs, these may be associated with two different sets of individuals. Some of this cost may be borne by those (habitual entrepreneurs) who are successful with a subsequent start-up, but two-thirds of all start-ups represent the first effort by those involved (Table 5.6).

The most pervasive image of business organizations is associated with the seventh assumption, that firms, particularly the new ones, are driven by economic or business considerations. Simply put, an emphasis on profits dominates. The major conceptual schemes have focused on the reactions of economic actors (workers or firms) to market forces (Storey, 1994). There has been virtually no attention to the family or kinship context of the owner/managers of firms, new or otherwise.

One of the more dramatic findings has been that over 90% of new start-ups are either sole proprietorships or controlled by a single family or kin group, which suggests that many of the decisions and the resource allocations may not be interpreted, or even identified, with a standard economic or business framework. Specifically, the focus has been on interpreting all business activity, now and in the future, in terms of potential monetary profits. While appropriate for prescriptions of what "should" be done by a rational player in a competitive market, it may not provide accurate interpretations of what actually is done. A full understanding of why firms take certain actions may require careful attention to family contexts and resources. (The great-grandfather of one author expanded his family firm to three, and only three, branches because he had three, and only three, sons.)

Without a more accurate conceptual framework for current market economies that takes into account the continuous shifts and high levels of turbulence among firms and jobs, it will be difficult to provide a full understanding of the changes or accurate interpretations for policymakers or participants. While this new framework has yet to be fully developed (Kirchhoff, 1994), it is clear that the constant renewal provided by the entrepreneurial engine will be an important feature of this new conceptualization.

THE ENTREPRENEURIAL ENGINE

For a mature market economy, the entrepreneurial process is continuous. At any given time there are—simultaneously—new cohorts of nascent entrepreneurs initiating the start-up process, start-up initiatives leading to firm births, and firms surviving infancy to become established businesses. This may be considered the "entrepreneurial engine"—a major mechanism of renewal and adaptation in market economies (Hall, 1995). We can consider the transitions and impacts at each stage in the process as a guide to considering appropriate government policy.

Table 9.1
The Entrepreneurial Engine and Job Dynamics

First Sales	Firm Start-up	Firm Births	Firm Infancy		
	< 1 Year	0	1 Year	2 Years	3 Years
Human population					
100,000 total					
74,000 18+ years					
Proportion nascent entres: 3.7%	2,755				
No. of start-ups					
2.2 per team	1,252				
Firm births					
Proportion of start-ups: 33%		413			
Firm survival		100%	96%	94%	83%
Firms per year		413	397	388	343
Jobs created					
Owner/managers (avg.)		1.8	1.7	1.7	1.8
Employees (avg.)		4.6	5.7	6.5	7.4
Total all firms					
Owner/managers		723	686	672	607
Employees		1,913	2,293	2,513	2,524
Jobs by firm cohort:					
0 time lag		2,637	2,979	3,185	3,132
1 year time lag			2,637	2,979	3,185
2 year time lag				2,637	2,979
3 year time lag					2,637
Total jobs: all cohorts		2,637	5,616	8,801	11,933
Labor force status per 100,000					
15 years and less: 23%					
16+ years, not in labor force: 25%					
Agriculture sector, all: 1					
Nonagriculture sector					
Self-employed: 3					
Unemployed: 4					
All government: 7					
Private sector: 37					
Total civilian workers		37,000	37,000	37,000	37,000
New firm jobs/total civilian workers, nonagriculture		7%	15%	24%	32%

Source: Data on U.S. population for 1992 from *Statistical Abstracts of the U.S.: 1994*, Tables 15, 614, 629, 630, and 642.

The workings of the entrepreneurial engine are demonstrated in Table 9.1. Results from the previous analysis are used to estimate the development of jobs by new firms and—assuming no major structural changes in the economic system—the proportion of those who would have jobs provided by firms one to four years old.

These estimates begin with a representative group of 100,000 U.S. citizens and finish with the proportion of workers that would be holding new firm jobs. In 1992, for example, about 74% of each 100,000 U.S. citizens would be at least eighteen years old. If 3.7% of those are initiating a new firm in a given year, that would be 2,700 nascent entrepreneurs. As each firm involves an average start-up team of 2.2 persons, this would be about 1,200 start-up efforts. If one-third complete the process and provide a firm birth, then about 400 new firms would be created.

Annual rates of survival and the number of firms in operation can be estimated for the first three years. Four in five (80%) of these firms would be providing jobs as they start their fourth year of operation.

In their first year, the average firm creates about six jobs, of which two are for the start-up team. After three years the average number of jobs has risen to nine. However, as some smaller firms have ceased to exist, the proportion of employees has risen from 73% to 81%.

Each year a new cohort of firms will emerge from the entrepreneurial process. The total number of new firm jobs can be estimated by considering all jobs provided by firms in their first three years of operation. This leads to an estimate of about 12,000 jobs per 100,000 population. We can expect that for each 100,000 persons in the population, about 37%, or 37,000, have private sector jobs. Based on this analysis, we would expect one in three (32%) to have jobs with firms less than four years old and 7% to have jobs with firms less than one year old.

Diversity in size among the new firms is very significant. A variety of studies have found that a small proportion of high-potential new firms provides a substantial proportion of all new jobs. This is illustrated in Table 9.2. In this analysis one in five new firms is considered to be high-potential. The contribution of such firms to the total number of new firm jobs is 45% in the first year, rising to 56% in the third year. It is reasonable, therefore, to assume that high-potential new firms are soon responsible for more than half of all new firm jobs.

The entrepreneurial engine is, of course, an ongoing process. Each year—each day, actually—another set of nascent entrepreneurs begins the process by working on an independent firm start-up. Established businesses may also create subsidiaries or expand by implementing a branch. Each year independent firms, branches, or subsidiaries—new and established—contract or disappear. The jobs created by firm and branch births, as well as firm and branch expansions, provide new opportunities for the individuals required to relocate to new jobs once they are released by businesses that are shrinking or deactivated.

Table 9.2
High-Growth New Firms and Job Dynamics

First Sales	Firm Births	Firm Infancy		
	0	1 Year	2 Years	3 Years
Firm births				
Firm survival	100%	96%	94%	83%
Firms per year	413	397	388	343
Jobs created				
Owner/managers (avg.)	1.8	1.7	1.7	1.8
Employees (avg.)	4.6	5.7	6.5	7.4
Total all firms				
Owner/managers	723	686	672	607
Employees	1,913	2,293	2,513	2,524
Total jobs	2,637	2,979	3,185	3,132
High-growth firms				
Percent all firms	19%	20%	21%	19%
Owner/managers (avg.)	2.1	2.1	2.1	2.1
Employees (avg.)	12.8	17.2	18.4	24.5
Total jobs	1,179	1,502	1,685	1,762
Percent all jobs	45%	50%	53%	56%

There are substantial geographic and national variations in the critical transitions in the entrepreneurial process—conception, firm birth, and firms that persist to become established. If a given region has a dearth of young adults, those twenty-five to forty-four years old, the overall proportion of nascent entrepreneurs may be less than 4%; a region with an excess of young adults may have more than 4% acting as nascent entrepreneurs. The proportion of start-up efforts that leads to firm births may also vary, higher in regions or sectors that are growing, lower in regions or sectors that are contracting.

The growth of new firms, or the proportion that may survive, may also be affected by other factors. Variations in the availability or cost of critical inputs (employees, funds, supplies, or raw materials), customer demand, the presence of competition, or the costs or complications in dealing with government regulations may have an impact. The nature of the critical transitions may be quite different in other countries, where attitudes toward entrepreneurial careers and the sanctions for failure differ. While it is not possible, at this time, to specify the many factors that affect these transitions with precision, a useful framework for assembling more precise information is now in place.

GOVERNMENT POLICIES

There is a limited range of actions governments may take to enhance the start-up process and the contributions of the entrepreneurial engine. It is much easier for governments to slow the engine than speed it up. The policy options that may accelerate the entrepreneurial engine vary in terms of feasibility and efficiency (the ratio of public costs to the aggregate social benefits). Government policy might, as outlined in Chapter 1, affect the entrepreneurial process at different stages: (1) by encouraging more individuals to initiate start-ups, or by providing (2) assistance to those in the start-up process, (3) assistance to fledgling new firms, and (4) assistance to high-potential new firms. The analysis completed in this book clearly suggests that any of these efforts, if implemented with enough resources, could affect business start-ups. But each strategy has its own advantages and disadvantages, potential benefits and costs.

One of the least-expensive and most popular government efforts is exhortations to "be entrepreneurial," usually accompanied by a proposal that individuals should take more responsibility for their own economic well-being. Such messages may reach a wide audience, but in the absence of other measures—development of government assistance programs, entrepreneurial training in the schools, subsidies to assist new venture start-ups—it is not clear how much impact they might have. There is, in addition, little evidence to suggest that public messages promoting entrepreneurship have a major impact on whether or not individuals get involved in starting a new firm. Judgments about the feasibility of a specific business idea, other career options, and the presence of a trusted network of family, friends, and colleagues may be much more critical in affecting decisions about getting involved in an entrepreneurial initiative. Promotional messages of local governments about the business climate may be seen as another form of political noise.

Attempts to improve the entrepreneurial climate, either by publicizing a favorable orientation toward start-ups or outright subsidies, are often very popular. One unexpected finding from Wisconsin is the lower and lower assessments of the quality of the entrepreneurial climate as people move through the start-up process. This is in contrast with substantial evidence that when nascent entrepreneurs and new firms receive information and assistance, they are generally considered helpful. Those start-up firms that move successfully through the process are more likely to have received some assistance. While it is clear that business assistance programs are probably a positive asset, the extent of their impact on the entrepreneurial engine is unknown.

Subsidies, whatever their form, are politically controversial. They are usually much more popular with those receiving them than with those paying for them. Given the enormous amount of time and substantial financial resources privately devoted to the entrepreneurial engine, perhaps over $100 billion each year in informal support, the rather modest contributions from public funds probably have a limited impact. For example, over 98% of all start-ups do *not* receive funding from Small Business Administration (SBA) sponsored programs for financial assistance. Government-sponsored venture capital funds, if managed in the traditional fashion, are likely to reach an even smaller proportion of new firms, as traditional venture capital support is received by less than 1 in 400 start-ups. They are, however, likely to go to the more promising new firms, providing opportunities for "media exposure."

It is possible to provide special programs or training. Programs may have some value for firms in the start-up process, but it is often difficult to reach the potential clients. Even if they are informed about government assistance, those individuals with new firms are often reluctant to seek assistance. One of the lowest-cost initiatives that may provide the highest gains would be a more systematic promotion of assistance programs of all types, preferably reflecting coordination among the many programs that have been put in place.

Formal educational training, in high schools and post-high school educational programs, is another option with promise, particularly since such programs have the potential to reach practically the entire population as they move through the educational system. However, even those who elect to initiate a new firm may do so ten to twenty years after completing high school. For most teenagers or young adults, the immediate practical value of a formal course in entrepreneurship may be modest. The presence of such programs may, however, enhance awareness of entrepreneurial alternatives as a work option among students, teachers, and vocational counselors. The *absence* of any entrepreneurial offerings in an educational program provides strong evidence that starting a new firm is *not* considered a legitimate work/career option.

So what about efficiency in using public policy to affect the entrepreneurial engine? A major consideration is the time required to complete the process. It may take six to seven years from conception to an established new firm. This is somewhat longer than many election cycles, which are typically two to four years. It would be hard for politicians to demonstrate the effectiveness of a new initiative before the next election.

Nonetheless, some informed speculation is possible about each stage of the process. Public messages and exhortations encouraging more individuals to initiate start-ups will be low-cost, highly visible, and likely to have modest or mixed effects. At worst, they will encourage unqualified people to devote time and money to a start-up that will never reach fruition. Sustained broad investments in educational programs may have substantially more impact and assist people in making informed judgments about the issues and benefits of starting a new business but are likely to require more resources and take some time to have an effect.

Programs of assistance for start-up efforts and new firms appear to be well received by those who make use of them, but they are not well known. Additional resources for continuous programs of coordinated promotion may be a low-cost, but high-payoff, mechanism for improving the output of the entrepreneurial engine. Long-term success will require continuous promotion and may substantially increase client demands for many programs.

Programs of assistance targeted to high-potential new firms offer the promise of reduced costs, as only one in five new firms may require attention, with greater payoff in terms of job creation. The difficulty in identifying, in advance, such firms makes a proactive implementation problematic. Widely publicizing such efforts may, in addition, be controversial, as those whose efforts are not considered "high potential" are not offered the assistance. It is possible, however, to provide reactive assistance, offering those who contact assistance programs and appear to have a high-growth potential an expanded range of programs and assistance. There is an indication that persons initiating high-potential new firms are more likely to seek and use assistance programs.

THE ENTREPRENEURIAL CAREER

What about those who are considering an entrepreneurial venture? Who should proceed with a new start-up initiative? When, in their career, should they do it? How might they go about it? What reactions should they expect from others, particularly government agencies and those in the financial community? How much work will it require? Will it be risky? What is the payoff? Should women or minorities expect to confront special situations? Some comments are possible with regard to all these issues.

For example, who should get involved in starting a new firm? Based on who actually gets involved, a very wide range of people probably have an adequate background and an appropriate setting. Those who have finished high school; have some financial resources; know an industry or business area well; are knowledgeable about a given geographic area; and have developed a network of business associates, friends, and relatives may find they can achieve their personal objectives through development of a new firm. It helps a great deal if they have a promising business idea. Those with the opposite characteristics, people who have not finished high school, have little background or experience in any economic sector, have little in the way of financial resources, are new to an area, and have poorly developed social networks may not be in a good situation for starting a new firm. Those in this situation should probably be careful about pursuing a new start-up, unless it is based on a very promising business idea.

Most involved in the entrepreneurial process seek to achieve a mixture of three personal goals: money, autonomy, and interesting work. While the mix varies for different people involved in the entrepreneurial process, almost all give some weight to all three. Almost half of all new start-ups appear to reflect a strong desire for independence, as they are owned by a single person. On the other hand, as the complexity of the new firm increases, or as size grows in importance, the necessity for a team start-up increases. More than half of new start-ups involve several persons who will share ownership of the business, and over 40% of new firms involve teams of relatives or kin. Less than 10% of new firms involve teams of unrelated individuals, although these firms are more likely to be high-potential.

The amount of work involved in the start-up phase is considerable. There is evidence to suggest that about one person-year of work (2,000 hours) is required to initiate the typical new firm. This may be one person working for a year, two persons working for half a year, or some other combination of effort. Those start-ups that do a number of things quickly, a half-dozen or more steps in the first six to nine months, are more likely to have a firm birth. Those that draw out the process, doing one or two things every four or five months, may find that trying to start a business is, in itself, a long-term hobby. They may never actually get an operating business in place.

Enthusiasm for a business start-up may decline as the team moves through the steps necessary to launch a new firm. Those just entering the process seem to consider the local context most supportive. But the complications and frustrations associated with dealing with multiple government agencies in different jurisdictions, to say nothing of coping with the financial community, are often time-consuming and frustrating. This may lead to a negative opinion about the local context as a good place to start a new business. Media hype about how much "Mudville loves business" may seem hypocritical at this stage of the process.

New firms with a higher-growth trajectory will have even more problems than a typical new firm. Higher compound growth may lead to compounded problems, as it becomes necessary to coordinate "everything at once." Only when a firm enters adolescence, about the fifth year of operation, do these problems appear to diminish, perhaps leading to a more positive judgment about the local context.

What types of risks are involved? There is always the risk that the personal investment of time may be lost. The amount of financial risk in the start-up phase does not seem large, as few people invest more than a few thousand dollars at this stage. Businesses that actually begin operation seem to provide less risk, for over 90% survive from year to year. That is not to say, however, that the financial rewards are great. Many of these new firms will not provide high incomes for the owner/managers. A good management accounting system will do much to provide information regarding the profitability of the venture and the capacity to distinguish between earnings as managers and equity payoff to the new business owners.

Are there special issues confronting minority ethnic groups? There is little evidence that minorities, per se, are more or less likely to become involved, once their situation in terms of educational background, personal resources, duration of residence in an area, and extent of social networks are taken into account. Institutional discrimination may exist, but evidence of such bias is hard to find in the data. On the other hand, there is substantial evidence of great diversity among American Indians, Asians, blacks and Hispanics. This is further confounded by great diversity within ethnic groups: American Indians and Asians are particularly heterogeneous. While new in-migrants to an area may be very active in starting their own businesses, the majority of businesses are started by established residents with well-developed personal networks.

The experiences of women may differ from those of men. Most are involved with start-ups with men. When they get involved on their own or with other women, they approach a new firm start-up differently from men. Women focus on a smaller range of economic sectors—retail and consumer service dominate—with much more conservative and modest aspirations. They also seem to be less likely to use existing assistance programs, even those designed for women. As a consequence, they may find the economic rewards more modest.

~

One of the strengths of the United States, from the very beginning, has been an acceptance of people who wished to try something on their own. We have much evidence that the entrepreneurial spirit—and activity—is alive and well and that it continues to be one major source of economic adaptation and change. The entrepreneurial engine is a powerful source of economic growth, and the more we know about it, the more we can fine-tune public policy for optimum performance.

Future Research
on the Entrepreneurial Process

M uch research on entrepreneurship and the development of new firms has a number of features that reduce its value for providing accurate information, including (1) the use of proxy variables that fail to provide a reliable indicator of the phenomena (e.g., self-employment, new incorporation filings); (2) cross-section analysis that fails to include those who have not completed important transitions; (3) samples of convenience or an unknown relation to the population of interest (entrepreneurs, new firms, venture capitalists, etc.); (4) short time frame, which does not allow completion of the critical processes; and (5) a limited set of variables, perhaps with a focus on testing the presence of any impact by a small number of independent variables.

The analysis of the five representative samples in this book makes it clear that the entrepreneurial process involves the complex interaction of a number of processes and takes a number of years to reach fruition and that accurate causal inferences will be a major problem. This suggests that significant advances may not be developed from small- scale, piecemeal projects but will require a more comprehensive approach. A research design with the following features may be required.

The complexity of the business start-up process—reflecting the impact of a wide range of contextual, personal, life course, economic sector, and procedural features—suggests that major progress will require a well-developed, broad-ranging program of research. This may be done through a series of related projects that gather data on a wide range of factors from large, representative samples. This implies a sustained effort, perhaps developed as a collective initiative. There is ample precedent for research programs of this scope, such as the longitudinal studies of family economic well-being (Morgan et al., 1991; Hofferth et al., 1996), national panel studies of labor force activity (Ohio State University, 1995), the ongoing national election studies (Rosenstone, et al., 1995); and the annual general social survey (Smith and Keaney, 1995). These projects develop samples representative of the U.S. population and are generally considered major national resources, reflecting consensus that the phenomenon justifies a sustained commitment to a research program. It remains to be seen if the entrepreneurial phenomenon and the study of business start-ups will achieve this status, a phenomenon worthy of a major commitment of resources.

The length of time it may take to complete the start-up process and identify an established new firm, which may vary from four to eight years, suggests that systematic research will require a medium-term perspective, perhaps projects lasting five to ten years. As experimental designs are not feasible with these phenomena, the major basis for causal inferences will be comparisons of different entities at different times—longitudinal or panel studies. It will be necessary to design research with a potential for starting with representative samples of those entering the entrepreneurial process and periodically follow both those moving through the process and those dropping out at different times.

Finally, the significance of complex interactions among a range of powerful processes suggests that the linear additive models implied in most multivariate analyses (such as linear regression models) may not be the most appropriate for understanding the critical causal influences. For example, it has been found that gender has no impact on participation in start-ups among those twenty-five to thirty-four years old but is important for those over thirty-four. Such interactions are pervasive in this preliminary analysis. A sophisticated understanding of how the different stages of the entrepreneurial process are completed may well require careful attention to a range of subtle interactions which may change for different types of firms in different contexts with different ownership structures.

Nonetheless, this preliminary analysis indicates that substantial progress can be made on one of the most important phenomena in the modern world—the creation of new business organizations. Assembling both the intellectual and financial resources for such projects—with substantial representative samples, a wide range of variables, and tracking over a significant period of time—is a major challenge to those committed to understanding the entrepreneurial process. It may require either a substantial government investment or a consortium of research centers and other interested organizations.

References

Acs, Zoltan J., and David B. Audretsch. 1995. "Technology, Productivity, and Innovation." OECD Working Party on SMEs (Small and Medium Enterprises) High-Level Workshop on "SMEs: Employment, Innovation and Growth." Washington, DC, June 16–17.

Aldrich, H. E. 1990. "Using Ecological Perspective to Study Organizational Founding Rates." *Entrepreneurship: Theory and Practice* 14 (3): 7–24.

Aldrich, H. E., and R. Waldinger. 1990. "Ethnicity and Entrepreneurship." *Annual Review of Sociology* 16: 111–35.

Aldrich, H. E., and C. Zimmer. 1986. "Entrepreneurship through Social Networks." In D. L. Sexton and R .W. Smilor, eds., *The Art and Science of Entrepreneurship.* Cambridge, MA: Ballinger, 3–24.

Armington, Catherine, and Marjorie Odle. 1982. "Small Business: How Many Jobs?" *Brookings Review* 20: 14–17.

Arzeni, Sergio. 1995. "International Seminar on Local Systems of Small Firms and Job Creation: Background Paper." OECD Working Party on SME Enterprises High-Level Workshop on "SMEs: Employment, Innovation and Growth." Washington, DC, June 16–17.

Barreto, Humberto. 1989. *The Entrepreneur in Microeconomic Theory: Disappearance and Explanation.* New York: Routledge.

Bates, T. 1985. "Entrepreneur Human Capital Endowments and Minority Business Viability." *The Journal of Human Resources* 20: 540–54.

Baumol, William J. 1968. "Entrepreneurship in Economic Theory." *American Economic Review* (Papers and Proceedings) 58: 64–71.

——— . 1990. "Entrepreneurship: Productive, Unproductive, and Destructive." *Journal of Political Economy* 98 (5, part 1): 893–921.

Ben-Ner, Avner. 1988. "Comparative Empirical Observations on Worker-Owned and Capitalist Firms." *International Journal of Industrial Organization* 6: 7–31.

Birch, David A. 1979. "The Job Generation Process." Unpublished report, prepared by the Massachusetts Institute of Technology Program on Neighborhood and Regional Change for the Economic Development Administration, U.S. Department of Commerce, Washington, D.C.

———. 1981. "Who Creates Jobs?" *The Public Interest* 65: 3–14.

———. 1987. *Job Creation in America: How Our Smallest Companies Put the Most People to Work*. New York: Free Press.

Birch, David, Anne Haggerty, and William Parsons. 1995. *Corporate Evolution*. Cambridge, MA: Cognetics.

Birley, S. 1986. "The Small Firm—Set at the Start." *Frontiers of Entrepreneurship Research: 1986*. Wellesley, MA: Babson College, 267–80.

Blanchflower, D. G., and D. B. Meyer. 1991. "Longitudinal Analysis of Young Entrepreneurs in Australia and the United States." *National Bureau of Economic Research*. Cambridge, MA: Working Paper 3746.

Blanchflower, D. G., and A. J. Oswald. 1990. "Self Employment in the Enterprise Culture." In R. Jowell, S. Witherspoon, and L. Brook, eds., *British Social Attitudes: The Seventh Report*. Aldershot, UK: SCPR, Gower.

Boeker, W. 1989. "Strategic Change: The Effects of Founding and History." *Academy of Management Journal* 32: 489–515.

Bonacich, E. 1973. "A Theory of Middleman Minorities." *American Sociological Review* 38: 583–94.

Bruderl, Josef, and R. Schussler. 1990. "Organizational Mortality: The Liabilities of Newness and Adolescence." *Administrative Science Quarterly* 35: 530–47.

Bruderl, Josef, Peter Preisendorfer, and Rolf Ziegler. 1992. "Survival Chances of Newly Founded Business Organizations." *American Sociological Review* 57: 227–42.

Brush, C. 1992. "Research on Women Business Owners: Past Trends, A New Perspective, and Future Directions." *Entrepreneurship Theory and Practice* 16 (2): 5–30.

Carroll, Glen R. 1983. "A Stochastic Model of Organizational Mortality: A Review and Reanalysis." *Social Science Research* 12: 203–329.

Carter, Nancy M., William B. Gartner, and Paul D. Reynolds. 1996. "Exploring Start-up Event Sequences." *Journal of Business Venturing* 11: 151–66.

Carter, Nancy, Tim Stearns, Paul Reynolds, and Brenda Miller. 1994. "New Venture Strategies: Theory Development with an Empirical Base." *Strategic Management Journal* 15: 21–41.

Cooper, Arnold C., William C. Dunkleberg, and Carolyn Y. Woo. 1988. "Survival and Failure: A Longitudinal Study." *Frontiers of Entrepreneurship Research: 1988*. Wellesley, MA: Babson College, 225–37.

Cromie, S., and S. Birley. 1991. "Networking by Female Business Owners in Northern Ireland." *Journal of Business Venturing* 7: 237–51.

Curtin, Richard. 1982. "Indicators of Consumer Behavior: The University of Michigan Surveys of Consumers." *Public Opinion Quarterly* 46: 340–62.

Davidsson, Per, Leif Lindmark, and Christer Olofsson. 1994. "New Firm Formation and Regional Development in Sweden." *Regional Studies* 28 (4): 395–410.

Davis, Steven J., John Haltiwanger, and Scott Schuh. 1993. "Small Business and Job Creation: Dissecting the Myth and Reassessing the Facts." Cambridge, MA: NBER Working Paper No. 4492.

———. 1996. *Job Creation and Destruction*. Cambridge: MIT Press.

Denison, D., Amand Swaminathan, and Nancy Rothbard. 1994. "Networks, Founding Conditions, and Imprinting Processes: Examining the Process of Organization Creation." Academy of Management Annual Meetings, Dallas, August 17.

Dennis, William J. 1997. "More Than You Think: An Inclusive Estimate of Business Entries." *Journal of Business Venturing* 12 (3): 175–96.

Dolton, P. J., and G. H. Makepeace. 1990. "Self-Employment amongst Graduates." *Bulletin of Economic Research* 42 (1): 35–53.

Economic Behavior Program, Survey Research Center, University of Michigan. 1993a. *Survey of Consumer Attitudes and Behavior, October 1993.* [Computer file]. ICPSR version. Ann Arbor, MI: Survey Research Center [producer], 1993. Ann Arbor, MI: Inter-University Consortium for Political and Social Research [distributor], 1995.

———. 1993b. *Survey of Consumer Attitudes and Behavior, November 1993.* [Computer file]. ICPSR version. Ann Arbor, MI: Survey Research Center [producer], 1993. Ann Arbor, MI: Inter-University Consortium for Political and Social Research [distributor], 1995.

EIM (Small Business Research and Consultancy). 1993. *The European Observatory for SMEs: First Annual Report.* Zoetermeer, The Netherlands: EIM Small Business Research and Consultancy.

———. 1994. *The European Observatory for SMEs: Second Annual Report.* Zoetermeer, The Netherlands: EIM Small Business Research and Consultancy.

———. 1995. *The European Observatory for SMEs: Third Annual Report.* Zoetermeer, The Netherlands: EIM Small Business Research and Consultancy.

Evans, David S., and Linda S. Leighton. 1989. "Some Empirical Aspects of Entrepreneurship." *American Economic Review* 79 (3): 519–35.

Finchman, M., and D. A. Levinthal. 1991. "Honeymoons and the Liability of Adolescence: A New Perspective on Duration Dependence in Social and Organizational Relationships." *Academy of Management Review* 16: 442–68.

Fratoe, F. 1986. "A Sociological Analysis of Minority Business." *Review of Black Political Economy* 15 (2): 5–30.

Freeman, John, Glen Carroll, and Michael T. Hannan. 1983. "The Liability of Newness: Age Dependence in Organizational Death Rates." *American Sociological Review* 48: 692–710.

Hall, Chris. 1995. "The Entrepreneurial Engine." OECD Working Party on SMEs High-Level Workshop on "SMEs: Employment, Innovation, and Growth." Washington, DC, June 16–17.

Hannan, Michael T., and Glen R. Carroll. 1992. *Dynamics of Organizational Populations: Density, Legitimation, and Competition.* New York: Oxford University Press.

Hannan, Michael T., and John H. Freeman. 1989. *Organizational Ecology.* Cambridge: Harvard University Press.

Hisrich, R. D., and C. G. Brush. 1987. "Women Entrepreneurs: A Longitudinal Study." *Frontiers of Entrepreneurship Research: 1987.* Wellesley, MA: Babson College, 187–99.

Hofferth, Sandra, Frank P. Stafford, Wei-Jun U. Yeung, Greg J. Duncan, Martha S. Hill, James Lepowski, and James N. Morgan. 1996. *Panel Study of Income Dynamics, 1968–92 [Cross-Year Individual File, 1968–92 (Waves I–XXV)]* [Computer File]. Ann Arbor, MI: Survey Research Center [producer], 1995. Ann Arbor, MI: Inter-University Consortium for Political and Social Research [distributor].

Kirchhoff, Bruce A. 1994. *Entrepreneurship and Dynamic Capitalism* Westport, CT: Praeger.

Knudsen, Kjell R., and Donald G. McTavish. 1989. "Modeling Interest in Entrepreneurship: Implications for Business Development." *Frontiers of Entrepreneurship Research: 1989.* Wellesley, MA: Babson College, 67–68.

Light, I., and E. Bonacich. 1988. *Immigrant Entrepreneurs.* Berkeley: University of California Press.

Loveman, Gary, and Werner Sengenberger. 1990. "The Re-Emergence of Small Scale Production: An International Comparison." *Small Business Economics* 3: 1–17.

Magidson, Jay. 1992. *SPSS/PC+ CHAID: Version 5.0.* Chicago: SPSS Inc.

Manson, Donald M., Marie Howland, and George E. Peterson. 1984. "The Effect of Business Cycles on Metropolitan Suburbanization." *Economic Geography* 60 (1): 71–80.

Morgan, James N., Greg J. Duncan, Martha S. Hill, and James Lepkowski. 1991. *Panel Study of Income Dynamics, 1968–88 [Waves I–XXI]* [Computer File]. Ann Arbor, MI: Survey Research Center [Producer]. Ann Arbor, MI: Inter-university Consortium for Political and Social Research [Distributor].

Norusis, Marija J. 1992a. *SPSS/PC+ Advanced Statistics; Version 5.0.* Chicago: SPSS.

——. 1992b. *SPSS/PC+ Professional Statistics; Version 5.0.* Chicago: SPSS.

OECD. 1994. *Employment Outlook.* Paris, France: Organization for Economic Cooperation and Development.

——. 1995. "Globalisation of Economic Activities and the Development of SMEs Synthesis Report." Industry Division, Working Party on Small and Medium Enterprises, DSTI/IND/PME(95)3. Paris, France: Organization for Economic Cooperation and Development.

——. 1996. *SMEs: Employment, Innovation, and Growth: The Washington Workshop.* Paris, France: Organization for Economic Cooperation and Development.

Ohio State University, Center for Human Resource Research [principal investigators]. 1995. National Longitudinal Surveys of Labor Market Experience, Youth Cohort: 1979–93 [CD-ROM version]. [Machine Readable Data File]. Columbus, OH: Ohio State University, Center for Human Resource Research. [Distributor]

Palit, Charles, and Paul Reynolds. 1993. "A Network Sampling Procedure for Estimating the Prevalence of Nascent Entrepreneurs. *Proceedings of the International Conference on Establishment Surveys."* Alexandria, VA: American Statistical Association, 657–61.

Phillips, Bruce D. 1995. "New Census Data on Women-Owned Businesses: 1982–1992." Washington, DC: U.S. Small Business Administration, Office of Advocacy, Presentation at National Women's Business Council Summit: 1996.

Phillips, Bruce D., and Bruce A. Kirchhoff. 1989. "Formation, Growth and Survival: Small Firm Dynamics in the U.S. Economy." *Small Business Economics* 1: 65–74.

Portes, A., M. Castells, and L. A. Benton, eds. 1989. *The Informal Economy: Studies in Advanced and Less Developed Countries.* Baltimore: Johns Hopkins University Press.

Preisendorfer, P., and T. Voss. 1990. "Organizational Mortality of Small Firms: The Effects of Entrepreneurial Age and Human Capital." *Organizational Studies* 11: 107–29.

Pyke, Frank. 1995. "Comparing Small and Large Firms in Europe: Prospects for Incomes and Working Conditions." OECD Working Party on SME Enterprises High-Level Workshop on "SMEs: Employment, Innovation and Growth." Washington, DC, June 16–17.

Reis, Paula, and Anne J. Stone, eds. 1992. *The American Woman 1992–93: A Status Report on Women and Politics*. New York: W. W. Norton.

Reynolds, Paul D. 1987a. *Minnesota New Firm Survey* [Computer file]. Minneapolis: Paul D. Reynolds, University of Minnesota, Department of Sociology [producer], 1995. Ann Arbor, MI: Inter-University Consortium for Political and Social Research [distributor], 1995.

——. 1987b. "New Firms: Societal Contributions or Survival." *Journal of Business Venturing* 2: 231–46.

——. 1989. "New Firms and Economic Growth: Policy Implications from Surveys of New Firms." *Economic Development Commentary* 13 (2): 4–11.

——. 1993. "High Performance Entrepreneurship: What Makes It Different?" *Frontiers of Entrepreneurship Research: 1993*. Wellesley, MA: Babson College, 88–101.

——. 1994. "Autonomous Firm Dynamics and Economic Growth in the United States, 1986–1990." *Regional Studies* 28 (4): 429–42.

——. 1995. "Family Firms in the Start-up Process: Preliminary Explorations." International Family Business Program Association Annual Meeting. Nashville, TN: Hermitage Hotel.

Reynolds, Paul, and Steve Freeman. 1987. "1986 Pennsylvania New Firm Survey." Philadelphia: University of Pennsylvania, Wharton School, Sol C. Snider Entrepreneurial Center. Final report provided to the Appalachian Regional Commission, Washington, DC.

Reynolds, Paul D., Steve Freeman, and Lauren Oshana. 1987. *Pennsylvania New Firm Survey, 1979–1984* [Computer file]. ICPSR Version. Philadelphia: Paul D. Reynolds, University of Pennsylvania, Wharton School [producer], 1995. Ann Arbor, MI: Inter-University Consortium for Political and Social Research [distributor], 1995.

Reynolds, Paul D., and Wilbur R. Maki. 1990. "Business Volatility and Economic Growth." *Final Project Report*. Small Business Administration, Contract SBA 3067–0A–88 May 1990.

——. 1991. "Regional Characteristics Affecting Business Growth: Assessing Strategies for Promoting Regional Economic Well-Being." Final Project Report to the Ford Foundation, November.

Reynolds, Paul, Wilbur Maki, and Brenda Miller. 1995. "Explaining Regional Variation in Business Births and Deaths: U.S. 1976–88." *Small Business Economics* 7: 389–407.

Reynolds, Paul, and Brenda Miller. 1988. *1987 Minnesota New Firm Study*. Minneapolis: University of Minnesota Center for Urban and Regional Affairs, Pub. 88–1.

——. 1990. "Race, Gender, and Entrepreneurship: Participation in New Firm Start-ups." American Sociological Association Annual Meetings, Washington, DC.

——. 1992. "New Firm Gestation: Conception, Birth, and Implications for Research." *Journal of Business Venturing* 7: 1–14.

Reynolds, Paul, David J. Storey, and Paul Westhead. 1994. "Cross-National Comparisons of the Variation in New Firm Formation Rates." *Regional Studies* 28 (4): 443–56.

Reynolds, Paul, and Steve West. 1985. *New Firms in Minnesota: Their Contributions to Employment and Exports, Startup Problems, and Current Status*. Minneapolis: University of Minnesota Center for Urban and Regional Affairs, June.

Reynolds, Paul D., and Sammis B. White. 1993a. *Wisconsin's Entrepreneurial Climate Study*. Milwaukee: Marquette University Center for the Study of Entrepreneurship. Final Report to Wisconsin Housing and Economic Development Authority.

———. 1993b. *Wisconsin Entrepreneurial Climate Study, 1992–93* [Computer file]. ICPSR Version. Marquette University, WI: Paul D. Reynolds and Sammis B. White [producers], 1993. Ann Arbor, MI: Inter-University Consortium for Political and Social Research [distributor], 1995.

Rosenstone, Steven J., Donald R. Kinder, Warren E. Miller, and the National Election Studies. 1995. American National Election Study, 1994: Post-Election Survey [Enhanced with 1992 and 1993 Data] [Computer File]. Conducted by University of Michigan, Center for Political Studies, 2d ICPSR Ed. Ann Arbor, MI: University of Michigan, Center for Political Studies/Inter-University Consortium for Political and Social Research [producers]. Ann Arbor, MI: Inter-University Consortium for Political and Social Research [distributor].

Schreyer, Paul. 1995. "SMEs and Employment Creation: Overview of Selected Quantitative Studies in OECD Member Countries." Paris, France: OECD STI Working Papers 1995/5.

Schreyer, Paul, and Michelle Chavoix-Mannato. 1995. "Quantitative Information on SMEs: OECD Approach, Data Collection and Examples of Analysis." OECD Working Party on SME Enterprises High-Level Workshop on "SMEs: Employment, Innovation and Growth." Washington, DC, June 16–17.

Shaver, Kelly G., and Linda R. Scott. 1991. "Person, Process, Choice: The Psychology of New Venture Creation." *Entrepreneurship: Theory and Practice* 16 (2): 23–46.

Smith, Tom W., and K. Keaney. 1995. "Who, What, When, Where, and Why: An Analysis of Usage of the General Social Survey, 1972–1993." Chicago: University of Chicago, National Opinion Research Center, GSS Project Report No. 19.

Sonquist, John A. 1970. *Multivariate Model Building: The Validation of a Search Strategy*. Ann Arbor: University of Michigan Institute for Social Research.

Sonquist, John A., and James N. Morgan. 1964. *The Detection of Interaction Effects*. Ann Arbor: University of Michigan Institute for Social Research Monograph No. 35.

de Soto, H. 1989. *The Other Path: The Invisible Revolution in the Third World*. Translated by June Abbott. New York: Harper and Row.

Stinchcombe, A. L. 1965. "Social Structure and Organizations." In J. G. March, ed., *Handbook of Organizations*. Chicago: Rand McNally, 142–93.

Storey, David J. 1991. "The Birth of New Firms—Does Unemployment Matter?" *Small Business Economics* 3: 167–78.

———. 1994. *Understanding the Small Business Sector*. London: Routledge.

Thurick, Roy. 1995. "Small Firms, Large Firms, and Economic Growth." OECD Working Party on SME Enterprises High-Level Workshop on "SMEs: Employment, Innovation and Growth." Washington, DC, June 16–17.

U.S. Bureau of the Census. 1992. *Statistical Abstract of the United States: 1992.* 112th Ed. Washington, DC: U.S. Government Printing Office.

———. 1994. *Statistical Abstract of the United States: 1994.* 114th Ed. Washington, DC: U.S. Government Printing Office.

U.S. Department of Commerce. 1995. *Regional Economic Information System (REIS).* Washington, DC: Economic and Statistics Administration, Bureau of Economic Analysis, Regional Economic Measurement Division.

U.S. House of Representatives. 1988. *New Economic Realities: The Rise of Women Entrepreneurs: A Report of the Committee on Small Business.* Washington, DC: U.S. Government Printing Office.

U.S. Small Business Administration, Office of Advocacy. 1994. *Handbook of Small Business Data.* Washington, DC: U.S. Government Printing Office.

Wagner, Joachim. 1994. "The Post-Entry Performance of New Small Firms in German Manufacturing Industries." *The Journal of Industrial Economics* 42 (2): 141–54.

Waldinger, R., H. Aldrich and R. Ward. 1990. *Ethnic Entrepreneurs: Immigrant Business in Industrial Societies.* Newbury Park, CA: Sage.

White, Sammis B. 1995. *Metropolitan Economic Development in Wisconsin. Wisconsin Policy Research Institute Report* September, 8 (7).

White, Sammis B., L. S. Binkley, T. J. Chefalo, W. F. McMahon, and M. M. Thomas. 1994. "Which Business Establishments are Really Generating New Employment?" *Environment and Planning C: Government and Policy* 12: 409–24.

White, Sammis B., Lisa S. Binkley, and Jeffrey D. Osterman, 1993. "The Sources of Suburban Employment Growth." *Journal of the American Planning Association* 59 (2): 193–203.

Index

Acs, Zoltan, 4
Adolescence of firms, 6, 131–34
Age of entrepreneur, 98, 136–37, 166–67, 197–98
Aldrich, Howard, 5, 98, 179, 181
Annual firm birth rates, 15, 72–74, 205
American-Indians. *See* Ethnic subgroups
Appalachian Regional Commission, xvii
Armington, Catherine, 3
Arzeni, Sergio, 3
Asian-Americans. *See* Ethnic subgroups
Assistance programs. *See* Business assistance programs
Attrition, 69
Audretsch, David, 4
Automatic Interaction Detection (AID) modeling, 52–56, 147–53
Autonomous (single site) employers, 3, 14, 15, 18–20, 26
Autonomous firms versus branches, 15, 18, 26, 210

Barreto, Humberto, 2

Bates, Timothy, 168
Baumol, William J., 2, 207
Ben-Ner, Avner, 7, 133
Benton, L. A., 179
Binkley, Lisa S., 14
Biological analogy, 42–43, 129
Birch, David A., 3, 14, 87
Birley, Sue, 168, 171
Birth of firms: annual rates of, 15, 72–74, 205; biological comparison and, 129; entrepreneurial process and, 6–7; growth analysis and, 125; job creation and, 1; regional variation and, 26–27; success analysis and, 129, 130. *See also* Start-up activities/process
Blacks. *See* Ethnic subgroups
Blanchflower, David G., 52
Boeker, Walter, 7
Bonacich, Edna, 179
Branches versus autonomous firms, 15, 18, 26, 210
Bruderl, Josef, 7, 133
Brush, Candida, 167, 170
Business assistance programs: awareness of, 35, 62, 64, 109, 111; ethnic subgroup use of, 193–196, 201–

About the Authors

PAUL D. REYNOLDS is the Paul T. Babson Chair in Entrepreneurial Studies at Babson College. He is the author, coauthor, or editor of three books, two conference proceedings, and over eighty articles and reports.

SAMMIS B. WHITE is Professor of Urban Planning at the University of Wisconsin-Milwaukee. He is the author or coauthor of two books and over 100 articles and reports.